COMMUNICATING WITH BRA

Communicating with Brazilians
When "Yes" Means "No"

TRACY NOVINGER

Illustrations by Donald Haughey

UNIVERSITY OF TEXAS PRESS, AUSTIN

Requests for permission to reproduce material from this
work should be sent to Permissions, University of Texas
Press, P.O. Box 7819, Austin, TX 78713-7819.

⊗ The paper used in this book meets the minimum
requirements of ANSI/NISO Z39.48-1992 (R1997) (Permanence
of Paper).

LIBRARY OF CONGRESS CATALOGING-IN-PUBLICATION DATA
Novinger, Tracy, 1942–
   Communicating with Brazilians : when "yes" means
"no" / Tracy Novinger.—1st ed.
     p.   cm.
Includes bibliographical references.
   ISBN 0-292-70194-2 (cloth : alk. paper)
   ISBN 0-292-70287-6 (pbk. : alk. paper)
   1. Nonverbal communication—Brazil.   2. Intercultural
communication.   I. Title.
   P99.5 .N68   2004
302.2'22'0981—dc21

                        2003013128

Para Glen

Reprinted with permission of Travelers' Tales, Inc. Copyright 1997.

Contents

Preface

"Brazil is open to all races and all cultures and . . . it is located in the most beautiful and luminous province of the earth." [1]

Brazil is the land of paradox.

Jorge Amado's description of Bahia can well be used to describe Brazil as a whole: "a land where everything is intermixed and commingled, where no one can separate virtue from sin, or distinguish the certain from the absurd, or draw the line between truth and trickery, between reality and dream." [2] Despite the many serious problems that must be confronted just to negotiate daily living in Brazil, Brazilians exhibit happiness and zest for life.

It is easy to fall in love with Brazil, with its rich culture and its amiable people, and it is also easy to be lulled into a false understanding. The general pleasantness of daily interaction between people representing the gamut of races and hues may veil a measure of racial discrimination. More significant, however, is the social discrimination between the haves and the have-nots. The easy friendliness of Brazilians requires commitment and imposes obligations that foreigners may find unexpected, unfamiliar, or undesirable. The sometimes informal style of communication is undergirded by a hierarchical system in which everyone has a place and keeps to it, to avoid striking any note of discord in personal interactions. The social hierarchy is unforgiving of transgressions.

Language difference can impede intercultural communication, but a more difficult hurdle is "speaking" a foreign culture. Communication specialists estimate that some three-fourths of our communication takes place nonverbally, through behavior. All behavior is communication, and because we cannot stop behaving, we cannot stop communicating. During all of the waking hours that we spend with other human beings, we "speak" volumes through the behavior inculcated by our culture.

Each of us is conditioned from birth by our culture. It teaches us to use the appropriate tone of voice, facial expressions, gestures, table manners, and posture, when to establish direct eye contact and when to touch, and proper forms of address and social rituals, to mention only a few cultural elements—so many, in fact, that it would be impossible consciously to remember all of our cultural rules when interacting socially. We learn these rules so well that we internalize them and they govern our behavior subconsciously. We then become aware primarily of deviations from the prescribed cultural norms. What is particularly significant in intercultural communication is that we tend to react *negatively* to any such deviations—because we ourselves were trained by negative feedback. One intercultural communication expert states that if left to chance, a person's chances of having a satisfying experience living abroad would be about one in seven.[3]

This book does not treat Brazilian culture exhaustively, nor does it compare Brazilian and North American cultures point by point. Rather, it is intended to help foreigners communicate effectively with Brazilians by highlighting Brazil's salient cultural characteristics and explaining their function within the culture. It should also make each of us more aware of the dictates of our own culture and how they mesh or clash with those of other cultures. This preparation to consciously negotiate cultural differences will accelerate bridging the culture gap. It is my hope also that Brazilians will benefit from this look across cultural borders.

One cannot reduce the culture of a nation to a book, and it is impossible to fix in static words on a page the living, dynamic aspects of culture. But such an exercise is useful nonetheless. Fixing generalizations in print provides points of reference from which to start our own dynamic, living process of comprehension.

In evaluating a book on Brazilian behavior, a Brazilian graduate student in the United States lamented that it attributed "stereotypical" characteristics of a few to the members of a whole nation and that it focused on Brazil's upper and middle classes, excluding a large portion of society. I would propound that consciously constructing a national cultural model provides a useful tool for achieving effective cross-cultural communication. Such a model is based on observation and is flexible; it is easily altered and supplemented. In these ways, it differs from a stereotype. And travelers to Brazil will benefit most from a model that has the characteristics of the stratum of Brazilian society with which they are likely to interact.

I was born in the Caribbean and lived part of my youth in Brazil, where I attended Brazilian schools. I have portrayed Brazilian cultural characteristics from my experience of living in Brazil, from subsequent visits, from archival research, and from recent focused interviews and conversations with more than one hundred individuals. I was privileged to stay in the homes of Brazilian friends on a number of recent occasions while conducting research for this book. Except for sources cited in the notes, to preserve their anonymity, I have changed the names of all of the persons from whom I gathered information.

Culture affects our communication in two major ways. The history and the experience of living in a culture shape our *perceptions,* which in turn filter how we interpret situations and understand persons. Culture also regulates the *processes* of communication interaction, both verbal and nonverbal. All of the elements of culture interact in communication. A change in one element affects all the others, just as a slight rotation of a kaleidoscope creates a new picture.

In this book, I first introduce Brazil, the concept of culture, and an outline of culture's perceptual filters. Second, to explain the Brazilian perspective, I present a portrait of Brazil's history, racial fusion, economy, and the experience of contemporary living. I address the nation's social organization and ranking systems and discuss preconceptions, worldviews, the values and identity of the Brazilian, sex and food as important cultural components, and thought patterns. Third, I examine nonverbal communication processes and the differences between common Brazilian and North American styles when negotiating, persuading, or conversing. The concluding chapter includes a list of the paradoxes of Brazilian culture, a culture-specific checklist, and eight prescriptive points to accelerate cross-cultural competence when communicating with Brazilians. I have endeavored to be objective throughout. But as the anthropologist Edward T. Hall points out, one can never entirely overcome the culture of one's youth.[4]

Boa viagem on your venture into Brazilian culture.

Acknowledgments

I am indebted to many individuals for their support, information, courtesy, and warm hospitality. I cannot possibly acknowledge them all. Nonetheless, I want to expressly recognize and thank some by name. It should be noted that this recognition does not suggest that these persons agree or disagree with the contents of this book, for which I take full responsibility.

My thanks—again—to my multifaceted friend Nancy Hamilton for insightful comments and constructive suggestions. I also wish to thank Marilyn Smolinsky for valiantly wading through a rough early draft, Brazilianist Ann Hart for her interest and comments, and Herb Brandt for his observations.

I want to thank Glaucia Helena Assmann, Luciano Kley Luz, Cláudia Joenck Cayres Pinto, Vera Lúcia Rahde, Dr. Pedro de Moraes Garcez, and Pastora and Celso San Guidette for their friendship and assistance. My thanks also to Cláudio Passos de Oliveira, Sônia Nicolai, Maria da Graça P. Ibañez, and everyone at the Instituto Cultural Brasileiro Norte-Americano of Porto Alegre, Brazil, who assisted me. All of them truly exemplify Brazilian graciousness, generosity, and warmth.

I also wish to express my appreciation to and admiration for Michael Dell of Dell Computer Corporation, who, at the "speed of Dell," had interviews with Dell executives scheduled for me in the United States and in Brazil. My thanks to many talented and accomplished persons at Dell for helpful information regarding communication and cross-national cultural differences. You know who you are.

To Donald Haughey, Professor of Art at St. Edward's University, Austin, Texas, my thanks for the illustrations he prepared for this book.

Finally, *um agradecimento especial* to Theresa May, Editor in Chief of the University of Texas Press, for her interest in this project from initial concept to completion.

COMMUNICATING WITH BRAZILIANS

PART I

Communication
Is Culture

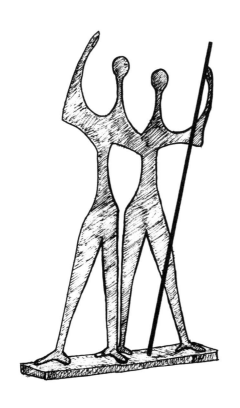

CHAPTER ONE

Communicating with Brazilians

A Brazilian will not say "no" (even if that is what is meant), a nicety that often confuses foreigners.

The South American Giant

When Brazil declared its independence from Portugal in 1822, the United States was the first country to recognize the new nation. The two countries have traditionally enjoyed a friendly and active relationship in both the economic sphere and the political sphere. Brazil is Latin America's dominant country, as measured by size, population, and economy. At the international level, Brazil has supported security efforts, from dispatching an expeditionary force to the Allied campaign in Italy during World War II to sending a battalion to Angola as United Nations Peacekeepers from 1995 to 1997.[1] Brazil is involved in a wider range of international issues and with a greater number of partners outside the Western Hemisphere than any other country in Latin America, and it backs up its interests with sophisticated diplomatic and organizational skills. In addition, Brazil has maintained more foreign policy continuity from administration to administration than is typical in Latin America.[2] Brazil has led political efforts for economic integration in the Southern Cone of South America through the Mercosul alliance of Brazil, Argentina, Uruguay, and Paraguay. And in 1998 Brazil was the United States' eleventh largest export market.[3]

Because of Brazil's great potential as an export market, many U.S. companies have established a presence there. All of the large high-tech corporations have been established in the country for years, and many newer companies are turning their attention to Brazil as an expanding market. In a 2000 interview in Austin, Texas, a Dell Computer Corporation executive stated that Mexico was Dell's largest export market but that the company anticipated Brazil would become its largest export market in Latin America. For this reason, Dell opened a plant in the metropolitan area of Porto Alegre.

With the inauguration of Brazil's internationally focused and reformist president, Fernando Henrique Cardoso, on January 1, 1995, and his reelection in 1998, unprecedented high-level contact and cooperation between Brazil and the United States began. President Cardoso visited Washington, D.C., in 1995, President Clinton visited Brazil in 1997, and First Lady Hillary Clinton, Secretary of State Madeleine Albright, Secretary of Defense William S. Cohen, Secretary of Commerce William M. Daley, and U.S. Trade representative Charlene Barshefaky visited Brazil in the late 1990s. Many other exchanges have taken place between U.S. and Brazilian cabinet and subcabinet officials.[4]

We can expect the interaction between Brazil and the United States to increase. According to the U.S. Commercial Service's *Country Commercial Guide Fiscal Year 2000*, Brazil's government has been increasing opportunities for the private sector through privatization, deregulation, and the removal of impediments to competition. U.S. exporters have been able to expand their sales to Brazil and to benefit from new business opportunities that are making Brazil one of the United States' strongest commercial partners.[5]

But despite this economic importance, the mental image most people have of Brazil, if they have one, consists of the exotic Amazon rain forest and Rio's bacchanalian *carnaval.* They are unaware of the country's disparate regions, such as colorful Bahia in the Northeast; conservative, colonial Minas Gerais; bustling, productive São Paulo in the Southeast; and the eco-city Curitiba and busy Porto Alegre in the South. Brazilians who live in the temperate climate of the country's industrious South say that North American visitors arrive fearful of giant snakes and expecting to see "the locals" swinging from trees. As one Brazilian said, many North Americans are hard pressed to say just where between Mexico and Cuba Brazil lies.

Brazil is an exciting and vital country, and its history and geography are such that it has salient national characteristics that are uniquely Brazilian. Much is known about the Spanish influence in the Americas, and Christopher Columbus is a familiar name to most North Americans. However, when one mentions Portuguese in the United States, the very word sounds exotic and unfamiliar. Certainly Pedro Álvares Cabral, who claimed Brazil for the Portuguese when he landed in Bahia in 1500, is not a household name in the United States.

The Spanish and the Portuguese both wanted to stake their claims in the Americas. The Treaty of Tordesillas between Spain and Portugal in 1494 gave land discovered west of the Line of Demarcation to Spain and land to the east to Portugal. Thus the intrepid Portuguese had laid claim to the large portion of Brazil that juts into the Atlantic Ocean. And since they subsequently pushed the boundaries, the western frontier of Brazil is not the straight line mandated but reaches far toward the western side of the continent. In fact, Brazil borders every country in South America but Ecuador and Chile. And to state the obvious, Brazilians speak Portuguese, not Spanish. As many language students will emphatically attest, the two are different languages.

As in most countries, in Brazil customs such as diet, dress, and attitudes differ from region to region. The most significant division in Brazil lies between the North and the South, causing some Brazilians to comment that their nation comprises two different countries. But along with the regional differences Brazilians hasten to point out, they also point to the many commonalities. Brazilians have many characteristics and perspectives in common, as Brazilians, that they do not share with North Americans. And, conversely, North Americans from very diverse regions of the United States share customs and beliefs that they do not have in common with Brazilians.

Beyond focusing attention on a nation's characteristics that seem exotic and foreign to outsiders, to communicate successfully across cultures it is sometimes important to just rely on common sense. Small towns in both the United States and Brazil, for example, are more conservative than are large cities, as is generally true throughout the world.

Embraceable Brazil

The prominent Brazilian statesman, politician, educator, and anthropologist Darcy Ribeiro states that Brazilians are the center of neo-Latin civilization in the New World, "better than the others because bathed in black and Indian blood, a people whose role from here on will be less a matter of absorbing European things than of teaching the world how to live with more joy and more happiness." [6]

Brazilians are a gracious people. The primary and ubiquitous rule for personal interaction for Brazilians is to remain courteous, pleasant, and cordial in all circumstances. Abrasiveness, friction, confrontation, loss of face, hostility, overt competition, and displays of individual ego are to be avoided at all costs. A Brazilian will not say "no" to you, a social nicety that can lead to more than a little confusion. If you learn little else about Brazil, remember the cordiality rule.

Like most customs, there are exceptions to the rule of cordiality. Perhaps the most significant involves the social discrimination of the haves against the have-nots. Brazil has a class system that clearly delineates the social location of its citizens. This class system is maintained in daily interactions. The culture's hierarchy governs Brazilian cordiality, and, consequently, it is first extended horizontally and upward in the social pyramid. Pleasantness is usually maintained when communicating down the social ladder as long as the person on the higher rung perceives that the person on the lower rung is properly deferential. A not inconsequential merit of this surface civility is the pleasantness it affords in daily interactions.

Brazilian culture is structured in two other distinct dimensions, *casa* and *rua*, as described by Roberto DaMatta. The first is the realm of the "house," that in-group dimension of trusted social relationships with family, kin, friends, and colleagues. This is the safe haven in what Brazilians often experience as a dangerous world. The other dimension is the out-group realm of the "street," where one faces the danger of the unknown, the foe, and the thief. The street is where one lives at risk. Cordiality is essential in the house and conditional in the street, although great care is taken to respect the street's hierarchical rules.[7]

Social interaction in general in the United States is conducted with more directness and bluntness than in Brazil. Brazilians experience unadorned North American directness of communication like a dash of cold water. But despite the difficulty that Brazilians sometimes have in coping with North American communication style, many Brazilians living in the United States express their appreciation of an underlying and more equitable respect of persons and human rights than they enjoy as Brazilian citizens living in their own country.

Brazil is a country where reality is perceived in a broad spectrum of color and all shades of gray. Things may be right, but maybe not, or they may be wrong, but maybe not. It depends. There is a great deal of latitude in the allocation and use of time. Civil law is broadly interpreted. And it is nearly impossible to catalog a huge segment of the population as to their "race"; they are Brazilian, which by definition is usually a mixture of races and ethnicities.

In contrast, the United States is above all a country of black and white. Things are right, or they are wrong. One is on time, or one is late. Business and law seek specific answers and concrete examples. People are categorized as either black or white. In the United States black/white segregation of the population was actually legislated, and a person who was "white" in phenotype was categorized as "black" if it could be determined that he or she had any black African ancestry, even if this was so far back that there remained no physical manifestation whatsoever— which is incomprehensible to a Brazilian.

The history, geography, experience, economy, and organization of a culture filter and shape the perceptions of its people, which in turn affect how they interact and communicate. Given that very different factors have shaped the two nations, communication between Brazil and the United States must bridge a vast cultural distance.

In Spite of Ourselves

Most of us think that we act through our own free will. But think again. For the most part, we do not.

All communication is a system of behavior. We cannot stop communicating, because all behavior is communication, and we cannot stop behaving in one way or another.[8] Communication specialists estimate that some three-fourths of all communication is nonverbal. Some have estimated a larger proportion. In addition, the proportion of nonverbal to verbal communication frequently varies from culture to culture. For practical purposes, however, what is significant is that a person communicates far more through nonverbal behavior—such as gestures, facial expressions, tone of voice, dress, body language, rituals, and courtesies—than through words.

Our behavior is taught to us from birth so that we will conform to the culture in which we live. We learn when we may speak and when we may not. We learn that some facial expressions earn approval while others provoke a reprimand. We are taught which gestures are acceptable and which are not; we learn whether we can eat food with our hands, which utensils to use at the table for what purpose, whether we need to hide the use of a toothpick with the other hand, when to shake hands, and whom we should kiss and in what manner. We learn how to address people with the words, honorifics, and titles approved by our culture, what tone of voice we should use, how close we should stand to people to converse, whether and where we should touch them, when and how to make eye contact and for how long, and countless other things that would be impossible to consciously remember and use at the same time when interacting socially. We learn this behavior well, because we must pass the ever-alert scrutiny of our peers in order for them to accept us and incorporate us into their social group.[9] The elaborately written subconscious cultural programming that we have internalized directs most of our social behavior; consequently, we govern only a small percentage of our actions by conscious choice and thought.[10]

We usually become aware of the culturally prescribed behavior that we expect from ourselves—and therefore from others—when someone *violates* the patterns we have been trained to follow. Such a violation raises our cultural rules to a conscious level of awareness. And we usually react negatively to any behavior that does not conform to our own norms, because we ourselves were trained largely through negative feedback. Negative evaluations cause dislike rather than like, avoidance rather than approach. They occur because the foreign culture deviates from the norms to which we are acculturated. The barriers are not necessarily reciprocal. They can be one-way, reflecting an unwillingness or inability to understand the norms of a foreign culture.

Most of us can clearly understand that we need to translate verbal language. We should therefore be able to understand unequivocally that we also need to translate the extensive nonverbal language that cultures use to communicate.

This does not mean that we all have to think, feel, and act in the same way. But to survive in a multicultural world, we need to be able to communicate with each other well enough to cooperate on practical issues.[11]

Some Definitions

Before proceeding to an examination of intercultural communication, let me first define some terms. I use a macro definition of "intercultural" that indicates differences between communicators relating to language, national origin, race, or ethnicity rather than a micro definition that, for example, might indicate the difference in "culture" between musicians and accountants. I focus on the obstacles that arise in communicating across cultures that are *inter*national, rather than target *intra*national subcultures (sometimes called co-cultures) that share the experience of living in the same polity. "Intercultural communication" means a transnational "transactional, symbolic process involving the attribution of meaning between people from different cultures."[12] I use the term "cross-cultural" synonymously with "intercultural."

"North American" refers to an English-speaking citizen of the United States who is an anglophone. An anglophone of northern European origin is sometimes called an "anglo" in the United States, but this latter term has a different, often pejorative connotation. One should note that the peoples of North, Central, and South America are all "Americans." When interacting with someone from the Americas, rather than say "I am an American," a citizen of the United States expresses this awareness and is somewhat more precise by referring to himself or herself as a North American, even though Canada and Mexico are also in North America. In past years Brazilians traditionally used the term "norte-americano/a" to refer to a U.S. citizen, but common usage in recent years has been simplified to "americano/a." "Norte-americano/a" now is usually confined to more formal language, or where specificity is desired, such as in the name Instituto Cultural Brasileiro Norte-Americano, a well-known Brazilian school where English is taught.

CULTURE IS A DYNAMIC, ongoing process that constantly creates, re-creates, and reinforces itself through its patterns of interpersonal communication. I will construct a model of Brazilian culture and national character and discuss how its distinctive features influence interpersonal communication. Because culture is central to the issue of intercultural communication, I begin with a map of cultural territory.

CHAPTER TWO

What Constitutes a Culture

Culture is how one does things. If one takes a list of everything one considers important, such as laws, family values, marriage and sexuality, money, political power, religion and morality, art, food, and pleasure in general, one can immediately identify a person's culture.[1]

Culture is communication and communication is culture. We constantly and silently communicate our real feelings in the language of nonverbal behavior, which our culture elaborately patterns.[2]

Cultural Interface

Intercultural explorations and exchanges may lead to mutual suspicion rather than mutual understanding, and to greater provincialism rather than greater sophistication.[3] One example of such an encounter took place in Santos, Brazil. An Englishwoman turned to a North American who was shopping in the same small grocery store that specialized in import items and commented, "I have been shopping here for twenty years, and these people have not learned to speak English yet." The opportunity to learn about a different society can shatter one's preconceived stereotypes, but many travelers cannot appreciate any country but their own and cannot seem to accept another society on its own terms.[4] Simple exposure to another culture does not guarantee better intercultural communication. Therefore, without adequate preparation, encounters between Brazilians and North Americans may result in cultural collisions, and negative stereotypes may be reinforced.

The Australian Jill Ker Conway, reflecting on English life in her autobiography, *True North*, observes, "[Like] every émigré, I was always keeping score, somewhere in the back of my mind, weighing and assessing what was good and bad about my new situation, testing the new society against my native one."[5] When some aspects of English culture irked her, Conway's husband recommended she objectively observe rather than react to English society. He urged her to mentally catalog and enjoy viewing their cultural traits as if the English were some exotic and interesting tribe wearing nose rings and elaborate tattoos.

Conway writes that there are climates of the mind. "Some expatriates never arrive spiritually in the new land."[6] The light remains foreign, and the climate is perpetually measured by the standard of another geographic zone. The senses of sight and smell continue to search for the familiar sensations of childhood. We irrationally tend to want other cultures to be like our own.

The sociologist Thomas Sowell maintains that isolated cultures stagnate, while cultures that communicate with others evolve.[7] If this is so, one would expect Brazil to evolve positively and rapidly, because of the Brazilian predilection for communication with other cultures. If some nations are renowned for their xenophobia, Brazilians are confirmed xenophiles.

Ray Birdwhistell, analyzing body motion communication, writes that we speak our own verbal language effortlessly, and only the most ethnocentric persons can believe that the verbal language of other societies is some distortion of their own "natural" human language. Yet when it comes to the nonverbal language of behavior, most people believe that their own behavior is a natural form of communication that foreigners have not developed, have learned badly, or have lost.[8] If we can clearly understand that we need to translate verbal language, we should be able to understand that we also need to translate the nonverbal language of behavior that is spoken by other cultures.[9]

The Concept of Culture

Culture is the logic by which we give order to the world.[10] It "is the whole view of the universe from which people assess the meaning of life and their appropriate response to it."[11] Put simply, culture is "the way we do things around here."[12]

Hall, in his catalyzing work *The Silent Language*, stated that culture is communication and communication is culture.[13] Culture governs communication and communication in turn creates, reinforces, and re-creates culture in a living dynamic circle.[14] In fact, the most important process in the survival of cultures is communication.[15]

From the day we are born, we are trained by our culture in every aspect of how we are expected to behave, in fact, how our society will permit us to behave.[16] It organizes not only how we behave but also how we think.[17] Ultimately a culture's goal is to make our behavior predictable enough that society can go about the rest of its business. In order to attain membership in our society, we must be incorporated into its communication system.[18]

Culture is the total communication framework for words, actions, body language, gestures, intonation, facial expressions, the way one handles time, decisions, space, and materials, the way one works, makes love, and plays—all these things and more are complete communication systems. We can only read meanings correctly if we are familiar with these units of behavior in their cultural context.[19]

Often, we realize that we do not understand the meaning of another culture's behavior. But when we think we understand when in fact we do not can cause problems. People may take offense when none was intended when they misinterpret such things as the use or omission of verbal honorifics, the dynamics of turn-taking, or the use of space, to name only a few possibilities from a potentially infinite list.

Anything that can properly be called cultural is learned, not hereditary,[20] and these learned ways of interacting gradually sink below the surface of the mind. They become hidden controls that an individual experiences as innate because they are ubiquitous and habitual.[21] Each one of us is a cultural expert in our own culture, but we do not consciously know what we know. Our trained subconscious antennae can read insincerity when verbal and nonverbal messages are incongruent, and we can anticipate aggressive actions from subtle cues. But this same ability will cause us to misread cues that have different meanings in another culture. When this happens, we may react in an inappropriate manner.[22] A North American woman may feel threatened by the intense and prolonged gaze of Brazilian men, while in Brazil this behavior is a common cultural expression of appreciation and general interest and is generally expected and welcomed by women. A Brazilian may be offended when a North American skips preliminary "small talk" because of a reluctance to "waste" another person's time.

Since we automatically treat what is most characteristic of our own culture as though it were innate, we are automatically ethnocentric. We are thoroughly trained to be so.[23] All groups tend to interpret their own nonverbal communication patterns as universal.[24]

Our informal and subconscious cultural rules are so familiar that we rarely need to express them. But in foreign cultural territory, an external guide will aid us greatly in finding our way.[25] By explicitly categorizing alien cultural patterns and rules, they can be more easily taught and learned.[26]

Tools for Understanding

Different cultures in the world have developed different skills according to the time, place, and circumstance in which they unfold, because cultural features evolve to serve a social purpose. The result is that today different people may confront in different ways the same challenges and opportunities with varying degrees of effectiveness. Cultures differ in their relative effectiveness for particular purposes.[27] *North Americans excel at detailed planning; Brazilians are masters at improvising in the face of impossible situations.*

To understand another culture better, we need to examine it from two vantage points. The external, *inter*cultural view does not consider the function of a culture's characteristics within its system. It tells us that a certain tribe pierces the nose, ears, and lips to wear bone and shell adornments. The external view simply *lists* alien behavioral characteristics or differences.[28]

The internal, *intra*cultural view considers cultural characteristics as units that have a functional purpose in a culture's communication system. It demonstrates how the wearing of certain bone and shell adornments by members of a given tribe makes clear statements about rank, rights, wealth, and marriage eligibility and is used by the culture to order daily interaction. It *explains* alien behavioral characteristics.[29] For the most successful intercultural communication, both the external and the internal approach should be used simultaneously.[30]

To increase our competency more quickly, it is helpful to know what kinds of obstacles we are likely to encounter when we attempt to communicate across cultural boundaries. We can most easily learn a new culture in manageable, categorized units, for this is how we learned our own.[31]

I begin by using a list of cultural categories to *identify* the characteristics of Brazil's culture from the outside (Table 2.1). These categories are those that are most likely to impede communication between any two cultures.[32] Sensitizing ourselves to the idea that differences exist is the first step toward attaining intercultural communication proficiency, and, at least sometimes, this exercise should engender the concept that we are different from others and not always that others are different from us. Next, we can increase our understanding of behavior that seems foreign or inappropriate by trying to comprehend its function within Brazil's culture.[33] Brazilian culture frequently mandates verbal and nonverbal behaviors for personal interaction that are quite different from those prescribed as appropriate and desirable in the United States.

TABLE 2.1. *Cultural Communication Categories*

Culture		
Perception	Behavior	
	Verbal Processes	Nonverbal Processes
CULTURE-SPECIFIC	• Oral	• Body Motion
• Collectivism versus Individualism	• Written	Communication
		Eye Contact
• Face		*Facial Expressions*
• Hierarchy		*Gestures*
• History and Experience		*Touch*
• Materialism		*Posture*
• Power		*Smell*
• Preconceptions		• Context
• Role		• Immediacy
Class		• Physical Characteristics
Gender		*Extensions of Self (Artifacts)*
Race		*Physical Appearance*
• Rules		*(Phenotype)*
• Social Organization		• Space Sense
Family		• Speech Characteristics
Government		• Time Sense
• Symbols		*Monochronic*
• Thought Patterns		*Polychronic*
• Values		
• Worldview		
CULTURALLY PERSONAL		
• Adaptability		
• Attitude		
• Ethnocentrism		
• Uncertainty		

NOTE: For a more detailed discussion of these categories, see Novinger 2001.

Considering culture by the categories that most affect Brazilian–North American communication will help us to anticipate, recognize, and surmount potential difficulties.

It is important not to lose sight of the fact that culture is active, not static, that it continuously evolves. Thus we should stand ready to add to and adapt any list of cultural characteristics that we use. Ideally, we will learn to suspend judgment about the unfamiliar or seemingly offensive verbal or nonverbal behavior of any person while we ask ourselves, How is this behavior useful, or how does it originate in culture? This will cause us to think before we hasten to judge. Occasionally, of course, we may conclude that a person is obnoxious, but we will understand that we are evaluating the individual and not the culture. And although I address here *inter*cultural communication, the concepts presented will be useful in everyday *intra*cultural communication in our own cultures.[34]

Differences in cultural characteristics can create communication obstacles in the *process* of verbal and nonverbal personal interaction. But because culture as a whole creates different ways of *perceiving* events and behavior, it is also important to broadly consider categories such as history, religion, form of government, and preconceptions that form the cultural matrix in which the perceptual filters of a people develop.[35] The interrelationships of cultural categories are complex.

The Culture Chasm

Richard Pells writes that many expatriates living in Europe after World War II found the experience an occasion for introspection. A number of writers and intellectuals spoke of an awakening to the strengths and deficiencies of their culture of origin. We may need each other for self-definition. How can we know what is distinctively British, French, or Mexican without describing what is distinctively German, Italian, or Japanese? How can we know what is distinctively Brazilian without defining what is North American?[36]

The great gift of intercultural interaction is the opportunity to catch a rare glimpse of the strengths and weaknesses of our own cultural system; it has value beyond simply experiencing an "exotic" encounter.[37] Freeing ourselves from the grip of our unconscious culture cannot be accomplished without such self-awareness.[38]

FOR PEOPLE OF DIFFERENT cultures to communicate, verbal language is an obvious and important ingredient. Many experts have competently addressed the vast subject of verbal language. Therefore, rather than focus on the verbal communication process, I examine the history, government, customs, and experiences that have shaped and continue to shape the perceptual filters of Brazilians and Brazil's nonverbal language of behavior.[39]

CHAPTER THREE

Perceptual Filters in Communication

We should be able to recognize that another culture is different, without judging it defective.[1] *It is all in how we perceive things.*

Communication is like a kaleidoscope. Many cultural units of different sizes, shapes, and color make up the whole picture. Any action, shift, or change adjusts the pattern and the relationship of all of the units to each other, thereby altering the picture.[2]

The Filters of Culture

We select, evaluate, and organize the stimuli of the outside world through an internal process of perception. From the time we are born, we learn our perceptions and resulting behaviors from our cultural experiences.[3]

Each of us has personal characteristics that developed in the matrix of our culture. These characteristics filter our perceptions of events and affect how we experience the world. We evaluate and take action in accordance with what we perceive. Our perceptions directly affect our verbal and nonverbal behavior.

The Brazilian anthropologist Teresa Pires do Rio Caldeira analyzes São Paulo, the city where she spent most of her life, in *City of Walls*. She is a native speaker of Portuguese, the language in which she studied up to her master's degree, wrote her first book, and conducted the research for *City of Walls*. But she wrote the latter in English. She recalls the constant complaint of a copyeditor: "What is the subject? Do not write in the passive voice!" She thought it useless to explain that a sophisticated academic style in Portuguese is frequently structured in the passive voice and often with an ambiguous subject. But as she wrote, she realized daily that, more than her words, her *thinking* had been shaped by her language and her culture.[4]

The question was not one of words and grammar alone. Anthropology has a corpus of theory, method, and literature that is shared by practitioners worldwide—an international style or reference point. But Caldeira became acutely aware that points of view have strong local and national biases and that the discipline of anthropology is, therefore, plural: there are "anthropologies." What North Americans think relevant and exciting often does not centrally concern Brazilians, and vice versa.[5]

Caldeira realized that just as her English has an accent, so does her anthropology, her thinking. At one point, the differences in perceptions between the two cultures became so acute that she considered writing two books, one in Portuguese and one in English, to address two culturally different audiences. She concluded, however, that since her own thinking and perceptions had been transformed by simultaneous immersion in both cultures, she could only artificially squeeze her subject into one cultural mold or the other by sacrificing important insight. Exposure to two different cultural perspectives had broadened her understanding of her subject, just as approaching any issue from multiple cultural perspectives broadens understanding.[6]

A North American engineer who worked at Lockheed for many years recounted that he had a customer who had to be treated with kid gloves. The engineers were told that if the customer perceived they had erred or misled him, then, in fact, they had—because perception is reality.

Personal Perceptual Characteristics

UNCERTAINTY

Most people try to avoid situations that are uncertain, because the unfamiliar almost universally causes discomfort. When we try to communicate with a person from another culture, often we are not sure how to act, and we are unsure as to whether we understand each other correctly. Because we are conditioned to expect others to behave and communicate as we ourselves do, another person's deviation from our cultural patterns makes us uncomfortable. We feel awkward. Because we cannot effectively use our native subconscious cultural programming in an unfamiliar behavioral environment, cross-cultural communication is more tiring and stressful than is communication with members of our own culture. The resulting anxiety compounds the problems of intercultural communication.[7]

To reduce uncertainty, a person involved in an initial encounter usually begins by trying to assess the similarity between herself or himself and the other party. In this process, there are two important goals: first, we try to predict the other's actions; second, we attempt to explain to ourselves the causes of the behavior we observe.[8] In cultures that are organized collectively, people often try to reduce uncertainty about a target person through in-group relationships.[9] Brazil is a collective culture, and people rely heavily on family, friends, and colleagues for information about another person's characteristics. Brazilians also reduce uncertainty by taking time to get to know and evaluate people before doing business with them. North Americans can improve their communication with Brazilians by obtaining introductions from mutual friends or business colleagues to initiate a relationship whenever possible and by consciously participating in the culturally important process of getting to know each other before attempting to initiate business discussions.

ATTITUDE

Goodwill and honest desire on both sides will overcome many intercultural communication barriers. A negative attitude interferes with communication.[10] Barriers to intercultural communication are not necessarily reciprocal, and animosity should not be assumed.[11] When one who is exposed to a new culture is adaptable, open-minded, and disposed to be friendly and curious, remarkable changes in thinking can occur.[12]

A positive attitude helps to bridge language differences. Just hearing a foreign accent negatively affects some people's motivation, as they anticipate that they will need to expend great effort to communicate.[13] The barrier to communication in such a case may be primarily one-way. A positive attitude will also mitigate clashes in cultural norms. Many people evaluate a foreign culture negatively only because it deviates from the familiar standards of their own. While people may be unable to understand fully the norms of a foreign culture, willingness to do so is crucial. Willingness is an attitude that one can choose.

A U.S. corporation sent two petroleum engineers to collaborate with Petrobrás in the city of Santos. One of the engineers was interested in Brazilian culture and willing to learn, and he enjoyed his stay in Brazil. The other judged negatively the many salient cultural differences he encountered; he was unhappy and less productive and soon left. The attitudes people bring with them to another country and how much they are willing to learn about its culture color the experiences they have.[14] Attitude works both ways in Brazil–U.S. communication. Brazilians visiting the United States will benefit most if they examine cultural differences in order to understand them rather than dwell on what they dislike about the differences.

Gary Althen, in *American Ways*, points out that foreigners often deplore those characteristics of North American culture that are related to qualities they admire. Impersonality and a rapid pace of life may contribute to the efficiency of organizations. Individuals can often avail themselves of better job opportunities when they are free to move away from their families, and this mobility may well be related to divorce. Aspiration to material well-being may motivate North Americans to hard work and productivity. And individualism is related to a sense of freedom.[15]

Althen points out that the characteristics of what we call a "culture" are interrelated. One cannot transplant one or two characteristics of North American culture into Brazilian culture (or vice versa) if the transplants are incompatible with other aspects of society.[16] Brazilians complain that North Americans eat dinner too early and that parties end too soon. But North Americans who pride themselves on their punctuality, work ethic, and arriving early at their jobs cannot continually stay out late and maintain their work patterns. Although many North Americans love Brazilian parties, the culture's spontaneity, and Brazilians' informal measure of time, they cannot always reconcile these traits with the unforgiving North American schedule.

Foreign visitors who make the effort will begin to see how various characteristics of Brazilian culture fit together and the function each serves, even though they may not like a particular characteristic. Focusing on objectively understanding behavioral traits rather than subjectively judging them permits visitors to interact more constructively with Brazilians to achieve their purposes.

Research has found that attitudinal similarity is an even stronger correlate of attraction than cultural similarity.[17] North Americans often comment about someone approvingly, "We speak the same language." Usually this does not refer to communication with a "foreigner," nor does it refer to verbal language. Rather, it indicates the attractiveness and ease of communication with a person who has the same ideas, values, behavior, and life.[18]

ETHNOCENTRISM

"People begin with different operating environments and run different [mental] software. People have different databases and they process information differently. As a result, they arrive at different results." [19]

Learned cultural perceptions that are narrow and cause rigid behavior are ethnocentric.[20] A fundamental human truth is that each of us expects everyone else to behave just like we do and thinks that we all perceive the world in the same way under normal circumstances.[21] Hall observes that many North Americans attribute cultural differences in other people to their not being fully "developed" according to the North American model.[22]

In recent years, the national sport in Argentina has been to blame Brazil, "the giant economy to the North," for its economic difficulties. Demonstrators carry signs that protest "Made in Brazil, No!" and declare "If we buy only Argentine shoes, the country will 'run' better." With the devaluation of Brazil's currency, the real, in 1998, Brazilian products became cheaper in Argentina, and Argentina's exports to Brazil dropped.[23] The uproar over Mercosul in South America is reminiscent of NAFTA controversies in North America.

We can point to many national cultures that are convinced of their own superiority. But although a person belongs to a culture or society that admittedly has expertise or dominance in some area, it is in his or her best interest to move past ethnocentrism to better communicate with others.

Gustavo Franco, Brazilian economist and former president of the Banco Central, states that the most serious foreign invasions of Brazil have been in the area of direct investments, which rather than bring suffering have brought benefits. He goes on to comment that Brazilian nationalism has never manifested itself in racism or hate; it is moderate and without rancor. Therefore, Brazilians view nationalistic demonstrations with a certain condescension. Europe is definitely not the same: caution and fear are widespread, and the wounds of the past are immense.[24]

There are many examples of ethnocentrism in Brazil–U.S. communication. Moacyr Pereira has a master's degree and is the comptroller for a high-tech North American company in São Paulo that I will call "Trexcel." It is not surprising that Moacyr is required to keep accounting records and financial statements in the format used by Trexcel worldwide to standardize company records and reports. But the Brazilian government also mandates a specific format for accounting and reports, and Moacyr must keep records as required by the government. When pushed by his manager to keep the records only in the format established by Trexcel, he explained the situation. Instead of discussing ways to streamline the workload necessary to do business in Brazil, the North American executives with whom he works retorted, "Change your government." Such a response is both unrealistic and unproductive. Further, it demeans both Moacyr and the Brazilian government.

Moacyr is bright and efficient, and Trexcel has to rely on his knowledge and experience to navigate the vast bureaucratic maze that constitutes doing business in Brazil. It would be in Trexcel's best interest for its North American executives to broaden their ethnocentric focus so as to collaborate with this key employee.

Lourenço Juvenal also works for Trexcel. He was the first Brazilian executive hired when the company established its operation in Brazil. He commented that North Americans usually have no comprehension of Brazil's economics, monetary changes, international exchange rates, and history of inflation, nor can they conceive of what it is like to work in Brazil's environment. Even in the United States it can be difficult to work out meaningful financial projections because of the many variables that must be taken into account. But in Brazil there can be such a large number of variables, each with a wide range of possibilities, that there have been periods during which it was impossible to make valid financial projections. Juvenal finds that this economic scenario lies outside the experience of most North Americans. This may be less of a problem in the future, as Brazil's rampant inflation has been tamed to single digits in recent years.

Jonathan Frieze worked for Procter & Gamble for many years. In addition to his administrative and business expertise, Frieze spoke Spanish and had traveled and worked extensively in Latin America. In addition, he had studied Portuguese and was well informed about Brazil because of his personal interest. He interviewed for a key position at Procter & Gamble in Rio de Janeiro and was selected from among several competent candidates. After being assigned the position, he inquired about whether his knowledge of Portuguese had been the deciding factor. The executive's response was, "Oh, do they speak Portuguese in Brazil?"

Pells writes that all societies view the differences they encounter in others negatively. Many North Americans assume that all foreigners secretly wish to emulate the United States and expect them to reorganize their institutions according to the North American model. They tend to evaluate other countries by how closely they resemble the United States, judging not only a nation's social institutions but also its plumbing and its kitchens. To communicate well, we need to accept that another culture can be different without being defective.[25]

A concomitant of ethnocentrism is the assumption of similarity. Unless this tacit assumption is made explicit, there is no chance of correcting resulting misinterpretations.[26] A North American may expect Brazil to be peopled largely by individuals like herself (more difference might be expected in Tibet, for example) and underestimate the effect of an unfamiliar cultural environment. You can never assume, for example, that addressing a multicultural or foreign audience is the same as speaking to a group made up of members of your own culture.[27] Whereas many North American speakers typically open with a joke, this is not customary in Brazil. Brazilians feel that joking in this situation is undignified and detracts from its seriousness.

People who demonstrate low ethnocentrism typically have a tolerant and strong personality. They think multidimensionally, are comfortable with uncertainty, and have high self-esteem. Ethnocentrism and empathy are opposites.[28]

ADAPTABILITY

Brazilians are cultural cannibals. They avidly consume the parts of foreign cultures that they like, assimilate them, and Brazilianize them. Whether fashion, a word, an attitude, or a trend, if they like what they find, they consume, digest, and transform the trait for their own benefit.

Adaptability is the capacity to alter the structure and attributes of one's psychic system to meet the demands of the environment and to suspend or modify one's cultural ways to manage creatively the dynamics of cultural difference.[29] To some degree, one can consciously choose to be more or less adaptable.

Brazilians exhibit forbearance and an extraordinary degree of adaptability in the face of discomforts and hardships that might drive others to protest or even to open revolt. The amiable Brazilian copes amazingly well under difficult circumstances. Page, in his comprehensive book, *The Brazilians*, writes that these qualities may have developed as a reaction to the futility of openly challenging Brazil's social hierarchy, rigid laws, and unresponsive bureaucracy.[30]

A salient national characteristic of Brazilians is that, individually and collectively, they have the ability to change with astonishing speed.

Brazilians embrace that which is foreign. The São Paulo theologian Lourenço Stélio Rega cautions that although this enthusiastic adoption is not undesirable in and of itself, Brazilians should take care not to disdain or reject a priori that which is national.[31]

In 1994 Brazil began its leap into the information age. The use of cellular phones, computers, and the Internet skyrocketed: Brazil is both wired and wireless. On a driving trip through the open, sparsely populated countryside south of Porto Alegre, visitors Annie and Carl Nimos were in the middle of nowhere on a deserted side road. They watched a beat-up old pickup truck (*um picape*) jolt along the road toward them. It traveled at a moderate pace only because of its rattletrap, dilapidated condition. As it passed by, they read with delight the announcement "www.churrasqueria.com (www.barbecue.com)" painted boldly on its side.

Brazilians can generally be described as adaptable, flexible, open, and curious. During the time Moacyr Pereira worked for Sousa-Cruz in São Paulo, the company participated in a worldwide executive exchange program, whereby an executive worked for a specified period at another company to broaden his (or, theoretically, her) knowledge and perspective of various aspects of business. With typical enthusiasm, some forty Brazilian executives from various companies volunteered to go anywhere in world. North American executives who participated in the program volunteered primarily for intranational exchanges. At the far end of the spectrum, German executives expressed their preference for only intracity exchanges.

As speakers of a relatively obscure language, historically Brazilians have had to learn other languages in order to communicate in the world. In learning other languages, particularly English and French, they also absorbed cultural perspectives and assumed some of the other cultures' postures.[32] Brazilians have a long history of being francophiles, but in recent years, for economic and practical reasons, the study of English has become a passion for many Brazilians. By 2000 ads everywhere in Brazil admonished the public to "learn English or perish." Brazilians' ability to learn the English language is remarkable. For example, while visiting the small town of Estrela in Rio Grande do Sul, Annie Nimos met Rosanne, who teaches and speaks English comfortably, although she has never traveled outside of Brazil. Rosanne speaks with a Brazilian accent and occasionally uses sentence construction and chooses a word different from those of a native English speaker, but her command of the language is excellent and she communicates without difficulty. She loves English. Through effort and interest, many Brazilians have attained similar proficiency, even though their exposure to English has been in their own country.

A former Procter & Gamble executive observed that in the 1980s in Rio, unlike in most Spanish-speaking countries where he had worked, Brazilian top executives and the elite rarely spoke English. Either one had a command of Portuguese or one's efforts to do business were seriously hampered. Recently this has largely changed, and it is not uncommon to encounter executives who speak English well. Even so, it is important for foreigners to understand that speaking Portuguese will open doors and cement relationships in a way that is not otherwise possible.

The capacity to creatively alter and adapt oneself is the metacompetence for intercultural communication.[33]

People are certainly more adaptable when they are motivated. Pedro de Moraes Garcez, a professor of communications, writes that empirical evidence indicates participants in cross-cultural communication "routinely gloss over major communicative differences when it is to their advantage." Research shows that both native and non-native speakers of a language will accommodate the party with whom they wish to communicate under certain circumstances; they can and do diverge from their usual language and interaction style when it is in their best interest.[34] In addition, when negotiating, motivated parties will try to keep the process going until they reach agreement. This may be more common when people step into a metaphorical neutral zone to conduct international business. There, each party tends to suspend some of their native cultural communication traits.

In general, Brazilians think that North Americans are ingenuous and not adaptable or street-smart. A Brazilian language professor in the United States said, "[North Americans] believe anything you tell them, even if you tell them you are going to bring them fifty kilos of something totally absurd." North Americans, in turn, think Brazilians are not "serious." To some extent, these perceptions have to do with North Americans expecting verbal language to be information-specific in content, whereas Brazilians often do not employ language in this way.

Culture-Specific Perceptions

"The idea itself does not really travel, only the code; the words, the patterns of sound or print. The meaning that a person attaches to the words received will come from his mind. His interpretation is determined by his own frame of reference, his ideas, interests, past experiences, etc.—just as the meaning of the original message is fundamentally determined by the sender's mind, his frame of reference."[35]

We need to become acquainted with some of the cultural factors that shape our perceptual filters. I begin below with some simple definitions and then expand on these concepts in subsequent chapters.

COLLECTIVISM VERSUS INDIVIDUALISM

One of the most fundamental ways in which cultures differ is whether they are organized collectively or individually. In some cultures, membership in a collective group is permanent and not subject to choice. Belonging starts with the self and the family at the core and includes extended family, close friends, and trusted colleagues. The responsibilities of membership come before the rights of individuals. Anyone with whom you wish to have a relationship needs to be incorporated at least at the fringes of your group. The essence of a relationship is to be able to incur reciprocal obligation.[36]

Collective cultures require close, very personal interaction, and people in these cultures are far more dependent on one another than those reared in an individualistic society.[37] Collectivists are best encouraged by appealing to their group spirit and by requesting cooperation, whereas persons in individualistic cultures are often motivated by individual competition.[38] Brazil is organized collectively; the United States is organized individually.

FACE

"Face" is a person's value, standing, or prestige in the eyes of others. In many cultures, the concept of face is of great importance, and one must take great care in disagreeing, criticizing, or competing.[39] Maintaining face is of utmost importance in cultures such as Brazil with steep social hierarchies; in the United States, it is less important.

HIERARCHY

All living things have a ranking order,[40] and all cultures have some degree of hierarchy. However, the steepness of the hierarchy differs from culture to culture. Steep hierarchy in a society encourages respect for rank, harmony, formality, and inflexibility and discourages social mobility. A less steep hierarchy is decentralized and more democratic and encourages participation based on declassification, equality, exploration, adventure, flexibility, and social mobility. There is, of course, some overlap.[41]

Generations of North Americans have been raised to believe that anyone can improve their status in society through hard work and that this improvement is desirable. This attitude toward class mobility is very different from that in countries where the dominant belief is that each person has a station in society and that station is where the person is most comfortable. To try to rise above one's station brings discomfort or pain, and to fall below one's station is undesirable.[42]

The use of language and ritual courtesies can change or reinforce the steepness or flatness of a society's hierarchy. For example, when Germans get angry, they may shout and their faces turn red. But typically they will maintain proper "distance" and hierarchy by using the formal and correct "Sie" for "you," even while hurling epithets.[43] Brazil has a steep and unforgiving social hierarchy, whereas hierarchy in the United States has a flatter profile.

HISTORY AND EXPERIENCE

The history of a country and the experience of its daily life mold individuals' perceptions. Some cultures maintain history as part of the living present, and this colors people's perceptions of their daily lives. Other countries are said to lack historical memory. Brazilians and North Americans have different histories and experiences, which causes them to perceive many aspects of the world differently, but both nations are said to lack historical memory.

POWER

Significant differences in power or status between groups often cause people to assume certain attitudes or to adopt certain positions for effect when interacting. This can be demonstrated in ways as diverse as defensive, subservient, or aggressive behavior. Such posturing tendencies interfere with successful communication between groups both within a nation and between nations.[44]

The strong and successful and the weak and poor perceive their relationship and positions differently. The strong attribute success or failure to individual traits and underestimate the influence of external factors. They tend to exaggerate their generosity and criticize the recipients' lack of gratitude. The disadvantaged attribute lack of success to the "system" rather than to themselves. They see the successful as demanding and selfish. They also seek recognition and respect, which the strong seldom give because they rarely understand the need.[45] One can see this phenomenon at work in interpersonal communication within cultures as well as in communication between cultures. The disparity in national power affects Brazilian–North American communication.

PRECONCEPTIONS

People tend to see what they expect to see and, further, to discount that which conflicts with these preconceptions, stereotypes, or prejudices toward persons or cultures.[46] In contrast to preconceptions, however, people can constructively categorize unfamiliar or complex data to make sense of it. One way to understand our own and other cultures is to create a model based on a culture's general characteristics. Such a mental representation, or model, will change with the introduction of new information. In contrast, stereotypes are fixed and rigid and stamp identical characteristics on all members of a group.[47]

ROLES IN SOCIETY

Cultures may prescribe roles for persons based on their gender, race, or social class.[48] One's position in society and the type of work he or she is expected to do or not do may be predetermined by these characteristics, and depending on the culture, it may be more or less difficult to act in another role. Gender, race, and social class can dictate whether a person takes a dominant or submissive role when interacting with others.

RULES

Cultural rules are based on ideas.[49] They govern formality and ritual and what types of interaction take place when and where.[50] There is not much flexibility in cultural rules, and one must learn the rules of a target culture to communicate effectively.[51] The rules arbitrarily set for formal attire in the Western world, for example, may be very different from those dictated for formal dress in other parts of the world.

SOCIAL ORGANIZATION

Cultures typically organize themselves into formal or informal institutions, such as government and family.[52] These institutions affect how the members of the culture communicate. Government and its representatives may be respected and honored, or suspected and feared. Families may primarily include the small nucleus of parents and children or may be defined as an extended network of several generations of relatives, including aunts, uncles, cousins, and in-laws and their relatives.

SYMBOLS

A culture often has abstract symbols that are agreed on and respected by groups.[53] If, for example, culture A is tightly organized around a political symbol, it may be difficult if not impossible for culture A to communicate effectively with culture B.

The Brazilian diplomat Lauro Moreira writes that the Brazilian has a certain disrespect for symbols. In 1964 a serious debate arose when the military dictatorship judged the public's attitude toward national symbols such as the flag and the anthem as lacking in respect and pride. But Moreira counters that the Brazilian easily separates the symbol from what it symbolizes. He explains that, for example, on the opening stanza of the national anthem at a public gathering, people usually stand and feel emotion, but by the time the second stanza is played people have lost interest in it. Moreira says that this is not lack of respect; it simply means that one stanza is enough. If Brazilians are gathered for a soccer game, what is important is life, the game, and the presence of friends and other people. For the Brazilian, symbols are only symbols, not the thing itself.[54]

THOUGHT PATTERNS

Different cultures arrive at their concepts of reality in different ways. One's perception of reality may come through faith or belief, independent of fact. It may come from fact based on evidence, which is the most predictive concept of reality. Or a culture may perceive reality primarily through feelings or instinct, the most common basis in the world.[55] Cultures also may organize their thoughts and communication starting with details and coming to a point, or starting with a point and then backing it up with details.

VALUES

We learn values through acculturation. Values are the learned organization of rules that we use to make choices and to resolve conflicts.[56] Differences in value systems can hinder intercultural communication.[57] Religious values are manifested not only in dogma but also in living patterns and outlook.[58] Materialism emphasizes money, work, and material success. To respect another culture's values can conflict with one's own values as a basis for judgment. There is a great deal of debate over relative and absolute values.[59]

WORLDVIEW

Worldview may well be the most important cultural perception and the most difficult to describe. It is a culture's orientation toward God, nature, life, death, the universe—the meaning of life and "being."[60] It affects how one views and confronts daily living.

WE USE OUR CULTURAL filters to assess what goes on in the world, and we then communicate our perceptions through both verbal and nonverbal behavior. We will next consider the history of Brazil so as to help us understand how the experience of being Brazilian influences communication with other cultures.

PART II

Resplendent Brazil
Land of Paradox

CHAPTER FOUR

A Capsule of History

A culture's history has everything to do with its style of communication. It molds the perceptual filters of its people; it colors attitudes; it often dictates rules that functionally affect communication in daily life.

"Brazil has created, beneath a facade of harmony, a contradictory society." [1]

Resplendent Brazil

Joseph Page recounts that the resplendence of Brazil has contributed to the ironic saying, "God is a Brazilian." Brazilians tell the self-deprecating joke that an angel complained to God that He had allocated disproportionate physical splendor and resources to Brazil and spared the country natural scourges such as hurricanes and floods. God replied, "But wait until you see the people I'm going to put there." [2]

It is difficult to encapsulate the salient characteristics of such a large, diverse, and dynamic country as Brazil. It is a country of continental dimensions, larger in area than the United States, if one excludes Alaska and Hawaii. It spans a wide band of tropics in the north and narrows to an area of temperate climate in the south. It is a rich, lush country full of crushing human poverty. It is a country where people immerse themselves in warm and gratifying human relationships with family and friends but go into the streets of the large cities always alert to the possible dangers that await. Smooth, friendly personal interaction predominates in Brazil's culture, but this pleasant surface dresses an exacting hierarchy and racial and social discrimination. Democracy successfully deals with some of the country's problems, but people constantly seek a way (*um jeito*) around laws that inconvenience them, as well as those that unjustly constrain them. Citizens' primary concerns revolve around personal safety, economic stability, health care, and education, especially functional literacy.

In some cultures, history is a part of the living present, and it colors people's perceptions of their lives on a daily basis. This would certainly be true in eastern Europe today in a way that is not the case in Brazil or the United States. Some Europeans complain that in the Americas there is lack of respect for the past; others declare that the people of the New World are emancipated from the shackles of history. Still others say that many in the New World rarely look back because they are certain that the best lies in the future.[3] Certainly, a characteristic that Brazil and the United States share is that neither society has the cultural and daily consciousness of the past that permeates society in Europe or even in Mexico.

Brazil's antecedent European culture is Portuguese, not Spanish. Since Portuguese culture is often referred to as Lusitanian, Brazil is frequently referred to as Luso-American or as a Luso-tropical country. Brazilians do not consider themselves "Latins." And in the Southeast and the South of Brazil, one sometimes hears people say that they have more in common with the United States than they do with the Northeast and North.

The Portuguese culture that influenced Brazil is called Lusitanian after the ancient Roman province of Lusitania on the Iberian Peninsula, which corresponded roughly to modern Portugal. Portugal's equivalent of the Iliad *and the* Odyssey *is the literary classic* Os Lusíadas *(The Lusiads).*

A Plantation Colony

The Portuguese crown divided Brazil into fifteen east-west strips of territory. These areas were called captaincies and were given to wealthy Portuguese families to govern and from which they extracted wealth to bring back to Portugal. The captaincies constituted an authoritarian, steeply hierarchical form of society that imposed stability on Portugal's colony in the Americas.

Bahia, in the Northeast, where Portuguese cultivation of sugarcane began, was initially the most significant economic and political region of Brazil. Brazil's well-known sociologist, Gilberto de Mello Freyre, writes of early colonial Brazil in terms of the "master's house" (*casa grande*) and the "slave quarters" (*senzala*), which are vivid symbols of the social development of the country, especially in the North and Northeast. Their development in this agrarian area established a semifeudal plantation society with all of the advantages and disadvantages of a patriarchy. Brazil's plantations created what Freyre describes as the most stable civilization in Latin America.[4]

Freyre writes that the slaves who were brought to Brazil came from the most advanced cultural areas on the African continent and that these slaves became an active and creative element in the colonization of Brazil. They were more than just labor; they had a civilizing function. From Africa came workers who were skilled in agriculture, mining, forging, and cattle raising and who were cloth and soap merchants, teachers, priests, and Muslim prayer leaders.[5]

In the United States an optimist is said to see the world through rose-colored glasses. In Brazil, the optimist says that "everything is blue" (está tudo azul).

Freyre seems to view aspects of slavery through rose-colored glasses, glossing over many of its horrors. Nonetheless, he points out the positive contributions of the Africans who were forcibly brought to Brazil, which has sparked a sense of pride and dignity in the many Brazilians who have African ancestors. Before Freyre, Brazilians of mixed race (a majority of Brazilians) had to contend with the then popular attitude borrowed from Europeans that the miscegenation of Amerindians and Africans with the Portuguese (and other Europeans in Brazil) resulted in a diminishment of positive genetic European traits.[6]

Freyre also points out the many Moorish influences that the Portuguese brought to Brazil. The Moors had occupied the Iberian Peninsula for some eight hundred years. Freyre refers to a Moorish "gentleness" in the treatment of slaves. He also notes as Moorish influence the love of the sound of running water from spouts and fountains. He recounts that in the nineteenth century children in Brazilian schools would chant multiplication tables and reading passages, just as is done in Moslem primary schools, and that in the interior of Minas Gerais and São Paulo women would cover their heads with *mantilhas* to go to mass, in the style of Arab women. But, of course, the Moorish influence that came via the Iberian Peninsula can be observed throughout Central and South America. The Jews also unmistakably influenced the Portuguese colonizers of Brazil. Freyre attributes the Portuguese love of commercial activities to Jewish influence.[7]

Slavery was a significant factor in Brazilian history. Following Brazil's discovery by the Portuguese in 1500, Brazil imported some 3.5 million Africans as slaves, and by 1800 Brazil had the largest slave population in the world. At that time the country's 1.5 million slaves equaled one-half of its population. British naval pressure finally forced Brazil to halt its

Atlantic slave trade in 1850, after it had flourished for three hundred years. Slavery took longer to dismantle in Brazil than in any other society in the Americas and finally ended legally with the Golden Law of May 13, 1888.[8]

Another factor in Brazil's racial mix was heavy European immigration between 1887 and 1914, when approximately 2.7 million people, primarily from Italy, Spain, and Portugal, arrived in southeastern and southern Brazil. By 1900 the majority of the citizens of São Paulo were immigrants or children of immigrants. These immigrants gradually replaced the slaves that had worked in the important coffee fields of the Southeast. The large, relatively recent influx of immigrants to this area turned southeastern and southern Brazil into a society quite different from the older mining region of Minas Gerais and the Northeast with its sugar plantations.[9]

From Colony to Republic

Although Spain had fought fiercely and futilely to retain what it could of its American colonies, in the early nineteenth century Portugal and Brazil took very different historical paths. When Napoleon invaded Portugal in 1807, the Portuguese crown preferred retreat to imprisonment. The monarchy recognized that Brazil *was* the Portuguese economy, and the royal family along with ten thousand Portuguese sailed to Rio de Janeiro, transferring the center of the empire to Brazil. This would be the only time that a European monarch would rule his world empire from the colonies. Dom João reigned over Portugal's Asian, African, and American colonies from his court in Rio, and while the Spanish American colonies warred with Spain for independence, Brazil flourished as the center of the Portuguese empire. The presence of the Portuguese monarchy and court in Brazil brought together the elites of the two nations and paved the way for independence. This also permanently moved the concentration of power from the Northeast of Brazil to the Southeast.[10] The presence of the royal family spread excitement and pride throughout Brazil. Although Portuguese officials controlled the bureaucracy in Rio at the top, Brazilians were integrated at the lower levels.[11]

ALTHOUGH DOM JOÃO might have returned to Lisbon when the Napoleonic wars ended in 1815, he remained in Brazil. But when in 1821 a new and aggressive Portuguese parliament, the Côrtes, threatened Dom João's power and returned Brazil to colonial status, he reluctantly returned to Portugal. Before departing he is said to have advised his twenty-three-year-old son, Pedro, to lead the emerging movement for

Brazilian independence if it became powerful, rather than oppose it. This would put father and son on two thrones rather than lose Brazil's throne to the revolutionaries.[12]

On September 7, 1822, Dom Pedro I received an order from Portugal challenging his authority. He brandished his sword and shouted, "Independence or death!" (known as the Grito do Ipiranga). He was proclaimed emperor of Brazil and crowned constitutional monarch of the new nation. The withdrawal of Portuguese troops was completed within a year with remarkably little bloodshed (which contributes to the belief that Brazilians are a nonviolent people).[13]

On achieving independence from Portugal, the Empire of Brazil maintained national unity despite its enormous size and even though Spain's South American possessions had split into nine independent countries. The Portuguese distaste for organization resulted in a lack of centralized control that allowed substantial local autonomy, so independence did not provoke separatism in outlying regions of Brazil. In addition, the presence of the royal family was a strong unifying influence.[14]

Although Pedro I had liberal sentiments, he ruled as an autocrat and also remained deeply involved with Portugal. Faced with rebellion in Brazil in 1831, he opted to abdicate. He thus twice spared Brazil from war: first when he supported Brazil's move for independence in 1822 and again when he abdicated in 1831. Pedro I returned to Portugal and left behind his eldest son, Pedro II, who was five years old and grew up a virtual orphan. The child received an extraordinary education from tutors, and in the meantime a council of regents ruled the country. In 1840, at the age of fourteen, Pedro II accepted the crown offered to him by Brazil's parliament, and he reigned as an enlightened monarch for forty-nine years. During this period, which was called the Second Reign, Brazil maintained an enviable political stability, in stark contrast to Mexico and Peru.[15]

The transition from monarchy to republic began initially with little bloodshed, similar to the transition from colony to empire. A small group of conspirators with support from high-level army officers initiated a coup d'état in 1889, and Dom Pedro II chose exile over resistance. The military ran Brazil's First Republic until 1894, when power was handed over to an elected civilian president, Prudente de Morais Barros.[16]

Brazil Today

To understand Brazil," you need to look at two sides of the coin: modern and electronic on one side, old and well worn on the other.[17]

Brazil encompasses half of South America and possesses one-third of the population of Latin America; it has immense wealth and widespread poverty; the South is heavily European, and the Northeast heavily African. It boasts modern industry, and although its agriculture has been outdated, it is in the process of modernizing. One Brazilian economist quipped that the country should be called Belindia because its modern industrial base resembles Belgium and its backward social structure is more like India. Brazil's social structure spans a wide gap—a small class of the rich and sophisticated and masses of the poverty-stricken and poorly educated.[18]

Brazil is the fifth largest country in the world in area and the fifth most populous. It is the world's largest Catholic nation. It is nearly 2,700 miles wide and 2,500 miles long. The major cities in the Northeast are physically closer to West Africa than to neighboring Peru and Colombia. In 2000 it had a population estimated at 170 million people, compared to a U.S. population of approximately 275 million. And in 2000 Brazil had the tenth largest economy in the world, just behind the seven major industrial powers—the United States, Japan, Germany, France, Italy, the United Kingdom, and Canada—and Russia and Spain.[19]

Brazil is a federal republic: A República Federativa do Brasil. It has twenty-six states and a Federal District. The federal government has executive, legislative, and judicial branches. The 1988 Constitution grants broad powers to the federal government. The Congress consists of two houses, the Senate and the Chamber of Deputies, and state representation in the Chamber is only loosely proportional to state population. The system is heavily weighted in favor of less populated states. In addition to this imbalance, Congress is characterized by a large number of political parties—sixteen in 1999.[20]

A coup in 1964 established a military dictatorship that lasted until 1985. The Brazilianist Thomas E. Skidmore writes:

> The military who seized power faced one extremely awkward political fact: They had no firm legal basis for their intervention.
> This would not have bothered many Latin American militaries, but the Brazilian officers had a strong legalist streak and they wanted legitimacy.[21]

In a very Brazilian paradox, an "institutional act" was issued to authorize extraordinary powers for the executive branch of government, that is, the dictatorship, in an effort to "legitimize" it. The use of torture by the regime was common and widespread and privately justified by military officers as necessary to obtain "hot" information immediately after arrest, but the torturers continued their work for weeks and even months after the victim's arrest, when justification could not even be pretended.[22]

In conversations with diverse educated Brazilians, Annie Nimos found that it is considered common knowledge that Brazil's military received training in sophisticated methods of torture from U.S. specialists. U.S. President Lyndon Johnson recognized the military government just hours after the coup.[23]

According to the anthropologist Teresa P. R. Caldeira, disrespect for individual rights and justice is the main challenge to the expansion of Brazilian democracy beyond the political system. This disrespect can be seen in the privatization of security, which is escalating because of public distrust of the police forces and the justice system. Caldeira states:

> Even under democratic rule, the police in Brazil frequently act outside the boundaries of the law, abusing, torturing, and executing suspects, and the justice system is considered ineffective by the population. As a result, an increasing number of residents of São Paulo are opting for types of private security and even private justice (through either vigilantism or extralegal police actions) that are mostly unregulated and often explicitly illegal. Frequently these privatized services infringe on and even violate the right of citizens. Yet these violations are tolerated by a population that often considers some citizenship rights unimportant and even reprehensible.[24]

The experience of violence is a violation of civil rights, and it affects the quality of Brazilian citizenship. Caldeira maintains that violence and disrespect for civil rights constitute one of the main dimensions of what she calls Brazil's disjunctive democracy: "Brazilian citizenship is disjunctive because, although Brazil is a political democracy and although social rights are reasonably legitimated, the civil aspects of citizenship are continuously violated."[25]

Regions

Brazilians identify closely with their regional roots. According to Eakin, a state of mind, as much as geography and culture, leads Brazilians to see themselves as northeasterners, as *gaúchos* (from Rio Grande do Sul), as *cariocas* (from Rio de Janeiro), or as *paulistas* (from the state of São Paulo). This is similar to North Americans' consciousness of the accent and cultural traits of southerners, Californians, and New Yorkers. Much like other nations of continental dimensions, such as Russia, Canada, the United States, China, and India, Brazil has endeavored to impose national unity on regional diversity. However, Brazil has perhaps been more successful at creating a stable and subtle balance between national and regional culture and identity than any other large nation.[26]

Ribeiro writes:

> No matter how differentiated they may be in their racial and cultural matrices and in their ecological-regional functions, or in respect of being descendants of old settlers or recent immigrants, Brazilians have come to know themselves, to feel themselves, and to act as a single people, belonging to one and the same ethnicity. They are, it must be said, a national entity distinct from all others, speaking the same language, differing only in regional accents less noticeable than the dialects within Portugal. They take part in a body of common traditions that is more meaningful for all than is any one of the subcultural variants that distinguish the inhabitants of a region, the members of a class, or the descendants of one of the formative matrices.[27]

There are certainly some parallels between Brazil and the United States. According to John Krich, both countries are continent-sized, frontier-driven, slavery-haunted, immigrant catchalls.[28]

Out of a complex collision of Europe, Africa, and the Americas, Brazilians have forged a nation of substantial achievement and with enormous potential. The mixing of races over centuries has resulted in an ethnic fusion that frees Brazil from the bitter racial divisions found in many societies.[29] It is estimated that some five million European immigrants have become integrated into Brazil's population, four-fifths of whom entered the country in the last century. Their numbers overall may be unimpressive, but their role was important in the South, where they created a white European environment. However, Ribeiro points out, by the time these immigrants began to arrive in great numbers, the national population was already so large numerically and so defined from an ethnic point of view that it was able to begin its cultural and racial absorption of the immigrants without any great changes in its makeup.[30]

Brazil does not have the racial division characteristic of the United States and South Africa. Although regional, social, economic, and political inequalities divide Brazilians, they nonetheless share a common linguistic and religious heritage, and few nations of Brazil's size have so successfully created such a strong sense of national culture and national identity. Contrast this to the fratricidal violence of India, which is divided by language, religion, and caste. As Freyre wrote, Brazilians have fashioned a new Luso-tropical civilization that is unique and that should be a source of great pride.[31]

Page points out that even though a common Brazilian identity unifies the nation, there have always been southerners urging the secession of the states of Paraná, Santa Catarina, and Rio Grande do Sul to form an independent republic. In fact, Rio Grande do Sul was an independent nation at one time, as was Texas in the United States. From time to time separatists in the South attract national attention, but any breakup of Brazil is not likely because of national and military opposition.[32]

If a Brazilian cannot get weekend or holiday reservations anywhere else, he should go to Brasília. One can always get a flight and hotel room there.[33]

Historically, some 90 percent of the population of Brazil lived within one hundred miles of the coast. But in the 1960s Brazil constructed a new capital on a barren plateau in the interior of the state of Goiás. The construction of this new capital succeeded in drawing people to and opening roads in Brazil's interior, as the project was intended to do. Page comments that Brasília is very much a city without a past and thus symbolizes the absence of historical memory, one facet of Brazilianness.[34]

Brazilian Legends

In Rio Grande do Sul, people recount the legend of the little black herd boy (o negrinho do pastoreio). His master's son maliciously scattered the herd of horses Negrinho was tending. The master, known for his heartlessness, whipped Negrinho senseless and put his bleeding body on an anthill. After he lay for three days consumed by ants, the blessed Virgin, godmother to those who have none, raised Negrinho up, made him whole, and brought back the horses. Now he can be seen galloping through the countryside with his herd, except for the three days a year that he returns to the ants. Gaúchos revere him as a legend or a saint and petition him to find lost animals and possessions. A Porto Alegre newspaper recently ran an announcement seeking a talented ten-year-old black boy to play Negrinho for a cinematic production of the legend.

The colorful origins of the Brazilian people weave many legends, superstitions, and beliefs into the nation's popular culture. During colonial times, the Brazilian child lived surrounded by frightful creatures of the imagination. Some came from stories told by African slaves, others were

modified from the Portuguese, and yet others from Amerindians. The Brazilian psychologist Roberto Gambini states that the more bizarre, menacing, abnormal, and anomalous an image, the more important and Brazilian it is. He writes that Amerindians and Africans in Brazil were never afraid of these images. As a result of this heritage and these traditions, the Brazilian psyche is peopled by beings of phantasmagoric appearance and attributes. They appear in religion, art, and music.[35] People today still widely believe in these creatures.[36] Some of these bizarre beings are

• *a māe-d'água*—mother-of-water, also called Iara, a Brazilian version of the universal siren, luring men into rivers, lakes, and the sea.
• *o saci-pererê*—a one-legged black imp wearing a red hat and with a pipe in his mouth, who hops around and plays mischievous or malevolent tricks on people.
• *a caipora* or *o curupira*—a gnomelike creature with backward feet who protects the forest. It punishes people who hurt plants or animals, allowing them to kill animals only for food.
• *o boitatá*—a giant snake that takes form and undulates through the night sky as a blue and yellow light. It feeds on eyes and devours those of any person who looks at it.
• *a cabra-cabriola*—a horrible monster evoked to scare children into good behavior.

- *a mula-sem-cabeça*—a woman who had a child or amorous relations with a priest was punished by a transformation. She is condemned to wander the night on Thursdays and Fridays as a terrifying headless mule that emits fire from its neck. (The priest is apparently not thus condemned.)
- *a peitiça*—a bird with such an endless and irritating call that it drives people to great extremes.

Legends often reflect the reality of the Americas. The United States perpetuates the story of the marriage (not just the physical union) of Pocahontas and John Rolfe. Their union was seen as exceptional; the pair was never viewed as being the "parents" of the nation's people. Brazil has

Nossa Senhora Aparecida (Our Lady of the Appearance), the patron saint of Brazil.

a contrasting Pocahontas story. The Amerindian woman Iracema (her name is an anagram of *America*) and the Portuguese colonist Martím are said to have produced the first Brazilian from their union. This is similar to the union of La Malinche and Cortés in Mexico, who are said, in local lore, to have produced the first Mexican. The majority of Brazilians have traditionally seen themselves as originating from a mixing of races and heritages.

Nossa Senhora Aparecida (Our Lady of the Appearance) is the patron saint of Brazil, and she is traditionally represented as black-skinned. She seems to have female counterparts in Iemanjá and Oxum as "mothers" or "patron saints" of the nation. Iemanjá is the goddess of the sea. She is black, like Nossa Senhora Aparecida, and originates in African lore. On New Year's Eve in Santos and Rio people gather on the beaches carrying candles to pay homage to and entreat Iemanjá as an intermediary to supreme deities. They cast white flowers into the sea as a tribute. Oxum is the goddess of freshwater rivers and lakes, and she also is petitioned for her favors. Nossa Senhora Aparecida, Iemanjá, and Oxum comprise a spiritual triumvirate of females who dwell in the psyches of most Brazilians.

BRAZIL'S DISTINCT HISTORY is such that it requires closer consideration of the country's racial makeup and the singular race relations that have evolved. Races and ethnicities have blended into a significant and essential "Brazilian" component of the country's culture and therefore of its communication style.

CHAPTER FIVE

Racial Fusion

In general, communication between people of different races in Brazil is more pleasant than in the United States. The cloud of defensiveness, or mutual dislike, or palpable hostility that often hovers over interracial contact in the United States is usually refreshingly absent.

Brazil's best-selling writer, Jorge Amado, remarked, "There may be individual racists in Brazil, but there is no philosophy of racism—an important distinction." [1]

A Racial Composite

In the 1440s the Portuguese initiated the Atlantic slave trade. By 1500 African slaves constituted approximately 10 percent of Lisbon's population of 100,000. Over the ensuing three hundred years, roughly 1550 to 1850, that Europeans transported human captives from Africa to the Americas, it is estimated that 10 million to 12 million Africans survived. Brazil was the destination of more than one-third of all Africans transported to slavery in the New World; the United States received approximately 6 percent.

The result of approximately 3.5 million slaves arriving in Brazil and approximately 750,000 black Africans being enslaved on the plantations in the southern United States can be seen in the racial mix of the respective nations today. African Americans comprise some 11 percent of the U.S. population; in Brazil some 45 percent of the population have African ancestors.[2]

When the Portuguese began the colonization of Brazil in earnest in 1532, they already had one hundred years of experience in tropical environments such as India and Africa. To the colonists, the dark-skinned indigenous woman of the Americas resembled the familiar and desirable Moorish woman, like the enchanting mermaid of Portuguese (Lusitanian) legend. The Portuguese had a propensity for miscegenation, first with the Amerindians and then with the black women they brought from Africa. The Portuguese were more open to racial mixing than any other European people.[3] A contributing factor was that the early Portuguese immigrants to Brazil were usually single adult men.[4] The later wave of European immigrants in the nineteenth century was more often composed of families.

What is most notable about the population of Brazil is that from its discovery by the Portuguese in 1500, the racial and cultural mixing of Portuguese, Amerindians, and Africans began. The first "Brazilian" is said to have been the son of a Portuguese father and an Amerindian woman. The superstar singer Caetano Veloso stated in an interview published in the *Washington Post*, "A Brazilian always says—always, even if he is blond and blue-eyed—'We Brazilians all have black blood.' It's a myth that has been taken up by everybody. Something like this would be unthinkable in the United States."[5] Today, when Brazilians speak about their forebears, they are likely to comment that they are of Portuguese, or Japanese, or Lebanese, or *Brazilian* descent. "Brazilian" in this context is by definition a person of mixed race. It is widely and matter-of-factly stated in Brazil, "If you marry a Brazilian, your children can turn out to be any color." It is not remarkable for parents to produce children each of whose skin is a different hue, from very light to very dark. Indeed, this racial blend is one of Brazil's most endearing qualities and frequently produces physical characteristics of sensual and exotic beauty.

Annie Nimos grew up in Santos, Brazil, where her father worked for Petrobrás. She attended local schools and swam competitively on a local team. She had known one of her swimming teammates, Marcos, for years. She ran into Marcos one day with his family on the beach near the Boqueirão. With mild surprise, she noted that his mother was clearly of African descent, while Marcos looked more Portuguese, like his father. Each brother and sister had a different complexion; some siblings were of obvious African phenotype, while others were not. She realized that she had never given any thought to Marcos's racial makeup, an attitude that prevailed among her friends and was common in Brazil.

As people swarm along the pedestrian Rua dos Andradas in Porto Alegre, or in downtown São Paulo, or on other central streets of Brazil's cities, skin color, hair texture, and eye color are randomly mixed. One might see two women in their fifties, walking arm in arm, one very European in appearance and the other very African. They might be sisters or dear friends—either combination would be common. In public places, one does not see ethnic groups or people of similar complexion segregate themselves in the way that one commonly observes in the United States.

One can say "Negro" in Brazil. Like Asian or Arab, blond or redhead, it is a descriptive, not a pejorative, word.

PERCEPTION OF RACE and color in Brazil is different from that in the United States. The film documentary *Nascí Mulher Negra* (I Was Born a Black Woman), directed by Maria Luiza Mendonça and Vicente Franco, presents a portrait of Benedita da Silva, the first Brazilian woman of African heritage elected to Brazil's senate. In this documentary, one sees a woman of African phenotype describing herself as light-skinned, although in the United States she would be perceived as quite dark. The documentary points out that in Brazil sports and entertainment personalities may be dark-skinned, but one does not often see dark-skinned people in the higher ranks of government, the military, or business. Because of her position, society tried to attribute white, male characteristics to Senator "Bené," and she said that she had to reclaim her public status both as black and as a woman.[6]

Through centuries of miscegenation between individuals of Portuguese and African descent, the Brazilian mulatto, considered a distinctively attractive variation of the nation's racial blend, evolved. In the Amazon region the union of Portuguese with Amerindians produced the *caboclo*. People of the Northeast often combine Amerindian, African, and Portuguese phenotypes, occasionally highlighted by traces of the Dutch who occupied the region during the eighteenth century. The population of the interior of southern Brazil is a mix of Amerindians, blacks, migrants from São Paulo, immigrants from the Azores, and people who crossed the borders separating Brazil from the Spanish colonies that became Uruguay and Argentina.[7]

Satomi Furuichi writes that Brazilians do not necessarily prefer "white" as a skin color. She found in studies of census reporting that fewer respondents selected "white" to describe themselves and preferred a mulatto category when the word *moreno* (dark) rather than *pardo* (brown) was used to describe race. *Moreno* implies beauty in Brazil, especially for women.[8] However, one North American woman with a forty-year history of working in and traveling to Brazil offers a counterpoint. She recounts hearing "incredibly racist" remarks made unselfconsciously by educated Brazilians, both in the North and in the South, and separated by at least a decade in time.

In a lecture on the conceptual design of the 2000 census, a Brazilian sociologist reported that in a preliminary field study the respondents did not understand the question when asked if they were of "African" origin, so this term was not introduced as a new racial category for census taking. The 1991 Brazilian census placed blacks at 5 percent, mulattos at 39 percent, Asians (under the category "yellow") at 1 percent, and white at 55 percent, with respondents determining their category themselves. Marshall Eakin points out that to be "black" in Brazil means to have no white ancestry, whereas to be black in the United States means to have any black ancestry.[9] In addition, the census classifications do not reflect the broad color spectrum and complex intermingling of the Brazilian people.

The No Prejudice Ideal

Brazilians often claim the most nearly perfect racial democracy in the world, blending white, black, Amerindian, and Asian without rancor and discrimination. Brazil does have an easygoing acceptance of different races, respect for the educated black, and extensive interracial friendships, courtship, and marriage. Darcy Ribeiro writes:

> This coming together of so many and such varied matrices might have resulted in a multiethnic society torn by clashes among differentiated and unmixable components. Quite the opposite has taken place: in spite of the survival of marks of their multiple ancestry in physical appearance and spirit, Brazilians have not split up into antagonistic racial, cultural, or regional minorities tied to their different ethnic loyalties.[10]

Nonetheless, analysts point out that a disproportionate number of blacks have low-paying occupations and power is concentrated in the hands of an elite that is lighter-skinned.[11]

Eakin states that for a long period, Brazil was fabled to have no racial prejudice. In addition to racial mixing, Brazil's blending of religions also helped to break down the distinctions between black and white. Not all blacks practice religions with African influences, nor do all whites adhere to European-style faiths. It is possible in Brazil to be a Negro without being African and to be both white and African at the same time. "Africa has been thoroughly integrated into the mainstream of Brazilian culture."[12]

Page recounts that Brazil's multiracial, multiethnic society appeals greatly to populations around the world and is exported via its *telenovelas* (serial soap operas that usually last less than a year). The good quality, universal themes, multiracial casts, and tropical sensuality of Brazil's *telenovelas* strongly appeal to Latin Americans, Europeans, Africans, and Asians alike.[13]

Brazil's multiracial makeup is evidenced in many venues. In Rio Grande do Sul, said to be the country's most "European" state, a crowd

Street children on a church outing in Rio Grande do Sul represent Brazil's racial mix.

assembled in the capital at the doors to the legislative assembly to attend a vote on wages. Even here in the far South, the mix of people who gathered had a heterogeneous physical profile, displaying skins of multiple shades and hues, and hair of diverse texture and color.

The Prejudice Reality

DaMatta writes that Brazilians have a special capacity to adopt and adapt things positively for their own use, and they have glorified the mulatto and *mestiço* as the perfect synthesis of all the best characteristics of whites, Amerindians, and Negros. Brazil is not a dualistic society that operates solely with the logic of in or out, right or wrong, black or white. DaMatta describes the mulatto as an intermediary between two racial extremes and as representing a synthesis of two opposites; such a synthesis, he remarks, has high value in Brazilian society, which abhors antagonism in personal relations.[14]

DaMatta explains that the racism of the United States and South Africa makes "black" and "white" mutually exclusive terms and that this is a brutal concept to the cordial Brazilian. Brazilians have an infinite and varied range of intermediate categories between black and white, and the mulatto represents the whole range. DaMatta also describes Brazilian racial prejudice as more contextualized and sophisticated than that of North Americans, which is direct and formal. He maintains that since Brazilian racial prejudice is variable, it becomes invisible—and, as a consequence, more difficult to combat.[15]

Page writes that in the mid-twentieth century Brazil continued to question the abilities of its racially mixed population and whether an underdeveloped tropical nation could compete successfully with the countries of Europe and North America, where Brazilians felt they were regarded as "savages." According to Page, miscegenation has significantly complicated the relationship between whites and blacks. Some Brazilians see miscegenation as the basis for a single, harmonious *mestiço* society, but others think it camouflages serious social and economic inequities between races.[16]

Ribeiro describes the huge sector of blacks and mulattos as possibly being the most Brazilian component of the population. He proposes that slavery de-Africanized them, and being neither Amerindian nor white, they could find identity only as Brazilians. Blacks do not cling together to fight for their ethnicity of origin but as persons integrated into one Brazilian people. In his opinion, in Brazil whites are becoming ever darker, and many are proud of this fact.[17] But one also overhears approving comments about interracial unions, on the basis that they will "whiten" the population.

Aside from the Portuguese, no other culture and people had more influence in Brazil than the Negro from Africa. Freyre states that almost every Brazilian is marked by this influence. The black woman nursed him, fed him bits of food with her fingers, and told him the first stories of creatures and monsters of superstition. Freyre believes that the African Negro generally had a culture that was superior to that of the Amerindian. He writes that the Negro was well adapted to the tropical climate and thus fared better than did the Amerindian or the *caboclo*.[18]

Freyre recounts that in colonial times black and dark-skinned boys studied with light-skinned boys in plantation classes and in schools, and sometimes they all learned to read from a black teacher. There was a great deal of socializing among plantation owners and slaves. Many slaves were baptized as Catholics while allowed to keep African customs. Some prayed to São Benedito or Nossa Senhora do Rosário, both of whom were black. According to Freyre, the black slave brought joy into the life of the Brazilian, who was marked by the melancholy of the Portuguese and the sadness of the Amerindian. Africans added vivacity to the celebration of saints' days, dances, carnivals, and feasts of the Magi. And though many slaves died or chose death because of hardship and homesickness, Freyre maintains that slaves filled the plantation homes of Brazil with music and life.[19] Freyre's positive presentation of the contributions of African culture to Brazilian society caused people to correctly attribute many of the negative legacies of slavery to the institution rather than to the race of the slaves.

The belief that racial discrimination does not exist in Brazil is the prejudice of not having prejudice.[20] Such a prejudice is a formidable weapon against blacks, because no criticism of society on this count can be made if Brazilians deny the existence of racism.[21] The overt and hostile racism in Europe and North America operates differently than Brazil's subtle, veiled racism.[22] Roberto DaMatta states that racism Brazilian-style makes injustice tolerable.[23]

Page points out that even in discrimination the Brazilian conducts his personal interaction with more gentleness. Even so, private social clubs for upper- and middle-class Brazilians regularly refuse admittance to blacks. Exclusion from the networking of these clubs is a great disadvantage because Brazilians personalize relationships in every aspect of life, with friends calling on friends for favors.[24] According to a Brazilian executive at the U.S. Commercial Service in a large city, Brazil's prestigious Fundação Getúlio Vargas does not admit blacks, and its administration protested when a gifted black student from the United States was to come with a group for a program being held at the Fundação. The journalist Lucy Dias declares that formal racial separation does not exist in Brazil. She maintains that it does not have to, because social exclusion takes care of separating the races.[25]

Statistics confirm that the skin color of people of the lower socioeconomic strata in Brazil is proportionately darker as one descends the social ladder. Furuichi points out that the waves of European (and Asian) immigrants in the nineteenth and early twentieth century had more education than native Brazilians, protection from the governments of their countries of origin, and sometimes more money. These and other factors contingent on their being immigrants contributed to their rise in economic status. That most of this wave of immigrants came as families meant that they entered into fewer interracial marriages, resulting in lighter-skinned persons at a higher economic level than the "native" Brazilian population who were in great part descendants of early Portuguese colonizers, slaves, and Amerindians.[26]

It is interesting to note that in this nation of immigrants, the Brazilian constitution of 1891 banned African and Asian immigration.[27] A later federal decree in 1907 restricted immigration from Asia but permitted admittance of Africans.[28]

Brazilians who have African physical characteristics can be called ne-gro, prêto (black), mulato, or moreno. The designation African Brazil-ian or Afro-Brazilian is not commonly used to describe people in Brazil.

Black Brazilians who have had contact with the civil rights movement in the United States debate whether affirmative action might be appropriate for Brazil. Aside from whether this would be politically possible, how would one apply such a measure in the Brazilian context?[29] As one Brazilian university professor commented, given the racial mix in Brazil, the concept is senseless and, furthermore, it would simply be impossible to figure out who would qualify for benefits.

Similarly, Page points out that with five hundred years of miscegenation, it is difficult to create race-based programs or establish a black movement in Brazil, because it is difficult to establish who would qualify. One consequence of Brazil's racial spectrum, as opposed to a color line, has been that political candidates who have sought to identify themselves with blacks have fared badly in elections, whereas blacks seeking office based on ability have won some important races. In 1990 voters elected three governors of African heritage, one of them in the state of Rio Grande do Sul, where a majority of the population is white.[30]

According to Gambini, when Brazilians say "we Brazilians" they are conscious of being a multiracial and multicultural people, a blend of races. But he feels that although Brazilians see themselves as being made up of various racial parts, they identify with some parts and not others, or value some parts over others. Some Brazilians say that of the three original races that practiced miscegenation in Brazil, only the Negro could withstand and survive slavery. Gambini opines that Brazilians grow up believing that the Negro was strong and could withstand anything and was therefore the builder of the Brazilian economy. He thinks that the Negro is consequently seen only as a material contributor to the nation and that the person's humanity and identity are therefore denied.[31]

Page explains that discrimination in Brazil is by color and not by race. Marshall João Batista de Mattos, grandson of a slave and the first black to achieve the army's highest rank, is quoted in a magazine article as saying, "If an individual is of Negro origin but this doesn't show in the color of his skin, he won't suffer any restriction."[32] Ribeiro writes that the distinctive characteristic of Brazilian racism is that it is based on color of skin rather than on racial origin. Black means coal black. The mulatto is brown and is viewed as half-white. With a slightly lighter skin, he or she integrates into the white community. In Brazil, "whitening" can be purely cultural or social. Successful blacks socialize with whites, intermarry, and in the end are considered white. A successful professional or artist cannot be defined as *black.* The black painter Santa Rosa talked with a young black man who was complaining about the color barriers that hindered his diplomatic career. Santa Rosa replied, very sympathetically, that he understood the young man's case perfectly, because he was black once too. To add to the complexity, the miscegenation of Portuguese with Amerindian results in a phenotype lighter than the Amerindian, yet still dark. According to Ribeiro, to the eyes and racial sensibility of any Brazilian, these mixtures are white.[33]

North Americans often ask why Brazilians of African heritage have done so little to protest discrimination. Skidmore explains that the dynamics of race relations in Brazil have been remarkably stable because blacks, mulattos, and whites have all believed in the "myth of racial democracy." The first element of this myth is that race is only a secondary variable in determining life chances. Most Brazilians believe that social class, education, or the luck of the clientelistic culture are more important variables. Second, Brazilians know that the patrimonial system works against mobilization from the bottom. And third, there is almost a complete absence of nonwhite solidarity, a problem unique to Brazil.[34]

Only in Brazil

Page recounts a remarkable story. Recently, three years after the fact, it was discovered by chance that two babies had been switched at birth in the hospital. Each family loved the happy little boy it was raising. Despite daily news coverage and avid public interest in custody considerations, no reports remarked on the fact that one of the boys was black and was accepted at birth by white parents and that the other boy was white and was raised without question by dark-skinned parents. This clearly illustrates that racial miscegenation is common and accepted in Brazil.[35]

But in this paradoxical country where a light- and a dark-skinned baby can be switched without question by the parents, a university professor in Rio Grande do Sul, European in appearance, describes how his sister, who is dark-skinned, suffers discriminatory treatment because of it.

In June 2000 Annie Nimos visited a small class for adults at an English-language school. The class focused on vocabulary for business and law and was attended by a judge, an attorney, an accountant, and a university student. In talking about the United States, the judge expressed his concern about the racial attitude of North Americans. He stated that democracy in the United States does not work as well as North Americans think it does, because it does not adequately deal with the country's problem of racism. He gave as an example of racism the abusive treatment of Mexicans trying to enter illegally along the southern border of the United States. He commented that people go back and forth freely across Brazil's southern borders with Uruguay and Argentina. The judge then informed the accountant in the class that should the accountant go to the United States, he would be considered black. The accountant had brown eyes and an olive skin, and North Americans would probably take him to be of Italian or Latino heritage.

The impressions that the people in one nation have of people in another nation are often based on highly publicized events and do not take into consideration more mundane daily activities. Certainly, the concern a Brazilian might have with racism in the United States, given Brazil's racial mix, is justified. However, to think that an olive skin categorizes a person as African American and that no Mexicans come and go easily across the U.S.–Mexico border is an inaccurate assessment. Watching the news on television in Brazil, it is easy to understand how people acquire such beliefs. As in the United States, any news about Mexico–U.S. relations seems to involve the most tragic incidents of undocumented migrants crossing into the United States. There certainly was not any footage of the multitude of people, Mexicans and North Americans, who on a daily basis go back and forth by car and on foot across the Laredo–Nuevo Laredo bridge. Gerardo Bernard stated that people in Brazil are not categorized by their physical appearance as drastically as in the United States. Brazilians are taught that they are first and foremost *mestiço*. This is taken for granted, and it is nothing to be ashamed of. Brazilians do not discuss multiculturalism and diversity, which are as much a part of their daily lives as the air they breathe. Bernard sees North Americans as extremists, pointing out that the United States is the only country in the New World where segregation was mandated by law.

Bernard also recounted that in recent years there was an attempt to form an organization of "black" musicians in Bahia. To join, the skin color of adherents had to be black, not a mulatto brown. In response, appropriately named Carlinhos Brown, an "African" Brazilian, organized Bloco Alternativo music to include all colors of skins. He wanted to get away from the very un-Brazilian concept of a color line, which dictated that only black skin warranted membership in a group.

Over and over, one hears from people considering the societal organization of the United States and Brazil that the United States divides its population into two parts on either side of a color line, whereas Brazilian society encompasses its whole population across a broad color spectrum. The racial makeup of the Brazilian people represents a major cultural difference between the United States and Brazil, as does each nation's perceptions of and attitudes toward race. And in Brazil, as with race, life and reality are perceived as a continuum, a spectrum of shades of color; in the United States not only people but ideas and events tend to be neatly categorized as this or that, as black or as white.

In Brazil, on the one hand, personal interaction across the racial spectrum is most often relaxed, unselfconscious, and enjoyable. This quality has an intrinsic positive value from which many nations can learn. On the other hand, any bias that underlies a surface of pleasant communication may still be prejudicial in proportion to the darkness of a person's skin. Race relations in Brazil are complex and, indeed, contradictory.

ONE CAN SEE HOW Brazil's history and racial makeup mold cultural characteristics that are peculiarly Brazilian. Another important facet of this giant country that colors Brazilian outlook and practices is the singular economic environment that people confront on a daily basis.

CHAPTER SIX

Surviving the Economy

"Brazil is a rich country full of poor people." [1]

Brazil is not underdeveloped. It is underdistributed.

Economic Profile

In June 2000 the United Nations released its report on the Index of Human Development, a measurement of the quality of life in 174 countries. Factors in addition to economic statistics are considered: per capita income is adjusted for purchasing power, and life quality takes into consideration access to health care and potable water, life expectancy, and education to arrive at a "misery," or poverty, index.[2]

This report, based on an analysis of 1998 statistics, indicates that in Brazil the poorest 20 percent of the population have 2.5 percent of the country's income, whereas the richest 20 percent have 63.8 percent of the country's income. This distribution is among the most inequitable in the world.[3] Life expectancy averages 67 years, as compared to 73.1 in Argentina, 74.1 in Uruguay,[4] and 77.12 in the United States.[5] Further inequality exists in Brazil based on region, for example, 80 percent of the inhabitants of the state of Maranhão fall below the poverty level, compared to 20 percent in the state of São Paulo.[6] Tens of millions of urban and rural poor are marginalized. Of Rio de Janeiro's population of 5.7 million, 1.2 million live in the *favelas* (slums), which were not included on the city's maps until 1994.[7]

Between 1870 and 1970 the only country in the world that grew economically more than Brazil was Japan, and from the 1930s to the 1980s Brazil became the world's tenth largest economy and the most industrialized among developing nations. This belies the widespread belief that economic growth and industrialism ensure a higher standard of living. The contrast between affluence and abject poverty in Brazil is stark and ubiquitous. The huge disparity between wealthy and poor is seen most strikingly in Rio de Janeiro. Rio's exclusive beach area has been described as two blocks of a tropical and affluent Paris surrounded by the stark misery of Ethiopia.[8] First and Third Worlds exist side by side.

Brazil's economy has taken its citizens on many a wild ride. Inflation in the early 1990s was astronomical, then improved. There was a financial crisis in the late 1990s, but the economy recovered and expanded by 4.5 percent in 2000. Then in 2001 the value of Brazil's currency, the real, had slumped 20 percent by August, and the Central Bank had pushed its benchmark lending rate to 19 percent to forestall the threat of inflation. Electric power was rationed, with consumers forced to cut back their usage by an average of 20 percent. Such economic vagaries are difficult to survive.[9]

Nonetheless, the country's recent prosperity is evident in the widespread embrace of technology. The Internet is growing rapidly, e-business is spreading, and during the last few years of the 1990s the number of telephone lines in Brazil tripled and the number of wireless phone users jumped from 5 million to 20 million. Vendors on street corners in major cities offer wireless Internet access via mobile phone. In just a few years, Brazil became a very sophisticated market.[10] Trudy Rubin of the *Philadelphia Inquirer* wrote in 2001, "This is a country with top-notch universities, high-tech exports and half of Latin America's Internet users. Cell phones and automatic teller machines are ubiquitous, and all Brazilians vote electronically on machines that do an instant tally."[11]

A July 2000 newspaper article ranked the ten largest fortunes in Latin America. Four of the ten were Brazilians: Roberto Marinho, Joseph and Moises Safra, Aloysio de Andrade Faria, and Antônio Ermirio de Moraes. Roberto Marinho and his family, owners of Rede Globo, also ranked among the one hundred largest fortunes in the world.[12]

An editorial in a Brazilian newspaper bemoaned the fact that advances in health care are available only to a small portion of Brazil's population. It cited examples from the World Health Organization's health care ranking for 191 nations affiliated with the United Nations:[13]

1st—France
2d—Italy
22d—Colombia
37th—United States
125th—Brazil

A newspaper article entitled "Inequality Grows in Brazil" emphasized the inequitable distribution of income in Brazil, citing some world rankings to give one perspective:[14]

2000 UN REPORT

The five poorest of 85 developing nations:

85. Niger
84. Burkina Faso
83. Ethiopia
82. Central African Republic
81. Mali

Brazil ranks 21st.

The five richest of 18 industrialized nations:

1. Norway
2. Sweden
3. Holland
4. Finland
5. Denmark

The most developed of 174 nations:

1. Canada
2. Norway
3. United States
4. Australia
5. Iceland

The least developed of 174 nations:

174. Sierra Leone
173. Nigeria
172. Burkina Faso
171. Ethiopia
170. Burundi

Brazil ranks 74th.

But, as a Brazilian journalist points out, all countries have their share of misery. In the UN reports released in June 2000, the United States ranks third in human development but ranks last among the eighteen industrialized nations on the poverty index, because the United States has some 40 million people with no health insurance.[15]

In the Southeast, the cities of São Paulo, Rio de Janeiro, and Belo Horizonte (Brazil's three largest cities) form an industrial triangle that produces 80 percent of Brazil's manufactured goods. Greater São Paulo alone manufactures more than half of the nation's industrial output. If the state of São Paulo were a country, it would have the second largest gross domestic product in Latin America, second only to that of Brazil itself. Southeastern Brazilians have a standard of living that is approximately one and a half times the national average and three and a half times that of northeasterners.[16]

The Brazilian authors Lucy Dias and Roberto Gambini state that the face of Brazil is one of social horror. By their measure, the social system excludes some 64 million people: 15 million poor, 24 million dispossessed, and 25 million miserable. They also state that Brazilians need to fight for the right to public education just as a Brazilian elite fought in the nineteenth century for an end to slavery. They maintain that to deny education is the same as denying bread and food and is the epitome of Brazilian cruelty and that Brazil's current social exclusion is as shameful as was slavery.[17]

Brazil's former president, Itamar Franco, stated to the nation in 1991, "In unjust societies like our own, the only thing distributed with equity is fear." [18]

Page explains that what is happening in Brazil is the evolution of a system of de facto social and economic "separatism." Brazilian society is adapting to further exclude the increasingly unmanageable poor. This can be seen in the proliferation of residential communities and apartment complexes walled off from the misery around them, so that affluent city dwellers can live in safety and comfort.[19] Even reading about such gross inequity from the comfort and safety of one's home in another country provokes horror.

There is no way to justify the economic chasm between the classes in Brazil, and all of society pays a price for the plight of the desperately poor. There is the "middle-class" citizen who rents or owns a residence and who must go to work every day to earn a living. Many Brazilians of the lower middle class especially struggle on a daily basis to ensure their physical safety and to protect material possessions they have acquired through great effort in a country with a history of rampant inflation. They sit on the brink of the economic chasm. In times of crisis, many of these citizens who border poverty lose ground and slip into the ranks of the impoverished. Fences, gates, walls, and bars do not protect only the super-rich. They are part of the defense that a working middle class erects to try to protect their families and belongings from the daily siege of crime. The economic disparity between the classes adversely affects the quality of life of all Brazilians to some degree.

Some attribute many of the problems and misfortunes of Brazil to its people's attitudes toward work. The psychologist John F. Santos explains that for the Brazilian, systematic planning and attention to jejune details detract from the appreciation of the present and from the spontaneity of life, while North Americans impress Brazilians as overly compulsive about work and emphasizing efficiency as an end in itself.[20]

There are, of course, individual and regional variations in how work is regarded in Brazil. While some persons assiduously dedicate themselves to several jobs, others are appreciated for having the "talent" to specialize in doing nothing. In São Paulo, Curitiba, Caxias do Sul, and Porto Alegre industriousness is prized in a way not typical of the rest of the country. Although this may be attributed to European influence, Santos points out that there are greater opportunities for work and a greater probability that hard work may lead to a better life, in contrast to the northern regions of the country. In the Northeast the work pace is noticeably slower, and in the interior the attitude toward work is influenced by a number of factors, including the scarcity of jobs and the fact that even a considerable expenditure of effort may not be rewarded. Here the possibilities for advancement and gain are so minimal that work practically has a negative reward value.[21]

Santos indicates that for many young Brazilians, the most desirable state of affairs is to be paid well and to have minimal obligations in work and effort. Responsibility for work accomplished is attributed to the employer rather than to the employee. In Santos's view, the driving, conscientious, ambitious individual in Brazil receives little support from the social system.[22]

Nonetheless, a talented Brazilian engineer who has worked for Dell Computer Corporation in both the Porto Alegre area and in the United States commented that Dell's key employees in Brazil work a grueling schedule. He maintained that in his department Brazilians certainly match and even exceed the production of their North American counterparts in the United States. "Dell pays well, but working for one year at 'the speed of Dell' seems like working for several years at another company," he reported.

The Heavy Hand of Government

Although Brazil has Latin America's largest economy, nonetheless, the size of the country's gross economic product belies its chronic and recurring acute economic ills. On March 15, 1991, President Fernando Collor de Mello temporarily froze the deposits of all persons and entities in Brazil's banks under the Plano Collor (Collor Plan). Although some individuals and businesses were able to gain access to their liquid assets through legal action,[23] freezing bank deposits was a catastrophe for most Brazilians. Many experienced financial ruin; many committed suicide.

César Guardini and his wife, Patrícia, live in the Serra da Cantareira, just outside the city of São Paulo. To the foreign eye, their situation appears idyllic. They have a home of some 4,000 square feet; lush, landscaped grounds with tropical plants and exotic bromeliads; a swimming pool; and servants' quarters with a live-in couple who work as maid and gardener and rotate their weekly day off because, for security reasons, the house can *never* be left empty when the owners are not home. The double doors to the grounds that open to allow the Guardinis' cars to enter are crafted of solid mahogany.

César is an electrical engineer and has his own company, LabElétrica, which installs and maintains electrical systems. The Plano Collor froze all of the Guardinis' personal and company bank assets. Their cash flow from accounts receivable was disrupted as well, because all of their customers were struggling to obtain cash, just as they were. The Guardinis were not faced just with their own problem of how to buy groceries and gas. They have financial responsibility for many people. The live-in couple who work for the Guardinis depend on their income not only to support themselves but also to support their family and relatives, including elderly parents. Patrícia's brother and sister-in-law are partners in the firm. The Guardinis' daughter and son-in-law work for the firm. All of their employees, many of whom average a third-grade education and whom the Guardinis have painstakingly trained over years, depend on their incomes from LabElétrica to survive and also to support extended families. The Guardinis feel keenly an obligation to provide for and to help sustain the collective, extended group of people who derive their livelihoods from their enterprise and through their efforts. Indeed, this system is indispensable to the survival of many in Brazil.

Patrícia is active in both a home owners' association and an umbrella coalition of associations that ensure basic services to home owners (water, trash collection, and road paving), services they do not receive from their municipality, although they pay mandatory taxes to fund them. (They point out that the mayor of their municipality of Mairiporã receives annual compensation that is greater than that of the president of Brazil.) Patrícia is also accomplished in fine arts and has had a number of her oil paintings exhibited in art galleries.

When faced with an urgent need to buy food for her family and provide for the needs of relatives and employees, Patrícia, her sister-in-law, and the maid started making fine chocolates by hand in Patrícia's kitchen. They crafted gourmet chocolates, set each chocolate individually in intricately hand-cut paper, and displayed them in elegant boxes. Patrícia then contacted wealthy families to sell the boxes of chocolates as gifts, to serve at parties, and for special occasions such as weddings. One can suppose that her customers lived in a financial stratosphere that gave them access to funds in bank accounts outside of Brazil, because they were able to pay her in cash. She says that she made and sold chocolates for close to a year to help her family and financial dependents survive. To this day, she cannot stand to smell or even look at chocolate.

As an investment, Vicente Almeida, an engineer from Rio, had just completed in 1991 a small bed-and-breakfast outside the city, a place for busy *cariocas* to get away from it all for a few days. When the Collor Plan froze all of Vicente's deposits in banks, he could not complete furnishing the facility or hire or pay his employees. Furthermore, there was not much demand from customers under the circumstances. Vicente and his wife, Lúcia, also worried about their two teenage sons. How would they get ahead or get good jobs in such an unstable economy?

Fortunately, the Almeidas had emergency savings they had placed in the United States. They decided to send their two sons to high school in Wichita, Kansas, thinking that if their sons became fluent in English they would have more job options in their future. Vicente himself enrolled in graduate engineering courses at Wichita State University, not that he needed them, but so that he could obtain a student visa, which would allow him and Lúcia to live with their two boys in the United States for the time that the young men were in Wichita.

Wichita is not Rio. The couple sorely missed their country, their culture, their city, the beach, their family, their friends, and their own home. They did not *want* to live in the United States; they wanted to live in their own country, as comfortable and familiar as a well-worn sandal. But the economy in Brazil was at a standstill, and they felt that this sacrifice was a constructive act in a situation in which they were almost powerless and had few options.

It is hard for North Americans to appreciate this experience. It would be traumatic to wake up one morning and find you could not access your bank accounts and that the business you had built had come to an abrupt halt. Imagine moving to a foreign country where you did not speak the language, where you really did not want to stay, and then living for several years with only the possessions you could bring with you in suitcases.

Inflation

Brazil had had chronically high inflation rates when the "Real Plan" stabilization program was launched in mid-1994. This plan featured the real as the new currency to replace the most recent version of the cruzeiro. It initially pegged the real to the U.S. dollar, it introduced a degree of governmental budget control, and real interest rates were high. The Real Plan reduced inflation, which peaked in 1993 at 2500 percent per annum, to only 2.5 percent in 1998.[24] More recently, in 2000, inflation was approximately 8 percent. But the cost of lowering inflation was high: interest rates of about 50 percent per annum prevailed in 1998, and unemployment hovered at 18 percent to 20 percent per annum in large urban areas in 1999–2000.

Brazilians tell North Americans that they have "dirty money" and that "Brazilian money is clean—because we change it so often." From the 1980s to the early 1990s the cruzeiro changed to the cruzado, from the cruzado to the cruzado novo, from the cruzado novo back to the cruzeiro, from the cruzeiro to the cruzeiro real, and from the cruzeiro real to the real.[25]

Annie and Carl Nimos were not novices at handling foreign currencies. They had lived in a number of countries, and Carl had traded foreign currencies for Citibank in the Middle East. On a 1994 visit with friends in São Paulo, Carl tried to pay for gas when the couple's hosts stopped to fill up on a drive to their mountain home. The cashier looked at the money Carl proferred and averted his gaze. He then readily accepted money from the couple's host. Later Annie and Carl privately discussed the incident. They had wondered whether they were missing some sort of unwritten cultural protocol that dictated payment could be accepted only from the "main" man. Maybe he who drove and appeared to be the owner of the vehicle thereby signaled his ranking in the group. But after leaving the gas station, Carl had discreetly examined some of the bills he was carrying and figured out that he was trying to hand the cashier the equivalent of less than a dollar instead of the thirty dollars he had intended. In 1994 there was more than one currency in circulation. In addition, stores had begun pricing in reals (the plural of the word *real* in Portuguese is *reais*), but since there was not yet a real currency (no pun intended), Brazilians had to calculate the "exchange" price to make daily purchases with the currency in circulation in their own country. Change was made in more than one currency, and the currencies in circulation looked similar. Annie and Carl were mortified. On arrival at the mountain *chácara* where they were to spend the weekend with their friends, they closed the door to their bedroom and in privacy spread out all their cash on the bed and sorted it. They each segregated the different currencies they were carrying into separate envelopes. At that time in São Paulo, you would see people glance at coins in their hands and toss them away in the street in disgust, because they had so little value.

On that June 1994 trip, the price of gasoline doubled in three weeks and the rate of inflation was some 45 percent per month. The Swiss owner of a restaurant outside of São Paulo commented to the Nimoses and their friends that the annual rate of inflation in Switzerland per year approximated the daily inflation rate that Brazil was then suffering.

Brazilians rely on statistics published by the prestigious Fundação Getúlio Vargas in São Paulo rather than those of the government's Instituto Brasileiro de Geografia e Estatística, whose results are likely to be politically motivated.

It is common for Brazilian newspapers to decry the manipulation of statistics. The economist Ronald Harry Coase was quoted in a São Paulo newspaper as saying, "If we torture statistics long enough, nature will always end up confessing." [26]

A July 2000 Brazilian newspaper article on the economy, "Six Years of the Real Plan," reported that in the six years from the time the real currency replaced the cruzeiro real, the Consumer Price Index (Índice Geral de Preços de Mercado da Fundação Getúlio Vargas) increased 106.18 percent, a far cry from an inflation of 2500 percent per year. Even so, this increase caused more hardship for much of the population than is at first apparent, because the increase in income during the same period was minimal, if there was any increase at all. [27]

The U.S. Commercial Service recommends that companies interested in doing business with Brazil establish long-term partnerships with local representatives or joint ventures with Brazilian companies or international consortiums. [28] It emphasizes that the complexities of the Brazilian business environment create formidable obstacles for U.S. companies. Doing business in Brazil requires intimate knowledge of local regulations and procedures. [29]

ON JUNE 13, 2000, Annie Nimos watched the legislative assembly of the state of Rio Grande do Sul approve proposal 122/2000 granting Dell Computadores do Brasil Ltda. a special deferment on taxes charged by the state on the purchase of materials, parts, and components acquired by Dell from companies in Rio Grande do Sul until Dell actually assembles the merchandise into computers.

Dell had been seeking this tax deferment since it had opened a plant in the state in 1999. The details of the tax deferment had been worked out with the state government, but there was a change in governor and political party before the matter came to vote before the legislative assembly. The vote was to have taken place on June 6, 2000, but had to be postponed because there was not a quorum of deputies present. At the June 6 assembly, Deputy Berfran Rosado of the Partido do Movimento

Democrático Brasileiro pointed out that fiscal benefits requested for Ford Motor Company at an earlier date had not been approved and that now special benefits were being requested for Dell.

This tax treatment was important to Dell's operation. The Dell proposal was the first item scheduled for consideration on June 13. It was approved in orderly fashion with no further discussion before the vote.

In Brazil June 13 is the Feast of Santo Antonio, the patron saint of marriages, lovers, and lost objects sought. Legislative approval of this tax proposal on this day boded well for the relationship between Dell and the state of Rio Grande do Sul, where Dell had committed itself to invest some U.S. $71 million (128 million Brazilian reals) in the next five years.

Personal Income

Joseph Page recounts that a director of Television Tupi had a salary of $5,000 a month but was never paid. At the end of the year, the director was informed that he was to receive a $2,000 raise. He politely refused, pointing out that he had steeled himself not to receive $5,000, but he could not bear not to receive $7,000.[30]

Brazilian bumper sticker: The Minister of Health warns that the minimum wage is injurious to your health.[31]

Brazil's patrimonial state has what Brazilians call "public functionalism" (*funcionalismo público*), or an entrenched bureaucracy. The federal, state, and local bureaucracies employed some 6 million people in 1997—one in every six salaried employees in the country. In 1989 public functionaries' salaries took more than 60 percent of the federal budget. Politicians have historically put people on the public payroll to get and keep their support, and legislation makes it very difficult to fire them. The biggest challenge to government reform is diminishing the power of the bureaucracy and making it accountable, which attacks the very nature of the system.[32] A Brazilian newspaper editorial commented that France has a tradition of state participation in the economy that has never led to the disastrous inefficiency observed in Latin America.[33]

Brazilians discuss wages in terms of monthly income and minimum wage. It is common to hear someone say that he or she pays an employee two minimum wages, or three minimum wages (*três salários mínimos*). In 2000 the minimum wage in the state of Rio Grande do Sul at then-current exchange rates was the equivalent of approximately $151 per month for a forty-four-hour week. At professional levels, such as for an engineer or an accountant, salaries are similarly discussed in terms of monthly income. A woman who has a master's degree in chemical engineering explained that through most of the 1990s, for example, inflation was so rampant that a person's salary by December of a given year might be many multiples of what it had been in January of the same year, and yet the person might actually be receiving less in terms of buying power. It was therefore meaningless to talk in terms of yearly compensation. A month was "long term" when inflation was high.

Overheard in Brazil: "If communism were such a good thing, they'd have it in the United States." [34]

Annie and Carl Nimos took a taxi to the Botanical Gardens in Porto Alegre to meet Márcio Efe, local coordinator for the conservation group PróAves, and to see local birds. On arrival they paid the taxi driver and got out of the vehicle. The taxi drove away. Carl then realized that he had laid his binoculars down on the backseat when counting out the taxi fare and that he had forgotten them. The binoculars were worth $200, about 133 percent of a month's minimum wage at that time in Porto Alegre. Carl was unhappy and disappointed at the loss of the binoculars. But about twenty minutes later, as they stood talking with Márcio, the taxi reappeared. The driver had noticed the binoculars on his backseat and had driven back to the Botanical Gardens (not an area where he would easily find a new fare, especially in winter) to return them. Carl and Annie were amazed that the binoculars had not already been sold and that the driver would go to so much trouble. The return of the binoculars was a significant act of honesty and consideration, given the driver's status in the local economy and the value of the item returned. This illustrates another paradox of Brazil, where such public kindnesses contrast starkly with ubiquitous street crime.

Civil War

To survive economically, people invent all sorts of commercial activities. The self-appointed title Car Guard has become practically an institution in Brazil. In fact, few Brazilians realize that in 1975 Federal Law 6.242 created the profession of self-employed Guard and Washer of Automotive Vehicles. In the city of Porto Alegre, a union for this activity was created. But, as reported in a newspaper article, only some 220 *flanelinhas* (as they are called because of the flannel cloths they brandish to hawk their services) of the city's estimated informal industry of 15,000 car watchers had joined. Paying for the services of a car watcher has actually become a necessity as insurance against the damage and theft that the car watcher can practically "guarantee" if his, sometimes her, services are not used.[35] One professional couple, both engineers, would not drive their vehicle (not a luxury car) to downtown Porto Alegre at night to go to a movie at the Casa de Cultura Mario Quintana because they feared the car would not be there by the time they came out. For special occasions, such as a concert or theater event, the *flanelinhas*—many of whom take up the profession just for the evening— flock to the vicinity and aggressively solicit R$5 to R$10 (approximately U.S. $3–6 in 2000), payable in advance, to park anywhere near the event—de facto extortion. Since so many poor flock to the area in the hope of making a few reals, the mood is overtly aggressive and hostile.

Many Brazilians resent car watchers taking over as their territory the public streets of a city that all citizens have the right to use and then blackmailing citizens into making payment to park "in safety." Payment, in fact, does not ensure safety, but nonpayment almost guarantees damage or theft. Even so, in the center of town where parking is scarce and many need to keep daytime business and government appointments, a few quasi-permanent *flanelinhas* organize street parking that is several cars deep; the *flanelinhas* even keep the owners' keys in order to jockey cars in and out. They function as an informal parking lot on city streets.[36]

In fact, "informal" commerce in Brazil is conservatively estimated to equal three times the total economy of the nation of Portugal, or one times that of Switzerland. A significant problem is that informal businesses pay no taxes.[37]

Rua Tuyuti is a street one block long in downtown Porto Alegre, with several apartment buildings along it. From her balcony, Annie Nimos could observe the whole block. For months, every morning at about eight o'clock Egberto, a man with frizzy grizzled hair, would arrive to take up his self-appointed position as the block's car watcher. Egberto would sit all day on a chair in front of a tiny storefront that sold sewing supplies, located midblock. Each day the owner of the shop set out the wooden chair for the man as a charitable act but perhaps also because Egberto's presence gave the shopkeeper some small protection from robbery. People who parked on the street would pay the car watcher on their return. Egberto would leave around nine o'clock at night. One day a woman appeared and began to work one end of the block. She harassed Egberto and at one point pounded on him with her fists. She said this block was her territory and that she was going to bring in her nephews. Apparently, in "the street" the rules of Brazilian cordiality can be suspended. Drawn by the ongoing commotion, apartment residents would placidly observe the daily turf struggle from their balconies or as they walked by, but no one interfered or commented. After a few days, the woman brought a young man with her who worked at one end of the block. She kept up a constant barrage of yelling and threats from the other end. After a week she brought another young man to work at the other end of the block, and she herself paced back and forth toward the middle. Every day the trio moved in closer and closer to Egberto, running out to make arrangements to watch the car of every person who pulled up to park. They squeezed the old man down to an area only a few yards wide. There was a heavy atmosphere of hostility. If asked, the Tuyuti Street residents would shrug their shoulders at what seemed an inevitable struggle in the streets. One morning Egberto did not show up to take his usual post. He was not seen or heard from again. When asked, the shopkeeper said he did not know if some mishap had suddenly befallen the old man, if he had just been intimidated and run off, or if he had succumbed to AIDS, from which the shopkeeper said Egberto suffered.

There is a civil war going on in Brazil, and the frontiers are social and economic. The estimated 70 percent of the population that is poor presses daily at the perimeters of the 28 percent that is middle class. The extremely wealthy 2 percent at the top of the pyramid are not affected in the same way: they can afford better guards and higher walls, and they live in less accessible enclaves; they can jet off to other parts of the world whenever Brazil's social ills press on them too heavily. It is the populace that is so important to the economy and the nation that is most affected: the middle class of small business owners, professionals, and working people who are fortunate enough to live well or reasonably well but who shop, go to work, and are in the streets every day. This is the class of people who are productive and who promote the personal safety of citizens, justice, and democratic process in a nation. Their material well-being, whether at the lower or upper end of the middle-class spectrum, is what is most visible to the have-nots and is, therefore, what is most assailed.

Skidmore points out that the rise in crime in Brazil has probably worked against greater awareness of social inequality. The elite classes have shifted their focus from the *trabalhador* (the worker who has a job and contributes to society) to the *marginal* (the hustler who lives by streetsmarts). Focusing on violent crime committed by the "marginal" criminals makes it easier to ignore the plight of the many millions of hardworking Brazilians at the bottom tier of society.[38]

The songwriter and gadfly Caetano Veloso complained in a much-noticed interview with *O Globo* newspaper, "The very idea of Brazil as a nation makes me tired."[39] In 2001 a California-style energy crisis forced the government to ration electricity. The worst drought in decades had seriously affected Brazil's hydroelectric production. In little more than three months, the value of the real fell more than 20 percent against the dollar. In addition, a judge, cabinet ministers, and two powerful senators had been forced to step down because of corruption (the good news is that they were forced to step down). Brazil even lost soccer games to "lightweights," Brazilian supremacy in soccer always having been the nation's psychological bulwark in times of trouble. There was a feeling of malaise, of depression, and of disenchantment. Workers were saying that they sacrifice and sacrifice for a "golden future" that keeps being pushed out of reach. Even so, Brazil's neighbors noted that it did not have to contend with Colombia's guerrilla violence, Argentina's crippling recession, Peru's political turbulence, or Venezuela's threatened dictatorial rule.[40]

Brazilians have always been motivated by visions of historical destiny and national greatness that any North American would recognize. But national events in 2001 eroded the conviction that "God is Brazilian" and that Brazil is "the Country of the Future."[41]

Eakin writes that Brazil must address its "social question" to become a truly modern nation. "The Brazilian masses must be enfranchised both politically and socially."[42] Income inequalities must be reduced, and all Brazilians must enjoy and exercise their full rights as citizens. It will take enlightened and pragmatic leaders to successfully address social inequity so that Brazil can proceed on the path to development. If this does not happen, the country may descend into social chaos, and Brazil will remain the country of a future that never comes.

THE ECONOMIC CLIMATE of Brazil colors much of what Brazilians live as their world. It affects the day-to-day circumstances, events, and activities that constitute one's experience of living in a nation.

CHAPTER SEVEN

Experiencing Brazil

"The situation in Brazil is not bad. It will have to improve a great deal to get bad." [1]

"Brazil: Love it or leave it. Last one out, turn off the lights." [2]

Give Us This Day

To effectively communicate with Brazilians, it is important to have an understanding of their world. Life experiences create filters through which one sees the world, which in turn affect one's behavior. Given the negative aspects of daily life in Brazil, it is remarkable that there are so many positive aspects as well and that Brazilians live with a heady joy and have a predominantly optimistic outlook.

Personal safety is an issue of primary public concern in Brazil. A 2000 newspaper editorial reported that according to Justice Department statistics, between 1979 and 1998 the population of Brazil increased 37 percent and the number of murders increased 273 percent. Fifty percent of the residents of capital cities report they avoid going out at night.[3] A 2000 study showed that the risk of being murdered in Brazil is three times greater than in the United States and forty times greater than in Japan. Murder is the second leading cause of death in Brazil.[4]

Today people in Brazil are engaged in an ongoing war, but it is not a war on a geographic frontier. The frontier is internal, between the haves and the have-nots, *entre a casa e a rua* (between the house and the street). In the nice *bairro* (neighborhood) of Auxiliadora in Porto Alegre, Claudina Junker, an attorney, lives in the freestanding home where she grew up. The house has the usual six-foot iron fence around the yard. Inside this exterior fence, there is another iron fence that encloses the front door and patio area, and inside the second fence an iron cage with bars on top encloses the front door as a third line of defense. Claudina also recently installed an alarm system. Nonetheless, she has been robbed five times in two years. The last time the thieves came in through the roof, while she and her family were at home. Fortunately, no one has been hurt. When her twenty-year-old daughter drops off the ten-year-old daughter at the front gate after a Sunday afternoon outing, they make sure that the eldest physically hands the youngest over to the mother and that all the gates and doors are immediately relocked. Claudina says that her daughter could be assaulted just standing in front of the house.

When Gisela Hauptman, an engineer, and her husband come home at night to their condominium, also in a nice neighborhood, they circle the block several times to see if there is anyone or anything that looks suspicious. Only if their drive-by inspections are satisfactory do they pull up to open an iron grill at street level where they lock their car in for the night in a space under the building. If they see someone or something they are uncomfortable with, they drive on.

In 2000 shopkeepers in downtown Porto Alegre understood that on a daily basis they risked being robbed of whatever cash they kept in their cash registers. It was practically impossible to get change for a R$50 bill (approximately U.S. $30 at the time) in almost any store, unless it was large and guarded—such as the Saffari supermarkets, protected by armed guards with two-way radios. In two months' time, some four banks and several supermarkets were robbed by groups at gunpoint, and on two separate occasions during this same two-month window, bank executives were kidnapped from their homes. The executives' families were held hostage while the executives were taken to their banks to withdraw cash. Yet the southern city of Porto Alegre is viewed by *paulistas* and *cariocas* as much safer than their own cities.

A young woman who is an engineer hired by Schlumberger to work on oil platforms said that when she goes home to São Paulo, she and her sister no longer go out at night without their parents because the city has become so dangerous. One evening the two young women went to a movie and were followed when they drove home. They called their house by cell phone. Their parents immediately turned on all of the outside lights, they and their gardener stationed themselves visibly to observe the arrival of the two sisters, and they ensured that the two young women had immediate access to the enclosed garage area.

In anticipation of the election of a new Porto Alegre mayor in 2000, a study was done to determine voters' main concerns. The highest priority, with a score of 29 percent, was public safety, up from the 16 percent that put this concern in leading position in 1996. (Inadequacies in health care were the next greatest concern.[5]) In the last two decades of the century, violence tripled in Brazil.[6] With 2.9 percent of the world's population and 10 percent of its homicides, the national Senate's Constitution and Justice Committee approved in 2000 the prohibition of the sale of arms in Brazil. The bill's principal backer, Senator Renan Calheiros, stated, "Violence is an epidemic and needs to be treated as such."[7]

The price of protection from street violence is high. In São Paulo, the person who has everything and wants to keep it is beginning to view as essential a house in a gated community with twenty-four-hour guards and a bullet-proof car as protection from robbery and kidnapping. Fear drives even middle-class citizens with more modest incomes to spend heavily on security. In 2001 business was booming for O'Gara-Hess's armor-plating works. Driving a cheaper car is a way to avoid attention, so humble Volkswagen Golfs are fitted alongside BMWs and Volvos. The cost of outfitting a VW with bullet-proof panels and windows is $30,000, more than the car itself is worth. Brazil's security forces worry that some of the increasing number of civilians driving armored vehicles are criminals. As implementation of a new state law requiring armor-plating firms to furnish lists of their customers to the police was pending, customers scrambled to reregister their cars in the name of especially created companies. They were terrified of the corruption that exists in the police force. In 2001 Brazil had overtaken Colombia, Mexico, and the United States to become the world's largest market for bulletproof cars.[8]

In the Serra da Cantareira, in the hills outside of São Paulo where people move to escape crime, the members of the home owners' associations have had to contribute to the cost of installing bulletproof glass in the main booths of the multiple layers of gated entries in the area. Without this protection, guards are unwilling to work there. In this suburban, gated community, most families have live-in servants to ensure that someone is always at their homes.

Iracy Saldanha went to Rio to work with a federal committee that administers medical benefits in the Região Sul, where she practices medicine and gives presentations on the program to other physicians. She is not a timid woman. On a nice day in Rio in 2000, with three female colleagues she set out to see the beautiful view from the top of Morro Santa Tereza. The *bonde* (streetcar) they were riding to the top began filling up with impoverished *favela* people who were clearly hostile. A man behind her commented, "There are four fish in the net." She understood instantly that she and her friends were the fish and that they were about to be assaulted. As the *bonde* slowed at the next stop, with no warning she jumped off, calling out to her friends that she wanted to take some photos. They were startled but followed immediately. She spoke to a police officer who was present (deeming him only somewhat less threatening than her situation) to help her procure a taxi. The four women returned to town as fast as possible.

Although Annie and Carl Nimos have never had a problem with assault or robbery in Brazil and do not feel threatened in the streets, they feel it would be foolhardy not to take note of the experiences of their Brazilian friends. It impressed them to hear that during a stay of several months in Porto Alegre, the sister of an engineer was carjacked at gunpoint and forced to withdraw money from various automatic teller machines. During the same stay, the same thing happened to a friend who was a teacher. Fortunately, neither woman was harmed. The teacher was mercifully put out at the entrance to a freeway leading out of town, and the carjacker proceeded to wreck her vehicle to the point of total loss within the hour.

Crime soared to new heights when carjacking escalated to plane hijacking, not for political or international purposes, but for domestic robbery. On August 17, 2000, five armed men hijacked a domestic flight out of São Paulo and got away with bank pouches containing R$5 million (U.S. $2.8 million) in cash. They did not harm the passengers. And in July 2000 a gang robbed a VASP plane on the runway at the Brasília airport of U.S. $500,000 in gold. Airport security and metal detectors were not a deterrent.[9]

The use of public space in Brazil is changing. Whereas Brazilians have traditionally interacted socially in the streets and *praças* (squares), today many urban areas have become cities of walls. Teresa Caldeira writes that in São Paulo,

> [c]ity residents will not risk living in a house without fences and bars on the windows. Physical barriers enclose both public and private spaces: houses, apartment buildings, parks, squares, office complexes, shopping areas, and schools. As the elites retreat to their enclaves and abandon public spaces to the homeless and the poor, the number of spaces for public encounters between different social groups shrinks considerably. . . . The idea of going for a walk, of naturally passing among strangers, the act of strolling through the crowd that symbolizes the modern experience of the city, are all compromised in a city of walls. People feel restricted in their movements, afraid, and controlled; they go out less at night, walk less on the street, and avoid the [dangerous] "forbidden zones" that loom larger and larger in every resident's mental map of the city.[10]

The Beasts at the Gate

Contemplating urban violence, the Brazilian journalist Júlio Mariani asked in a newspaper opinion piece why Brazil cannot build a truly civilized country. In Brazil, he writes, poverty is synonymous with barbarity. The rural exodus of the poor to large cities in the 1950s, 1960s, and 1970s seemed to cause their disassociation from society, resulting in a country without moral limits. He states that even thirty or forty years ago Brazilians of intellectual honesty already had sounded the alarm that the country was engaged in an undeclared civil war. The same level of misery exists in Asia, but violence is contained there by a tradition of solidarity. He writes that in Brazil poverty is associated with a complete absence of conscience and needs are filled by the assassin's arm. The money that is not being spent to educate people will have to be spent two times over to keep the beasts outside the gate.[11]

If crime is not contained through official measures, Brazil risks increasing police and vigilante extralegal remedies. In a letter to the editor in a Brazilian newspaper, a historian comments that any nation's official death penalty is totally and absolutely unacceptable because of one fact: the possibility of judicial error. He maintains that the death penalty tarnishes the image of the United States as a bastion of human rights. But then he goes on to ask what should be said of Brazil's extrajudicial death penalty, whereby the police, with public support, judge, condemn, and execute criminals. Who in Brazil does not fear the police? He comments that the English periodical *The Guardian* had recently categorized the Brazilian military police as assassins in uniforms.[12]

The Democratic Environment

Some Brazilians comment with irony that at least dictatorship was more stable than their current pseudo-democracy.

Gary Althen commented that North Americans like to keep politics out of their conversations; they tend to separate politics from the rest of their daily lives. North Americans also participate in elections at a lower rate than citizens of any democracy.[13] The economic success of the United States and the relatively effective functioning of its governmental institutions have lulled the general population into a sense of complacency.

In contrast, Brazil now mandates voting for everyone between the ages of eighteen and seventy. Anyone who cannot produce proof of having voted cannot obtain the permits and licenses needed to function and conduct business in everyday life. This puts some teeth into the legal voting requirement. The rationale is that mandatory voting will force citizens to participate in self-determination. Some Brazilians believe that this system is ineffectual. A large number of needy voters who are uninformed cast their ballots for whichever candidate or party that last stopped by with a case of beer and a hearty greeting to influence them.

Consequently, these people may not vote in a manner that is consistent with improving their lot in life.

Taking Action

Residents of a subdivision in the Serra da Cantareira are engaged in a struggle to secure the services they need for their homes, even though they pay for these improvements through taxes. Home owners in one subsection pool funds to pave their streets, little by little. The president of their home owners' association, Patrícia Guardini, maintains a running dialogue with the city to ensure trash removal. Patrícia worked with a retired professor of hydrology to put in a deep well to provide a reliable water source for a large number of residences, funded by the home owners. In her cul-de-sac, a home that was being constructed as the owner's funds permitted has been taken over by a multitude of squatters who bootleg access to electricity and water and let their sewage run open into the street, a common occurrence. Home owners of the association and of a coalition of associations in the area also pool funds to legally fight the squatters who bring open sewers, garbage heaps, and crime into their neighborhoods. In spite of the drain on their time and financial resources to ensure basic services, Patrícia also leads a number of concerned area residents in conservation efforts. Regulations have been passed and a natural conservation park established. Patrícia commented to Annie Nimos that North Americans can step into "ready-made" environments that are safe and salubrious as a place to build their homes.

When they visit or take up residence in the United States, Brazilians immediately note a stark contrast with their own experiences in daily living in their home country. The Brazilian sociologist Ana Cristina Braga Martes published a study in 1999 on Brazilian immigrants in the Massachusetts area. When she set out to interview these immigrants, she expected them to complain about discrimination because of their nationality, complexion, and language. However, these Brazilian immigrants did not necessarily find the environment of the United States hostile. They were pleasantly surprised to find that they have rights. Although they do not have political citizenship in the United States, they nonetheless benefit from a dimension of citizenship they did not experience in their own country.[14]

Martes points out that people do not participate in citizenship only through the right to vote but through receiving assistance in the public sector, by being respected by a policeman, or by being treated like other customers when they enter a bank poorly dressed. These positive experiences make the Brazilians in Massachusetts feel that they are part of a polity. This appreciation of North American civic life is surprising when one considers that most of the Brazilians interviewed were undocumented immigrants. They also feel that they are citizens because they can be consumers, not just of superfluous goods that they did not have access to in Brazil, such as athletic shoes or a good car, but of public or collective goods such as access to schools, health care, and a telephone at home.[15]

These rights are extended to them under the principles of the U.S. institutional system that is based on human and social rights. In other words, many of these Brazilians felt they were respected as persons and that they had access to basic social services that are superior to those available to them in Brazil.[16]

Respect for the Law

DaMatta observes that in countries where the legal system works effectively, laws are respected as serving a purpose or they are repealed. Where this parallel between laws and daily life exists, a person stops for a red light. The person accepts the usefulness of the law in society and does not view it as a specially created inconvenience for the citizen. A Brazilian finds this absurd, because he or she does not believe that laws are made to be obeyed. He or she distrusts any rule made by the government.[17] The Brazilian government assumes there will be a certain amount of disobedience. The people filter the laws, and government officials great and small make up their own interpretations in applying them. Brazilians say that laws exist to be broken. *Jeito*, finding a way around things, takes care of the "no" of the law and the "yes" of the individual.[18]

One Rio resident gives the following instructions for dealing with traffic lights. One should always stop at a red light, right? Wrong! First, there is a way to approach a light. If it is red, you slow down some on the approach, trying to time your arrival at the intersection for the same moment that the light changes to green, which means that you will actually have a green light when you go through the intersection. In any case, it is always advisable to slow down a little to go through an intersection. Look for other cars and the police, then step on the gas. After 10:00 P.M. ignore all lights and intersections and go for it. Besides, it is dangerous to stop late at night. If you stop at a red light, you will probably be assaulted while you wait for it to change. If you are supposed to go through red lights, you must be wondering what you should do for green lights. Use the same tactic, but blink your headlights so other drivers know you are going through. Usually, people with a red light will yield to those with the green light. All this takes some finesse if you are to survive.[19]

Lúcio Lara worked at Dell Computer Corporation in Austin for a time. He likes to regale his Brazilian friends with a story to illustrate the cultural difference between Brazil and the United States. He had been working late every night on a team project. One afternoon he was driving back to his apartment and in accordance with North American custom, stopped at a red light on a major street. He was so tired that he dozed off for an instant, and when he looked up he saw that the light was green. Glancing in his rearview mirror, he flinched when he saw the number of cars behind him. He did not know how long the light had been green but quickly drove off. He was amazed. "No one honked!" he tells his friends. "In Brazil all the drivers behind me would have been honking, and someone would probably have driven right over the top of me."

Diz-se em Brasília que a internet pegou no país porque aqui todo mundo @ e fica por isso mesmo. [In Brasilia, they say that the Internet caught on in the country because here everyone steals, *and that's why the Internet will stay.]*[20]

Corruption also undermines Brazilians' regard for the law. Corruption is so flagrant that *Imprensa* magazine published an alphabetized "Guide to Corruption in Brazil." It was as if the whole country were trying to confirm the statement attributed to De Gaulle: "Brazil is not a serious country." But in Brazil, the memory of the public is short in regard to even recent problems about which no more is heard. Rega comments that impunity is safe when complicity is general.[21]

A Democratic Process
Porto Alegre, Rio Grande do Sul, Brazil
31 degrees south of the equator

On June 13, 2000, the legislative assembly of the state of Rio Grande do Sul in Brazil voted on a cost of living increase in the wages of state judiciary employees. Instead of people walking in at will to be seated in a half-empty visitor's gallery as they usually did, Annie Nimos found herself waiting at the entrance of the building in a press of more than a thousand people who had traveled from all over the state to support the wage increase.

The assembly's doors were locked, and the crowd was becoming
impatient to gain entrance to a session scheduled to commence at
2:15 P.M. The crowd had a heterogeneous physical profile, and there
were no clusters of hyphenated Brazilians. Becoming impatient, a few
persons began to chant "abra, abra [open, open]" but were amiably
hushed by their neighbors and told to be patient and orderly. People
were relaxed and talkative, not tense or angry, despite the fact that
they had not received even a cost of living increase in wages in some
seven years. They stood body pressed to body, in part because of the
press of people toward the entrance and in part because Brazilians do
not require as much personal space as North Americans. When a quo-
rum of state deputies finally arrived to vote, the doors opened. People
entered slowly and the gatekeeper counted them one by one, admit-
ting only the same number of persons as seats available.

The assembly approved the wage increase, which was not equiva-
lent to the increase in the cost of living. The democratic process had
proceeded in orderly fashion.

Despite the many shortcomings of the governmental system, Brazil
has dealt effectively with a critical national concern. Of Brazil's 175 million people, an estimated 580,000 were HIV positive in 2000. In the early
1980s, when the first cases of AIDS were documented, health experts
predicted that by the end of the millennium HIV would affect at least
1.2 million Brazilians. But by 2000 AIDS death rates were dropping
rather than going up.[22] Even so, in 2000 Brazil had 41 percent of the HIV
positive population in Latin America.[23]

At the heart of Brazil's success is its AIDS drug distribution program,
begun in 1992. This program became far-reaching when the Brazilian
government decided to manufacture its own anti-AIDS drugs. Critics in
Brazil and abroad had predicted that a lack of health care infrastructure,
corruption, and inefficiency would doom the program, but its effectiveness has been praised. The government role has driven the price of AIDS
medicines down, and in 2000 a typical treatment of antiretroviral drugs
cost Brazil $4,152 per patient per year, while in the United States simi-
lar treatment usually cost $15,000. Brazil has demonstrated the politi-
cal will to effectively attack a serious domestic problem and has served
as counsel to some African nations in combating their own epidemics.[24]

Education

Education is another area of prime concern for Brazil. In 2000 Cuba
had an agreement to assist with postgraduate studies in seven Brazilian states (Piauí, Maranhão, Ceará, Minas Gerais, Espírito Santo, Bahia,

and Santa Catarina). Cuban Consul Guillermo Vias Rodrígues visited a number of states to promote a pedagogical conference that would take place in Havana. One of Fidel Castro's notable successes has been in education. He has completely eliminated illiteracy in Cuba, a goal that is of utmost importance in Brazil.[25] A number of Brazilians express admiration for the Cuban model. But, typical of the polemical discussions on political systems that inevitably ensue, a Brazilian accountant wrote in a letter to the editor of a newspaper that his friends on both the left and the right say that if they were to leave Brazil, they would want to live in the United States, Germany, or England. "Have you ever heard of someone from the left saying they want to go and live in Cuba?"[26]

In a letter to a newspaper editor, an engineer cautioned that Brazilians should not forget that the dictatorship of the right in Brazil was as bad as the dictatorship of the left in Cuba. Both impose extremist ideas and totally disrespect the rights of a large part of the population.[27]

Page states that those who are realistic about Brazil's future do not envision a superpower in the making. They cautiously laud the development of effective government and relative prosperity in some of the country's less populous states and municipalities. The city of Curitiba, for example, in the southern state of Paraná, has become well known nationally and internationally as Brazil's livable, ecological, and model city.[28] And amid myriad national problems, many laud their local government's accomplishments. A student in the state of Rio Grande do Sul, with characteristic *gaúcho* pride, wrote in a letter to the editor of *Zero Hora* that although state deputies sometimes argue about trivial issues, one does not hear talk of the corruption that is so common in the rest of the country. He appreciates what he terms at least a minimum of seriousness in local politics.[29]

IN ADDITION TO THE INFLUENCE of history, the economy, and the daily experience of living in a nation, the organization of a society significantly affects the culture, and therefore the communication, of a people. The structure of a society determines in great part how its individual members relate to one another.

CHAPTER EIGHT

Social Organization

In Brazil, everything is relative, and everything seems to involve relatives.

We, unlike the people of the United States, never say "separate but equal"; instead we say "different but united," which is the golden rule of a hierarchical and relational universe such as ours.[1]

Collectivism versus Individualism

Brazilian society is organized into collective groups, which fundamentally differs from the individualistic organization of United States society. Collectivists are conditioned by their culture to provide emotional and material support to each other. They nurture mutual ties of dependence; conversely, individualists are independent and distant in their personal interactions.[2] Collectivists are best encouraged by appealing to their group spirit and by requesting cooperation, whereas individualists tend to be self-motivated and typically can be stimulated to achieve through individual competition.[3] Further, collective cultures are usually less tolerant of variation in culturally prescribed behavior than are individualistic cultures.[4]

Individualist cultures hold people responsible for their own actions and teach problem-solving skills at an early age. They discuss problems as "bugs" to be worked out, or "wrinkles" to be smoothed away. Collectivist cultures do not hold individuals responsible for problems, although they may identify and blame an individual for a problem the individual points out. This makes individuals reluctant to report bad news in collective cultures. Collectivists do not see problems as external nuisances that interrupt and interfere with the accomplishment of a goal. They see them as an inevitable part of the situation and the process in which a group operates. The dynamics of the group relationship, that is, working on a problem together, is as important as solving a problem.[5]

Brazilians are obsessed with being connected because of their internal schisms.[6]

The French anthropologist Raymonde Carroll wrote on the cultural differences between individualistic and collectivist cultures. She observes that a North American believes that "I" exists outside of all networks. This does not mean that social networks do not exist or have no importance for the North American but rather that each person makes and defines his or her own identity, as expressed in the familiar North American expression "a self-made man." In contrast, in a collective culture such as Brazil, a person is always a product of networks that give the person his or her identity. Jean-Paul Sartre wrote that other people create one's hell. But others are not always or only hell, because a person's network of relationships does not just trap, stifle, and oppress; this same network also feeds, supports, defines, and makes a person significant.[7]

Brazilian society is organized primarily into discrete, collective in-groups of *parentela* (kin) and close friends. This explains the relative absence of voluntary associations such as parent-teacher associations, garden clubs, and civic clubs. Greater value is placed on kinship relations than on those based on common interest or occupation.[8]

Brazilians learn to take care of themselves because no one else will. They learn by being forced to adjust to difficult circumstances. Their financial security is constantly threatened by the unstable economy and the lack of social agencies. They become used to depending on few people and inured to misfortune and poverty, even citing U.S. social agencies for the poor and needy as examples of the impersonal North American way. The concern of the Brazilian for his or her well-being extends to concern for extended family and close friends.[9] Lauro Moreira writes that although Brazilians rarely identify constructively with the suffering of others, they are profoundly sentimental and generous, particularly with friends and family.[10]

DaMatta says that the Brazilian practices a self-centered individualism without limits that reduces collective values to no more than an appendix to personal happiness. He describes the Brazilian as always trying to get special treatment to the detriment of the collective good.[11] But, in fact, the Brazilian only disregards the good of anyone who does not belong to his or her in-group, "the house." The rest of society, "the street," comprises out-groups and is therefore of no concern. One of the many paradoxes of Brazilian culture is the frequently voiced observation by Brazilians themselves that the Brazilian is self-centered, when it is more accurate to say that Brazilian society is a mosaic of self-centered in-groups, each of which functions as a collective unit.

DaMatta explains the difference between his concepts of *a casa* (the house) and *a rua* (the street). In the home, persons are "persons," but in the street they are people, the masses. Theoretically, in the street there is no love, consideration, respect, or friendship; it is a dangerous place. The house and the street are the two basic spaces in which Brazilians live, and DaMatta cautions that to survive, it is unwise to confuse the two.[12]

In the house, harmony should reign. Individual opinions are banned from the table, living rooms, and bedrooms. If opposing views must be expressed, these discussions take place in marginal parts of the home, such as the veranda or the yard. The exterior world, the street, is governed by struggle and competition. There, DaMatta states, the cruel anonymity of *individuals* and *individualism* prevails. Brazilians are members of a perpetual corporation, the Brazilian family, with its network of *compadres* (godparents), employees, servants, and friends. This network is much more vital and permanent than the government and public administration, which must always compete with the family for loyalty and respect.[13]

Collective cultures place less value on relationships with out-groups (strangers, casual acquaintances, etc.) than do individualistic cultures. Therefore, persons of a collective culture tend to focus most of their appropriately positive behavior on persons in their in-group, to maintain group cohesion, cooperation, and harmony.[14] This value can be manifested in how Brazilians relate to and treat people in out-groups. Individualistic cultures like the United States do not differentiate as much between out-groups and in-groups and are more likely to form voluntary alliances and treat all people in the same manner. Brazilians say that they can deny nothing to their families. Therefore, family matters and celebrations, even the needs of friends, will often be put before obligations to an out-group such as an employer. North Americans frequently misinterpret this focus and these cultural obligations as a lack of seriousness about work commitments.

In Brazil it is important to make an effort to get to know an individual with whom one wants to interact. Over time, one can earn a position at least at the fringes of the individual's in-group. Persons belonging to an in-group receive preferential treatment and those from an out-group are discriminated against to some extent. Therefore, although expending the time and energy to get acquainted seems unnecessary or inefficient to many non-Brazilians, doing so is a wise investment that is likely to determine whether they are able to conduct business at all in Brazil.

North Americans differ substantially from collective cultures in their devotion to individualism. Althen writes that North Americans are trained from childhood to consider themselves responsible for their situations in life. They are not conditioned as members of a tightly interdependent family or other collective group and commonly use phrases that emphasize individualism: "Do your own thing"; "You made your bed, now lie in it."[15] This learned individualism explains some aspects of North American behavior and thinking that may not otherwise make sense to persons from collective cultures.

Although Brazil is fundamentally a collective culture, Brazilians share with North Americans an admiration for daring and solo feats. The motivation may be different, however. Some say that the penchant in Brazil for individual daring and grandiosity is an attempt to escape one's fixed social station. Many of the disadvantaged admire foolhardy, symbolic feats—such as "surfing" on top of a moving bus. And even though this behavior deviates from the prescribed norm, it is tolerated by much of society because it does not threaten the hierarchy, nor is it confrontational.

North Americans believe strongly in social mobility, that one can accomplish anything through personal effort, no matter how humbly born or disadvantaged, and they do not see one's station in life as fixed. The reverse side of this coin is that North Americans tend to hold the unfortunate responsible for not changing their lot in life, and they find it difficult to appreciate the great difficulty for a person who is humbly born to advance in a rigidly hierarchical society such as Brazil.

Privacy

North Americans and Brazilians differ in their concept of and need for privacy. Closely associated with the value North Americans place on individualism is the importance they assign to privacy. They assume that people need some time to themselves to recuperate from social and business interactions.[16] In contrast, Brazilians need a great deal of time with other people, and they seem to recharge through interaction.

Claudina Junker went to stay for two weeks with good friends in the United States. They gave her the bedroom where she had stayed for a night or two on previous visits. The couple ordinarily kept their computer set up in that bedroom. On this visit, Claudina noticed that the computer had been moved to a different room. Finally, she asked why they had moved it. They explained that they wanted to give her privacy. She responded, "But it makes me feel isolated and excluded. I feel cut off from your normal life. I *want* you to bother me. I am Brazilian—I don't understand privacy." Certainly, this may be an individual's reaction, but it illustrates well an important difference between collective and individualistic cultures in the personal interaction that people expect, prefer, and "need."

A São Paulo writer commented to Annie Nimos that the concept of privacy in Brazil and in the United States is quite different. "We don't need 'privacy' like North Americans. Of course, we have privacy in Brazil. But the concept of privacy is very narrow, maybe limited to some aspects of bathrooms and bedrooms. We don't understand what the boundaries are for North Americans in their daily lives. I feel like I invade North American privacy even with my eyes, because in Brazil we look at people more in public, and I see that I make North Americans uncomfortable with my gaze."

Ana Carolina Ecósteguy, a Brazilian professor who had studied in England for a time, said that the English are very polite and attentive but distant. She found it difficult to tell how close she could get, what help she could ask for, what questions she could ask professors without crossing the boundary that constitutes an invasion of privacy. She needed support for her studies and to adapt to living with her three-year-old daughter in a foreign culture. In Brazil she was accustomed to a closer and more personal relationship with her professors.

North Americans' attitudes about privacy can be difficult for many foreigners to understand. Their houses, yards, and offices can seem open and inviting, yet there are boundaries that others are not supposed to cross. If someone crosses these invisible lines, a Brazilian observes, one can see their bodies stiffen visibly and their manner will become cool and aloof.[17]

Family

Eakin explains that the ideal of the Brazilian affluent and powerful has been to have an extended family or clan. Such a family network constructed across generations and through marriage alliances with other families has historically been a visible demonstration of power in Brazilian society. Small or fragmented families indicate a lack of economic or political power. The Iberian practice of multiple surnames reflects the concern with family ties: your identity depends on your family connections. Anyone who cannot demonstrate family lineage is considered unimportant.[18]

Ritual kinship builds on biological kinship, and godparenting is an important social institution. Parents usually choose godparents from their own social level to reinforce powerful social and family networks, although sometimes parents try to persuade the more powerful to serve as godparents in an attempt to improve their and their children's lives.[19]

Page relates that personal relationships—a person's ties to family, clan, friends, and the people one knows—structure Brazilian society. The family is perhaps the most important of Brazil's contemporary institutions. The extended family, in particular, defines personal, social, and economic relations for most upper- and middle-class Brazilians.[20] In North American culture, the term "family" generally refers to a unit of father, mother, and children; grandparents, aunts, uncles, cousins, and others are more often called relatives. In contrast, in Brazil "family" usually means a network of people extended across generations and by marriage.

In Anglo-Saxon countries, such as England and the United States, the individual is raised to be his or her own master and is not possessed or encompassed by parents and family. Nepotism has a negative connotation. But in Brazil the network of family relationships and friendships is an imperative and affirms the importance of the network over the individual. A person is important or of value because he or she belongs to a family and has friends. Personal relationships define the person as a significant social entity.[21] And in Brazil the family takes on a great deal of responsibility for the welfare of its domestic employees.

A São Paulo sociologist, Noêmia Kobeh Ferreira, stated in a conversation with Annie Nimos that Brazilians *need* their families. Noêmia elaborated, "[This need is] hereditary, in our blood, and in our genes. We need parents, grandmothers and grandfathers, aunts and uncles, and cousins involved in our lives. We need full-body hugs and we need touch. We need to spend time with our children. We only want them in school half days. And we don't want our children to move away when they grow up." Gisela, an engineer from Rio Grande do Sul, confirms that adult children do not often move away from their families in Brazil. One middle-management employee at Dell in the state of Rio Grande do Sul commuted from São Paulo because, "of course," it would be too difficult for his wife and children to be separated from family and relatives.

Noêmia is of Lebanese descent on her father's side. The family went to live in Beirut for a few years, and her Brazilian mother was upset when Noêmia went to school all day. Her mother was unhappy about losing the time that she was accustomed to spending with her daughter. In Porto Alegre a professional woman with a master's degree who serves on a board of directors broke away from a meeting that included a North American. She explained to the visitor that she needed to go home to be there when her son, who was twenty-three, arrived for lunch. It was not that he needed her to be there; she liked to be with him at lunch time. Close family ties are forged and maintained.

Birthday parties in Brazil evidence the ties that Brazilians have with family and friends and the ties between generations of the family. A birthday party in Brazil is an event that includes both family and friends of all ages. Not only the child's friends but also the friends' families and the child's relatives are invited. Also, birthday parties for adults are much more common in Brazil than in the United States, and they also include extended family, friends, and people of all ages.

A North American family living in Santos had a party for their youngest daughter, Cathy. It was her fifth birthday. The mother, Alice, sent the eldest sister to invite some Brazilian children about Cathy's age whom the family knew because they lived on the same block. The party was scheduled from 2:00 P.M. to 5:00 P.M. Something must have been missed in the translation and cultural assumptions made. There was considerable confusion when the children came to the party accompanied by family members, all of whom sat down and stayed on until evening. Alice had carefully counted the number of cupcakes and party favors needed for the children she had invited. She had not prepared enough food or appropriate beverages for the brothers, sisters, and adults who came. There was considerable scrambling in the kitchen, and the maid came up with some stopgap measures. Fortunately, there was a large cake in addition to the cupcakes.

Subsequently, when Alice's whole family was invited to a birthday party for a neighbor's daughter, Cybele, Alice felt very embarrassed about her daughter's gathering. At Cybele's party there was a full table of delicious, individual sweets (*doces*) and delectable salty treats (*salgados*), such as little fried meat and cheese pies and individual pastry shells with shrimp filling. In addition, there were Guaraná (a soft drink), beer, coffee, a wonderful cake, cousins, aunts, uncles, friends, and grandparents. Music played. People talked and laughed. Children ran in and out. The party lasted all afternoon and into the evening. It would not occur to a Brazilian to designate a time for a party to end. The party would be over when the last guest had gone. Maria Brasil remembers the first birthday party her daughter had when she moved to the United States. She says she felt very sad because the only adults present were Maria and her husband. After that, she made sure to invite the children's parents, so that Maria would feel it was a "real" party.[22]

In the United States parents place great emphasis on teaching their children to make independent decisions and to take care of themselves. They raise them to loosen the close child-parent tie. As soon as their children get out of school, they expect them to get a job and support themselves, and society considers the children failures if they do not do so. Adult children who live with their parents usually pay something for the privilege, which in North American culture evidences individualism and responsibility.[23] In contrast, unmarried sons and daughters in

Brazil will frequently live with their parents, even though they may be in their twenties or thirties and have good jobs.

A woman in São Paulo who has a close relationship with her nieces related that they often visit her and bring their boyfriends. She is actively involved in their lives and makes decisions that in the United States might be seen as usurping parental authority. When one of the nieces started sleeping with her boyfriend, her aunt allowed her to use her guest room. "Better to have them in my home than off somewhere," she explained. In contrast, in one North American family, for example, the parents were resentful that their son's aunt and uncle presumed to interfere in the problems the young man was having with his university studies and managing his finances. They felt that this was a "family" matter and that the aunt and uncle were trying to usurp their authority.

North Americans do not relate to their parents in the same way that Brazilians do. João came to study for a year at the University of Texas and lived with a North American family. He was shocked to see that the wife's elderly mother lived by herself in an apartment, and once a week the family took the mother grocery shopping. He did not realize that both the family and the mother enjoyed their privacy, and the mother wanted to maintain her independence. João judged this culturally acquired behavior negatively, which hampered his communication with the Bensons and interfered with his learning about customs in the United States from them.[24]

In Brazil, Claudina Junker's grandmother lived alone in her own house, one block from her two grandchildren and her daughter and in the same neighborhood as various other relatives. As she got older and less capable, it became more difficult for her to live alone. She was asked, many times, to move in with her daughter and granddaughter, but she wanted to stay in her own house, which is unusual in Brazil. Her daughter and two grandchildren went to her house every day for eight years to visit and look after her. It would have been easier on the family to have had her move in, but since she lived so close and family members were in and out of her house on a daily basis, her situation was tantamount to living with the family. In addition, she had a live-in maid and gardener who watched over her. Such domestic assistance is far more affordable in Brazil than in the United States.

In response to a North American visitor's comment that the family was very kind to the grandmother, Claudina responded that the family certainly took care of the grandmother out of love. However, she stated, going to see the grandmother every day was more than kindness or an option; it was a duty and an obligation about which there is no choice in Brazilian culture. Patrícia Guardini took in her mother-in-law's sister who was confined to a wheelchair and required constant care for the two years before her death. Again, this was not just a question of compassion but an obligation and a duty.

This obligation extends beyond family to servants and employees. Life with servants in Brazil appears luxurious and carefree to the visitor from the United States. But it is not as carefree as it appears; most North Americans do not understand that many of these relationships are long term or for life and that there is an obligation on the part of the employing family to ensure that the servants (and frequently their families) have food, clothing, and sometimes medical care.

Friendship

Culture governs the closeness of personal relationships. People from collective cultures are conditioned to nurture close, dependent relationships with extended family and friends, whereas those from individualistic cultures maintain more distance from anyone who is not an immediate family member. Brazilians feel they can count on a friend for assistance at any time, no matter what the situation. Obviously, deep friendships require time to establish, but Brazilians who have had the opportunity to become well acquainted with North Americans in Brazil or the United States feel that North Americans do not extend the same unconditional friendship that they rely on in Brazil.[25]

With friendship in Brazil come both expectations and responsibilities. For example, Marisa, a thirty-six-year-old divorcée in Porto Alegre who had begun a serious relationship, started to receive complaints from her friends after about six weeks that she was not contacting them often enough, that they did not see her or talk to her enough. She explained to them that between work and several evenings out every week she did not have much time left over. They responded that her friends were as important as work and her new love and that she should not neglect her *obligations* to her friends. She organized a dinner for her friends at her apartment the same week because, "of course," she could not neglect this *responsibility*.

Althen explains that while to many foreigners North Americans seem relatively warm and approachable on first encounter, with their smiles and friendly hellos, they later come to seem remote and unreachable. Many Brazilians describe North Americans' relationships with other people as superficial. Some also believe it is only with foreigners that Americans tend to be slow to make friends, if at all. But most North Americans relate the same way among themselves. They are very private and tend to keep personal thoughts and feelings to themselves.

"They seem cold," one Brazilian woman said. "It is hard to get to know them—to know what they really think and feel."[26]

Most North Americans are simply not available for the close relationships that Brazilians take for granted, in part because they value self-reliance. They usually avoid becoming too dependent on or involved with other people, and except for immediate family members, they do not want others to be dependent on them. They withdraw from relationships if they become too demanding.[27]

Of course, most North Americans do have a few close friends with whom they discuss personal matters and to whom they feel some obligation, but they have more "acquaintances," who require less intimacy and mutual obligation. In the United States, the word "friend" is used loosely to include acquaintances, which is confusing to a Brazilian.[28]

For years after Maria Brasil moved to the United States, when she complained that she did not have any friends, her husband would exclaim in frustration, "What do you mean, you don't have any friends? You have lots of friends." She finally realized they were not talking about the same thing. "Amigo" in Brazil signifies a much closer relationship than "friend" does in the United States. A North American friend is more like an acquaintance in Brazil. Maria had a multitude of acquaintances, but she did not have the close, mutually obligated friendships she was accustomed to nurturing in Brazil.[29]

Interaction Is Personal

If you want to know Brazilians, you must get to know them personally, because they are a most personal people. It is the individual who interests them.[30]

Emotion—that is, like and dislike—is the ethic that dictates all forms of personal association (*convívio*) in Brazil. Rega thinks that few foreigners can understand this important aspect of Brazilian life. A purely economic relationship has to be mixed with a personal relationship, so that in Brazil, to win over a customer, the seller has to establish a friendship. A Philadelphia businessman was shocked to find that in Brazil, to win a customer he had to win him first as a friend.[31]

Bernard was emphatic that ultimately personal feelings dictate with whom Brazilians will associate and at what level. As an example he explained that at Companhia Val do Rio Doce where his brother, Emil, works the people in the company will associate and socialize with the persons whom they *like*. They do not select their personal associations because of job protocol or because they are supposed to periodically "socialize" with coworkers.

Lourenço Juvenal, who worked for Unilever in São Paulo, confirmed the importance of personal relationships in the workplace. He remarked that if a key person moves to another company, the whole group that works with him or her will go too. Annie Nimos commented that this can also happen in United States. Lourenço agreed but pointed out that in Brazil it is expected that the entire group will move; it is the norm rather than an occasional occurrence. When Dell Computer Corporation was interviewing to fill key positions for their operation in the Porto Alegre area, the interviewer would dwell on salary and job description with a promising candidate. However, candidates constantly returned to questions about their immediate managers and asked to meet the manager and the people with whom they would be working. While the Dell interviewer concentrated on compensation and job description as incentives, the personal relations aspect of the position was paramount in the candidate's mind. Carol Hart, who has been traveling to Brazil for forty years and managed an office in Rio, confirmed that relationships in the workplace are much more personal than in the United States.

Bernard stated that in the United States his colleagues invite him to dinner approximately every six months because this is a social protocol of their *professional* relationship; in Brazil, he pointed out, you are invited because of your personal relationship to the host, not because of professional ties. He would trust good daily interaction with a colleague in Brazil as a sign of friendship much more than in the United States. In the United States, you may get along smoothly at work with colleagues, because this is what you are supposed to do, but the relationship usually does not extend beyond the workplace. In Bernard's view there is a basic hypocrisy in communication in the United States. North Americans and the British are extremely polite and well mannered in their communications with each other, but this is a facade. Bernard maintained that it is difficult to establish friendships.

Social organization also affects how people are motivated. Members of individualistic and collective groups will be motivated differently. In the United States, teachers may assume that most children want to get ahead and may try to encourage students with contests. Children of some minority cultures often appear lazy to them because they seem not to want to make the effort the teacher expects. This stereotype takes on new meaning when we learn that to stand out from one's peers in collective cultures is to place oneself in jeopardy, and it is to be avoided.[32] The teacher is steeped in the individualism of North American culture, but some children have been conditioned by the collective culture of their families.

Verónica Ribeiro, a teacher, explained that there is no such thing as a contest or competitive approach as a motivation for learning in Brazil: "We have never heard of a spelling contest as seen in movies here. Students are encouraged, of course, to beat their own scores, and there is always a ranking as far as grades are concerned, ranging from the top students in a class to the poor ones." Collective cultures generally train their members to be motivated by cooperation rather than competition.

That Brazilians are a very personal people affects the medium by which they prefer to communicate. Lourenço Juvenal commented that today North Americans want to communicate by e-mail, even if the person they wish to communicate with is sitting in the next cubicle. Lourenço is not unsophisticated or inefficient. He has an MBA and has worked for several multinational corporations. He thinks it is silly to send an e-mail communication to someone in the next cubicle when you can speak to him or her personally. His order of preference for communicating with people in the workplace is first to speak with them in person, then to use the telephone, and only then e-mail. Lourenço's preference reflects Brazilian culture's personal style. He first prefers the personal contact that is so rich in nonverbal communication cues.

DaMatta explains that Brazilians personalize all relationships to the greatest extent possible. They use *jeito*, finding a way, to personalize a situation ostensibly governed by an impersonal norm. All social interaction is governed by personal relationships. In negotiation and conciliation, intermediaries—persons who can reconcile all that society irremediably divides—play a significant, ubiquitous role.[33] Getting anything done in Brazil depends greatly on intermediaries and therefore on one's network of social relationships. To do business or to meet people in Brazil, it is important to obtain introductions through a mutual acquaintance. The importance of having personal contacts in Brazil cannot be overemphasized.

CONSIDERING THE SOCIAL organization of Brazil into collective in-groups, the very personal nature of relationships, the importance and nature of interaction with family and friends, and the out-groups of Da-Matta's "street" leads us to the subject of hierarchy. The steep hierarchy inherent in Brazilian society governs many aspects of communication style and is not always apparent to foreigners.

CHAPTER NINE

Ranking Systems

A Brazilian will say imperiously, "Do you know who you're talking to?" whereas a North American will challenge, "Who do you think you are?" [1]

Hierarchy

All living things have a pecking order. Therefore, all cultures will have a system of ranking their members as to status and privilege.[2] The acceptance of hierarchy in a society is, by definition, an acceptance of inequality.[3] When the hierarchy of a culture is steep, with significant differences in people's rank in the social order, the inequality among its members will be significant. Communication between a person from a culture with steep hierarchical organization and one from a culture with a shallow hierarchy presents many difficulties.

Persons can be ranked in a culture by such factors as order of birth, order of arrival, or order of status. Hall states that societies will order people, situation, or station—but not all three simultaneously.[4] Therefore, depending on the culture, people requiring a service might be attended to according to their age, in the order of their arrival—first come, first served—or in keeping with their perceived social rank. Different factors determine a person's rank in the hierarchy of different cultures.

The cordiality of the Brazilian can easily mislead a foreigner into thinking that Brazil is a more egalitarian society than it is and that one can assume easy access to persons in all venues. But it masks an unforgiving ranking system. Eakin writes that Brazil's style of communal Catholicism reinforces the culture's hierarchy. It sees society as an organic body whose component parts must work in harmony to function and remain healthy. These parts are not all equal as individuals, but each has its assigned place in the social pyramid.[5] According to Ribeiro, hidden beneath Brazilian cultural uniformity is a profound social distance. The class antagonism that corresponds to all social stratification is exacerbated and sets a very restricted and privileged stratum in opposition to the masses. Social distances are more unbridgeable than are racial differences in Brazil.[6]

When Teresa Caldeira was conducting research in São Paulo, she found that her middle-class, academic position framed her relationships with members of all the social groups she studied. Working-class people felt obliged to grant interviews and give detailed answers about crime in their neighborhoods even when their fear and insecurity justified refusal and silence. She recounted, "Refusals increased as I talked with people farther up the social hierarchy, who felt confident in saying no to a middle-class person. Interviews with upper-class people were hard to obtain and required introductions." Upper-class people frequently dismissed some of the questions that all working-class people answered. Elites assumed she shared their own views and knowledge and would answer requests for explanation with, "You know what I mean!" She found that politicians and businessmen gave her the attention her position as a university professor commands, even when they strongly disagreed with her on matters such as human rights.[7]

Caldeira pointed out that Brazil's elite can employ both personal ties and statutes to avoid the violence that the Brazilian police use to control the population. Conversely, the police apply an unwritten code of inequality to the working class, and in some instances, this inequality is codified. Caldeira explains, "Brazilian legislation guarantees preferential treatment by the police and the prison system to anyone with a college degree."[8]

David Mayberry-Lewis writes that the disadvantaged in Brazil perpetually search for vertical, patron-client relations. These vertical ties provide the surest, sometimes the only, form of security and advancement in a society where upward mobility is difficult and restricted and where the majority of the population lives in wretched conditions.[9]

Roberto DaMatta describes Brazil's social structure as putting each monkey on its own branch.[10]

DaMatta says that as a hierarchical society, Brazil has numerous criteria for the classification of persons. They can be ranked according to skin color or money; they can be ranked according to the power they exert or the ugliness of their faces, by their family name, or by their bank account. The possibilities are unlimited.[11] In Brazil, the shade of one's skin generally corresponds to one's rank in the hierarchy. The persons darkest in color are generally found at the bottom of Brazil's social ladder, and complexions become lighter as one moves up the rungs.

The communication style in a steep hierarchical society serves to re-inforce or create hierarchical difference among individuals. Hierarchical distance, which can also be conceived of as interpersonal power distance, affects the degree of formality used in communication.[12] In a culture with a steep hierarchy, individuals use a communication style that maintains social distance. In recognition of the hierarchy, they tend to display positive emotions or behavior to persons who have higher status and negative emotions or behavior to persons who rank lower in status.[13]

"There is not and never has been a free people here, one that ruled its own destiny in search of its own prosperity. What there has been and what there still is, is a mass of workers exploited, humiliated, and offended by a dominant minority that is frighteningly efficient in the formation and maintenance of its own plan for prosperity, always ready to squelch any threat of reform of the effective social order." [14]

Brazil is aristocratic in its culture and politics, with the upper classes demanding deference from those considered social inferiors. People of "high rank" maintain an authoritative distance and use formal, although personal courtesy. North Americans, in contrast, strive for democracy and egalitarianism in relating to others and as a result employ a far more informal style of communication[15] across the spectrum of society's social levels than do Brazilians.

An individual's communication style in a flatter hierarchical society, such as the United States, strives to decrease status differences. A North American will tend to demote the rank of persons at higher echelons and promote that of persons at lower ones, communicating in a manner that both advocates and maintains equality. This communication behavior is the opposite of that employed by cultures with a steep hierarchy.[16] Nonetheless, Christopher Richards comments, although Brazil's social classes are clearly separated, the tension between them in interpersonal communication is not commensurate with the great social inequality that exists.[17]

The United States is organized with smaller distances in its social hierarchy than exist in the steeper social organization of many world cultures. The apparent lack of respect that North Americans express toward persons in authority and the familiarity with which they interact with persons of lower status than themselves can confuse or offend persons from cultures with a steep hierarchical organization. They frequently think that North Americans are communicating in a manner that is disrespectful or too familiar. For the purposes of successful—and enjoyable—communication, people from other cultures should understand that North Americans are conditioned by their culture to communicate in a manner that will decrease the hierarchical distance in the social ranking system. This is not to say that North Americans cannot or do not ever defer in their communication style. Although there is only one form of "you" for both formal and informal address in English, one can communicate deference by use of a title and last name, "Mr. Benson," and through such means as dress, posture, expression, tone of voice, and demeanor.

Shallow hierarchical organization affords an open and mobile society, whereas a steep hierarchy constricts social advancement. European intellectuals have observed that the authority of persons in government and large corporations in the United States stems from the weight of public opinion in a democratic environment rather than from hierarchical organization. North Americans in authority therefore strive to appear benevolent and democratic. In general, the United States is a fluid society where anyone can climb to the apex of the social pyramid, in contrast to the more rigid class divisions of Brazil.[18]

Hierarchical organization of a culture affects communication within a society on a daily basis. The United States' shallow hierarchy encourages participatory communication between persons of lower and higher ranks, while the steep, authoritarian hierarchy of Brazil discourages input from those at lower levels to those at higher levels. Furthermore, in Brazil's steep hierarchy, information slows down as it moves up the levels of authority, ending up in a bottleneck as it reaches the decision maker who is overloaded with information.[19] On the way down, information moves quickly but is manipulated as a resource that enhances status and authority. Steep hierarchies breed concealment and misrepresentation of information.[20] In a flatter hierarchy, information flows more quickly and freely and with less distortion.

Nonverbal Communication Cues

Studies of gender differences in the United States suggest that women are more skilled than men at nonverbal communication. One of several plausible explanations is that women more often have passive or submissive roles and learn to read nonverbal communication cues to appease those in positions of power.[21] Brazil's steep hierarchical organization equates to high interpersonal power distances, and, in fact, Brazilians are highly skilled at interpreting nonverbal communication cues.

A senior North American executive working at Dell in Brazil commented that Brazilians constantly scan nonverbal cues for information and meaning, particularly those of a person who is high on the ladder of authority. He became aware that his employees attached great importance to anything he said. Any negative comment he might make about how things were progressing, and which he would consider a normal expression of frustration during the course of a day, would be interpreted as a portent of doom. If he was tired from working long hours, he had to look energetic and optimistic rather than show it, because of the strong effect it had on his staff. He found that he influenced the outlook, morale, and rumors in the workplace to a far greater degree than in the United States; Brazil's steep hierarchy weighted his demeanor, his affect, and his words with far more communicative power than he was accustomed to. Since he was being overinterpreted and misinterpreted, he found he had to consciously monitor all of these channels of communication in a way that was not necessary in a North American setting.

Power

L. F. Veríssimo insists that the de facto president of Brazil is not the president of the United States, as Brazilians often say, but the U.S. secretary of the treasury.[22]

Brazilians live in two systems of relations that are superimposed—one is personal and one is legal. Personal power comes from the strong network of personal relationships.[23] The small power discrepancies within this network encourage communication.[24] Any person who does not have such a network must defend himself or herself through a legal system that is impersonal. The legal system is steeply hierarchical, and large power distances discourage and impede communication. Interpreting nonverbal communication cues becomes important for survival. DaMatta writes that in Brazil the law keeps only the weak in their place, because the powerful use their personal networks of communication to rise above the law.[25]

DaMatta comments on the fact that in Brazil a university graduate and a laborer will receive different punishments for the same crime. He contrasts Brazil to the United States, France, and England. It appears to him that the latter have justice systems that operate on the basis of right or wrong, whereas in Brazil laws are interpreted according to one's rank in society.[26]

In the international arena, power differences also affect communication. During negotiations between a Brazilian leather manufacturer and North American importers, for example, one reason that the North Americans had more power was because they were citizens of the most powerful country in the world. In contrast, the Brazilian team, in the words of Brazilian communications professor Pedro de Moraes Garcez, were citizens of a "troubled third world country."[27]

Garcez reports that a result of this imbalance of power was the use of interruptions by the negotiating parties. The North Americans both interrupted (more than they would normally) and resisted interruptions more than the Brazilians. Power or conversational control is an important communication issue because the interruptions of the Brazilian presentations by the North Americans triggered and magnified communication problems during the course of negotiations.[28] (See Chapter 14 for a fuller discussion.)

Many nations are ambivalent about the United States. While they respect U.S. wealth and military strength, they fear U.S. motives and interference in domestic affairs. They often envy U.S. preeminence, which causes them to exaggerate the nation's deficiencies. The United States is sometimes seen as a savior but more often as a necessary evil.[29]

Brazilians believe that the United States is superior to Brazil in a number of ways. The culture industry and consumer patterns of the United States greatly influence society in Brazil. Signs in São Paulo announce Brazilian businesses and products in English, to gain greater acceptance in the Brazilian market. This does not mean that Brazilians do not criticize various aspects of North American society. They characterize North Americans as cold, hard, too serious, distant, excessively formal, and interested only in money. In contrast, they describe Brazilians as happy, warm, friendly, informal, and always able to "find a way." Ana Cristina Martes finds that what Brazilians appreciate most are citizens' rights in the United States.[30]

Roles

Althen writes in *American Ways* that North Americans tend to relate to the specific role in which they know a person—physician, mechanic, or colleague. Personal behavior and character traits are less important. North Americans rarely spend the time that is the norm in Brazil to meet, greet, and get to know an individual, and unless there has been some public scandal, North Americans are less likely than Brazilians to be aware of a person's identity outside of his or her role in society.[31]

Race may contribute to determining a person's role in society. In Brazil, as discussed earlier, the elite generally have lighter skins and the poor darker skins.

The Galpão Crioulo restaurant in Porto Alegre serves the traditional grilled meats of the South and entertains patrons with traditional dance

Gaúchos converse at a Freio de Ouro competition in Rio Grande do Sul.

and song. The female dancers are beautiful, clad in traditional long dresses. They provide a pretty backdrop for the male dancers, who are flashy, sensuous, and display machismo. The men perform vigorous dances and show off intricate use of the boleadeira, *southern Brazil's equivalent of the lasso. A reflection of the region's* gaúcho *culture, the men dominate the show. And mirroring Brazil as a whole, the* gaúcho *performers represent a wide range of phenotypes.*

Gender is a fundamental determinant of roles in most societies. Traditionally, Brazilian culture has been male dominated. Gambini states that Brazilian society was founded on and is maintained by the masculine principle. He describes it as "phallic, domesticating, penetrating, conquering, and full of impunity in its excesses."[32] But in recent years the role of women has gradually begun to change.

By 1997 in São Paulo, for example, 44 percent of newly registered doctors and 63 percent of practicing dentists were women, and there were a large number of female engineers as well.[33] This trend can be seen in all of Brazil's major cities.

In October 2000 Marta Suplicy, fifty-five, was elected mayor of São Paulo, a city with a population of more than 10 million, plus 8 million in the suburbs. São Paulo is not only the largest city in Brazil, it is the largest and richest urban area in South America and the Southern Hemisphere. Suplicy has been called "mayor most rare." In a city traditionally governed by lawyers, engineers, and bankers, she is trained as a sexologist. She is a monied aristocrat whose strongest following is among the poor, a socialist in a financial center with the largest accumulation of wealth in Latin America, and a feminist competing in a political domain that still values rough machismo. She took office with a daunting task ahead of her: a debt-ridden and corrupt municipal government and many other grave urban problems. Still, she was elected to office with 58.5 percent of the vote.[34]

According to Maria Brasil, one should expect differences among social classes and geographic locations and expect some families to be more traditional than others. But a desire for change and the economic realities have dramatically altered a woman's role in Brazil. Many women now have college degrees, work outside the home, and are involved in politics. In addition to São Paulo, several large cities, including Santos and some cities in northeastern Brazil, have had female mayors in recent years. Women work at high levels in banking and big business, and more daughters are taking over their fathers' companies. The general attitude among many young women is that there is nothing they cannot do. The last two decades have seen implementation of new divorce laws, extended maternity and paternity leaves, and changing attitudes toward single and separated women.[35]

Maria Brasil has traveled alone throughout Brazil, on airplanes and buses, staying at hotels and small inns, going out to eat at night, taking taxis, buses, and the metro. She says that a male escort is sometimes advisable, but in general Brazil is a country where women traveling alone are not harassed, although people may stare.[36]

In the past the Brazilian woman has been treated like chattel, with virginity and fidelity fiercely guarded. The journalist Lucy Dias has followed research regarding the fidelity of today's Brazilian woman, with a focus on married women of the middle and upper-middle classes. If the woman does not have to reveal her identity, she readily admits that she has betrayed her husband. This betrayal most often occurs during a long marriage, and the woman confesses that these "exceptions" are what help her endure the tedium of years. Dias states that everyone knows that a Brazilian man's greatest fear is being cuckolded. And what he fears most is what happens.[37]

Noêmia Kobeh Ferreira, a sociologist, stated that despite the recent increase in the number of professional working women, in general marriage is still more important than a career for Brazilian women. She said that their dilemma is that they do everything by halves. "They work

half time, they are a wife half time—and they end up half satisfied."
Children in Brazil are in school half days. In fact, Noêmia volunteered,
"Brazilians do half-everything."

Annie Nimos talked with two teachers in Porto Alegre, Mariane and
Inge. It seems to them that the male/female ratio in the city is one available man for ten to fifteen available women, in the twenty- to forty-year-
old range. They say the men are either taken or gay. Because of this, there
has been a reversal of traditional roles in this urban setting. Men and
women meet and exchange numbers, and if the man does not call, the
woman calls him, or the woman might not wait but make the first call.
She might ask the man to go to dinner or to the movies. Sometimes the
woman pays for both; often they split the bill. "But," Mariane says, "the
men don't want any commitment." A male Brazilian professional transferred by his company to Porto Alegre confirms this dating protocol.

Both Mariane and Inge said that in recent years women have bettered
themselves and become more modern but men have not. They say that
women now want a partner who adds something to their lives. Men and
women come to Porto Alegre from smaller towns and the country to
work and to study. The women stay and cannot find partners. The men
study or work and then go back home to find young wives to bear their
children and often to settle down. Mariane and Inge think this helps to
ensure that the men get more traditional and submissive wives.

In Brazil the women of each household where the Nimos couple
stayed monitored Carl Nimos solicitously. They seemed to want to discern his mood and humor, as if concerned that he might be disgruntled
or dissatisfied in any way. Although Brazilians are consummately hospitable to all of their guests, the satisfaction of men in a household is
clearly a central concern. It was important not only that Carlos want for
nothing as a guest but also that he be pleased and satisfied. It seems as
though there is a latent fear of a man's displeasure.

IN BRAZIL IT IS ESSENTIAL to consider a person's station when communicating so that one can discern the many overt as well as subtle cues
in personal interaction. This awareness will greatly aid a foreigner in
communicating more effectively in Brazil. And since we all have preconceived notions about what some behaviors signify, whether or not
they derive from ranking, we need to consider how preconceptions affect
communication.

CHAPTER TEN

Preconceptions

Cultural Profiles

Prejudices and stereotypes are preconceptions, which our cultures engender in every one of us. These preconceptions filter our perceptions. We expect others to conform to our behavioral patterns and carry these subliminal expectations into cross-cultural encounters.[1] A deviation from our standards of conduct leads to a negative reaction stemming from our subconscious cultural rules and impedes communication.[2] We need to learn to suspend our negative reactions because the person from another culture may be behaving according to his or her own cultural rules.[3]

Because people are thus programmed in their behavior, stereotypes primarily express the culture of the person who espouses the stereotype. A Brazilian person who says that North Americans are rude because they leave a party without saying good-bye to everyone is basing that judgment on the Brazilian ritual of leave-taking, and the North American who maintains that Brazilians are rude because they always arrive late is basing his or her judgment on the North American conception of time and conventions regarding its allocation.[4]

People who use stereotypes make reality fit their preconceptions. Stereotypes are rigid. People tend to see what they expect to see and to *discount* that which conflicts with these preconceptions, stereotypes, or prejudices toward persons.[5] The different cultural identities of two persons attempting to communicate will encourage each to perceive the other as having the group attributes of the other's foreign culture rather than see the person as a unique individual.[6] Preconceptions can be positive or negative, but usually we are not aware of them[7] unless someone's unexpected behavior raises them to a conscious level.

People who grow up in a particular culture, whether Brazilian, North American, or another one, share certain values and assumptions. This does not mean that people from the same culture all share exactly the same precepts but that most of the time they agree on what is right and wrong, desirable and undesirable. A culture can be viewed as a collection of principal values and assumptions that shape the way a group of people perceive and relate to the world around them.[8]

Heaven is where the police are British, the chefs French, the mechanics German, and the soccer team Brazilian, and it is all organized by the Swiss. Hell is where the police are German, the chefs British, the mechanics French, and the soccer team Swiss, and it is all organized by Brazilians.[9]

Although preconceptions frequently are misleading, there is nonetheless a wealth of evidence provided by anthropologists, sociologists, psychologists, and others that a culture shapes national character traits. There are reasons why we perceive national or cultural identities:[10]

1. Members of a culture share common early experiences and from birth are trained in behavior by their culture.

2. These common experiences and training produce similar personality profiles.

3. Since the early experiences and training of individuals differ from culture to culture, personality characteristics and values differ from culture to culture.

4. Because there is a wide range of individual differences in persons, not all members of a culture have the same personality or behave in exactly the same ways. Even so, most members of a given culture share many aspects of personality and behavior to varying degrees.

A young woman who worked at the reception desk of the Flat Collins apartments in Porto Alegre told Annie Nimos that in her experience of working in hotels in the city, different nationalities seem to have different personalities. The Japanese are extremely polite, and in general North Americans are quite exigent. She laughed and said, "The Italians are charmers. Even when I know they just want to get me to do something for them, I enjoy them."

Because a majority of members of a given culture share many aspects of personality and behavior, useful mental representations of national character can be compiled to construct a national model. One can add to and build on this model through experience and observation. Although the model may not apply to each individual, it will fit the majority. Stereotypes, on the other hand, apply to only a few members of a culture but are attributed to most.[11] It does not take many stereotypical "ugly Americans" to tarnish the reputation of all the North Americans who travel unobtrusively and interact well with foreigners.

Understanding Others, Understanding Ourselves

Page points out that people in Brazil have developed regional characteristics because of the country's vast size. *Paulistas* are seen as hardworking, *cariocas* as fun-loving, *mineiros* (residents of the state of Minas Gerais) as frugal, *nordestinos* (northeasterners) as introverted, and *gaúchos* (from the extreme South) as fiercely independent. But Portugal has a history of remarkable tolerance for cultural, religious, and racial diversity and passed this tolerance on to Brazilian society as a centralizing force. Over the past century and a half Brazil has demonstrated this characteristic by its welcome and assimilation of non-Portuguese immigrants as varied as Italians, Germans, Spaniards, Syrians, Lebanese, and Japanese. The children of these immigrants have melted into Brazilian society, including the Brazilianized descendants of North American southerners who resettled in São Paulo after the fall of the Confederacy. Brazil's amalgamated diversity unifies rather than divides the country.[12]

Althen writes that to understand others, it is helpful to understand how they see themselves. Most North Americans see themselves as individuals who are different from all others, compatriot or foreigner. They generally believe they choose their own values and way of life rather than that they learn these from their culture. They often comment on the different traits that characterize the people of the diverse regions of the United States, such as New York, the South, the Midwest, and California. But although they willingly generalize about subgroups within their own nation, they resist generalizations that apply to North Americans as a whole. Because they are acculturated to see themselves as individuals, they generally believe that regional and ethnic differences are more pronounced in the United States than in Brazil. They frequently deny that there is an "American culture" because they often conceive of culture as a set of arbitrary and foreign customs to be found in other countries.[13] What is closest to us is what we know least well.[14]

North Americans generally believe also that the United States is a superior country because it is economically and militarily powerful and exerts its influence throughout the world. They consider its democratic political system the best because of its citizens' rights. They also avidly advocate their country's free enterprise system because many Americans enjoy a high standard of living. Since North Americans consider their country superior, by definition they consider many other countries inferior. They assume that people in those countries are not quite as intelligent, hardworking, or practical as they are, and they tend to be condescending. They generally respect Canadians and northern Europeans and esteem outstanding individuals of any nationality, whether a Kenyan runner, a Brazilian singer, or a Russian scientist. However, they often perceive foreigners as underdeveloped North Americans whose primitive economic and social systems and quaint customs prevent them from achieving what they could if they would learn the North American way of doing things.[15]

Maria Brasil lives in the United States. Her daughter, Inês, was born in Rio de Janeiro and visited Brazil during every North American summer as she was growing up. Inês decided to seek a "compromise" between Brazilian and North American cultures. She went to live in Europe for a few years, which, she says, combines the best of her two worlds. Inês returned to the United States with a better understanding of North American culture, perhaps because of her exposure to several others. This exposure seems to have given her more understanding, patience, and tolerance for the quirks of North American culture that her "Brazilian side" dislikes.[16]

Looking North

Annie Nimos visited an evening class on cultural differences at the Instituto Cultural Brasileiro Norte-Americano (ICBNA) in Porto Alegre. The participants included young people and adults, and on the chalkboard they prepared a model of their conception of the average North American family:[17]

- John Smith has an office job.
- Mary Smith is a kindergarten teacher.
- Both husband and wife have university degrees.
- Together they earn U.S. $100,000.00 per year.
- They have two children, Paul and Julie.
- They live in a very nice house in the suburbs. The house has three bedrooms and thin walls (no doubt a reference to wood and drywall construction).
- They worry about tornados.
- Their house is full of candles that they light.
- They go on vacation two times a year.
- They have all the latest technological gadgets.
- The Smiths have two cars, which are always dirty inside.
- They do everything with the car.
- They do not exercise or participate in sports.
- They are fat.

- John does not have time to sit down at a table and eat.
- They eat unhealthy food.
- Typical foods they consume are eggs and bacon, pancakes, cereals, pizza, hamburgers, and Chinese food.
- The community has a lot of churches.
- The Smiths are very religious but only in appearance.
- They are superficial in the relationships they have with others.
- They are polite, but they lack human warmth.
- The Smiths are very materialistic.
- The Smiths don't like people from the rest of the world.
- They don't take a shower every day.
- Their parties finish too early.
- They think that every person's job is important, no matter what the person does.

This composite was constructed from impressions gathered on visits to the United States, encounters with North Americans, and from reading, television, and Hollywood movies. These perceptions affect expectations and interaction between Brazilians and North Americans and therefore affect communication.

Another group Annie Nimos visited with was a chapter of the Friendship Force in Brazil. The Friendship Force has chapters around the world and promotes intercultural understanding through the exchange and hosting of visitors in homes. Annie asked this group what they thought were the salient characteristics of North Americans. These were their impressions:

- North Americans don't make much effort to learn another language.
- They are not well informed. They arrive in Brazil knowing little about the country, even though they are given culturegrams before coming. They expect to encounter snakes and "people in trees" everywhere, even in Brazil's temperate South.
- They wear funny shorts, T-shirts, and caps. They don't care how they look.
- Although they make a poor initial impression, when you get to know them, Americans are very nice.

The preconception of many Brazilians that every North American is racially prejudiced also interferes with successful communication. U.S. society has elements of racism by any standards, but it is an inaccurate perception that anyone who does not have a light complexion is classified as "black" and that every light-skinned person is racist. Such a prejudgment can hinder a Brazilian's personal interaction and communication with North Americans, and it interfered with Annie Nimos's communication with one class member at an English-language school. This person, European in phenotype, was the only Brazilian with whom Annie talked who allowed any hostility to show in interacting with her.

Many Brazilians form their impressions of the United States from news fragments, whether in print or on television, just as many people throughout the world form their impressions of other countries. And international news, like most news, focuses on problems and incidents whenever they occur. Television has a large impact on societies everywhere. In Brazil, as in many countries with a low functional literacy rate, television has a disproportionate impact over print. A number of Brazilians' comments indicate that from news reports they perceive Mexico as a country full of desperately poor people, all pressing to cross the border into the United States. They believe that Mexicans as a whole are poorer and more destitute than Brazilians, although statistics show that most of Brazil's population is poorer than that of Mexico. In general, their impressions of Mexico are as inaccurate as the general impressions that U.S. citizens have of Mexico, which again illustrates the difficulties of understanding and communicating across cultural borders.

While in Brazil, Annie Nimos commented in a conversation that the United States was colonized by families of men, women, and children who came to make better lives for themselves and that they were basically poor members of the working class. In contrast, Brazil was colonized primarily by men: soldiers and men of noble and important families who were sent with the mission to extract wealth. Many grandees were given great power and large tracts of land. One of the persons in the conversation group was a Dutch national who was living and working in Brazil. He remarked on Annie's use of the word "poor." In school in Holland he was taught that the United States was colonized by materially privileged persons from western Europe and that they brought with them western Europe's technology. He was taught that this class of people is what made the United States great and why the country developed so fast.

Some North Americans react strongly to the perspective of this young Dutch man. Marilyn, a North American of Swedish descent, referred to Emma Lazarus's poem on the Statue of Liberty, which "stands clearly on fact." "Witness my grandparents (poor, uneducated) arriving at Ellis Island and my Jewish husband's parents (poor, uneducated) arriving there. I wish I knew if this man's account is typical [of a foreign attitude]. Very tempting, I'm sure, to assume that this country's greatness can be attributed to those super-civilized western Europeans."

Brazilians frequently comment about living in a third world country and often wonder what North Americans think of them. In fact, even

Schoolchildren in São Paulo are excited to meet foreign visitors on a field trip.

children have this self-consciousness. When Annie and Carl Nimos were visiting the Butantan Institute in São Paulo, they encountered a group of schoolchildren there on a field trip to see the snakes used to develop antivenin. The children, who ranged in age from ten to thirteen, asked where the couple had come from. When the word passed that they were from the United States, the children flocked around to ask questions. "What do Americans think of us? Do they say we are a third world country?" Annie did not want to give the most accurate response, which was that most North Americans do not think of Brazil at all; they would be hard pressed even to locate the country with much accuracy. She was surprised that children so young would be conscious of Brazil's image to the outside world and concerned about its being labeled a "third world" country. The children were curious, engaging, and friendly. They wanted to try out words and phrases in English that they had learned, and they gathered with delight to talk to the couple and comment among themselves.

Stereotyping

Cultural caricatures, that is, stereotypes, get in the way of perceiving and successfully communicating with a person as an individual.

Juan Mario Sandoval is a Mexican who was trained in social psychology in the United States. He has taught intercultural (or, more accurately, *intra*cultural) communication training courses for corporate employees in the United States. In a male-female group of mixed ethnicities, he intentionally started out by presenting stereotypes of gender and ethnic groups. As he spoke, he could see each group that he targeted react negatively. He watched the tension build. When someone finally challenged the stereotypes presented, which is exactly the response he was trying to provoke, he pointed out that this is how people simplify ethnicity and gender. He then encouraged the participants to talk about themselves. They began to emerge from their "classification" of gender and ethnicity as individuals. He pointed out, and the group concurred, that as the person speaking began to take on individual characteristics to the others in the group, that person began to shed a simplified, stereotypical image.

Juan Mario commented that at the beginning of the class he himself had been guilty of stereotyping. One participant, who looked Latino, registered as Jaime Martinez. Unconsciously, Juan Mario began to speak and relate to him like a Latin. Standing very close, he greeted Jaime, "Mucho gusto." Jaime backed up, extended his hand at arm's length, and replied, "I'm pleased to meet you. My name is Jimmy MAR-tinez. I don't speak Spanish." Jimmy only looked Latino; his acculturation was that of a North American anglophone, and he was uncomfortable with Juan Mario's unconscious cultural switch.

Donald Lacy, an older, upper-middle-class white man who had had little contact with African Americans, except for what he called a few bad experiences, was one of the people in Juan Mario's training class. Lacy confided to Juan Mario that he was having difficulty dealing with a multiethnic workforce in his company, which is why he was participating in the class. Lacy ended up seated next to Steve Williams, a very large, very black man. Lacy was obviously uncomfortable. One by one, the participants were asked to talk about themselves—their school experiences, their family, and whether they came from a rich, middle-class, or poor environment. They were asked about their career paths. It turned out that Lacy and Williams came from very similar family and economic backgrounds. They both worked in marketing. Both were Roman Catholic. As the two men emerged as individuals from their ethnic and racial "categories," they were drawn to what they had in common. During the training course, they were given the opportunity to see each other as individuals, and because of this they forged a friendship that lasted beyond the classroom.

Two sisters who grew up in Salvador da Bahia are very Anglo-American in appearance. Their parents are North American, but the sisters were raised in Brazil and attended Brazilian schools. Although they are bilingual (Portuguese-English), culturally they are Brazilian. They always surprise both Brazilians and North Americans, because their appearance belies their command of Portuguese, as well as the way in which they relate to people.

CULTURE NOT ONLY PROGRAMS our expectations of people's behavior, it also trains us how to evaluate our experiences. Since culturally learned values profoundly affect one's attitudes and interactions with others, to communicate effectively with Brazilians, it is helpful to consider the characteristic ways in which they see the world.

CHAPTER ELEVEN

Worldview

Worldview is arguably the most important perception that a culture in-stills in its population.[1]

Perceiving the World

A person's worldview synthesizes many of a culture's categories of per-ception. Worldview has to do with whether one sees oneself as master of one's fate or views the human condition as a product of destiny, whether a person should act individually or collectively as part of a group, whether people are basically equal or have a predestined hierar-chical rank in life, and what daily activities and attitudes are most val-ued and praised by the people in a culture. In each of the world's cul-tures, a different set of such concepts makes up individuals' perceptions of the universe in which they live.

Symbols, religious beliefs, and a quintessentially Brazilian character-istic called *jeito* are three important filters among many that combine with other cultural factors to shape how Brazilians perceive and view the world.

Symbols

Symbols connect the people of a country. A culture may have a strong central belief system. As a result, an abstract symbol will often emerge that is agreed on and respected by groups. Such a symbol and the belief system supporting it affect perception and communication style.[2]

The important symbols of two cultures can be mutually exclusive. If the social structure of a culture is tightly organized around a particular religious or political symbol, it will be difficult or impossible to share perceptions cross-culturally.[3] A number of symbols can be said to repre-sent important aspects of Brazilian culture. But with the salient Brazil-ian cultural traits of adaptability and cordiality, there is probably not one symbol that so completely dominates the Brazilian psyche that it would close off communication with a foreigner who is unfamiliar with the culture.

Obviously, to insult a person of any culture will usually shut down communication. In the United States, a reference to "red, white, and blue" usually refers to the national flag, patriotism, or the quality of being North American. In Brazil, the comparable reference is to "yellow and green," the dominant colors in the Brazilian flag. It is offensive for an outsider to disrespect symbols such as the national flag of a country, or even its colors, although Brazilians seem particularly capable of separating the symbol from the thing itself.

BRASÍLIA

Some foreigners cite Brazil's capital, Brasília, as a national symbol and believe that Brazilians take great pride in its architecture and the feat of building this modernistic city in the interior of the country. Many Brazilians, however, do not consider Brasília as important a symbol as do foreigners.

Annie Nimos discussed with three Brazilians what Brasília represents to them: Angélica, a fourth-year university student in journalism; her mother, Claudina, a forty-seven-year-old attorney; and Dona Ermínia, Angélica's seventy-year-old grandmother. All three volunteered that Brasília is a symbol of corruption and was a shameful waste of taxpayers' money.

Angélica: "The city is in the shape of a plane. This is fitting, because there were no roads when it was built, so all materials had to be flown in at huge and wasteful expense. Brazilians have no special pride in the architecture; foreigners think it is supposed to be special."

Dona Hermínia: "I could shoot [former President] Kubitschek for his grandiosity in building Brasília."

Claudina: "Brasília represents the corruption, thievery, and inefficiency of the Brazilian government to Brazilians. The city itself is not so bad, but any novelty was immediately eclipsed by association with corruption."

The wife of a judge stated that building Brasília was a waste of taxpayers' money that should have been put to use for people. The government was already functioning, for better or for worse, in Rio, and it was not necessary to move it at huge expense.

A schoolteacher commented that she had seen a television interview of people who lived approximately one hundred miles from Brasília. They had no education or even television. When shown a film of an elephant, they asked what the strange animal was. The national capital did

not bring anything to them, she said, although it was supposed to develop the backward interior. In addition, a large number of government officials fly in from Rio and other cities, work the shortest week possible, and then fly home again to live in comfort in a city they love.

These are harsh comments about a major achievement, and the construction of Brazil's new capital did contribute positively to the construction of roads and the opening up of the country's vast and sparsely populated interior. Many Brazilians undoubtedly appreciate many aspects of their capital. But the attitudes expressed here have to do with "symbolism," and, clearly, a large number of Brazilians associate the futuristic, modern city with the disappointment and dissatisfaction they have with their government. For these people, Brasília is not a symbol of pride.

CARNIVAL

Brazil's Carnival, especially as celebrated in Rio, is world renowned and symbolizes the spontaneity and sensuality of the Brazilian. DaMatta writes that special celebrations planned by a culture reflect its society and help to explain it. Civic and religious festivals are rites that celebrate a culture's order; they reinforce its hierarchy; they maintain the status quo. In a rite of order, a president, judge, senator, priest, or professor appears in her or his precise role. These rites are structured to ensure that everyone immediately knows "who is who." No confusion of roles or positions is acceptable.[4]

Carnival is a festival, an orgy, that celebrates disorder. Most Brazilians find it irresistibly seductive. During Carnival, people live a utopian fantasy of freedom from work, obligations, sin, and misery. Life's daily rules are turned upside down. Carnival distributes sensual pleasure equally to all, without discriminating between rich and poor. It especially gives people an incredible sense of freedom in a society where they are dominated by a hierarchy that imposes a complex scale of rights and obligations applied from the top down—as DaMatta says, every monkey on the right branch, a place for everything, and everything in its place.[5]

DaMatta explains that the universe of individuality, assiduously avoided in Brazilian daily life, takes over during Carnival. Everyone can surface as an individual from the sea of collectively organized groups that Brazil's culture imposes, and can interpret the world in his or her own way.[6]

DaMatta describes Brazilians as a people sorted and ranked by a traditional order such as family name, professional title, shade of skin, home neighborhood, the name of one's godfather, personal connections, or being the friend of an influential politician. Carnival, however, permits movement in a society that restricts social mobility and exhibitionism in a society where everyone normally adheres to their roles. Public competition, which Brazilian culture normally abhors, is acceptable during Carnival. Participants compete in music, costumes, exhibitionism, and, of course, the samba groups (*escolas de samba*) compete for coveted first place. DaMatta explains that the basic objective of carnivals and orgies—festivals of disorder—is to bring people together and equalize them, abolishing all rank and difference.[7]

During Carnival, things are not what they appear. This paradox symbolizes much about Brazil.

SOCCER

Page thinks soccer may symbolize Brazil even better than Carnival. It unifies the nation; the country eats, drinks, and dreams *futebol* (FOO-chee-ball). Newcomers to a community can join its social life (if they are male) by becoming fans of a local team or by playing soccer themselves.[8] When Brazil's national team nimbly orchestrated a sound 2–0 victory against the precision of the German team to win the 2002 World Cup, the resulting euphoria lifted the national morale burdened by the falling value of the real and other social concerns.

On the beach in Santos, the city for whose team the great Pelé first played, one can see fathers beginning the typical initiation of their young sons into the game of soccer. Squealing with delight, a teetering toddler will attempt to kick and maneuver a ball that is half his height. Young boys will stand in a circle and keep a ball in the air for minutes at a time, with agility and grace passing it back and forth to each other with every part of the body they can muster, except, of course, the hands.

A number of scholars attribute universal respect for soccer's rules as the reason for the sport's hold on the Brazilian masses. In a society where the rich and powerful ignore or change inconvenient laws, everyone knows and observes the rules of soccer, a game in which personal talent, rather than money or connections, prevails. The sport demonstrates the possibility of social justice to people who are often powerless in their everyday lives. For this reason, they love the game.[9] Brazilians also play soccer with an exuberance, agility, spontaneity, and creativity that are representative, in great part, of their national character model.

Religion

For the most part, Brazil is homogeneously and culturally Catholic, and religion is taken for granted. Some 90 percent of Brazilians are said to adhere at least nominally to the Roman Catholic Church, whose rituals and traditions unify the nation.

Brazil is the largest Catholic country in the world, but the New World Catholicism practiced in Brazil is complex and diverse. The mixing of Portuguese Catholicism with Amerindian and African religions has produced uniquely Brazilian traditions that survive to the present day and attract followers of every race and social class.[10]

Eakin writes that in colonial Brazil, the Catholic Church was tightly controlled and regulated and by the end of the nineteenth century held virtually no economic or political power. In contrast, Spain's Catholicism was aggressive and militant when the Americas were discovered in 1492 because of its seven-hundred-year struggle to expel the Islamic Moors; Portugal had completed its reconquest by the mid-thirteenth century. The malleability and tolerance that were traits of the Portuguese softened their Catholicism, whereas the Spaniards implanted in Spanish America an unforgiving and trenchant form. These factors may help to explain the Brazilian church's historical tolerance of other religions.[11]

Because of Brazil's vast size and a shortage of priests, a folk Catholicism evolved without supervision, especially in the interior. Lush tropical regions tempted the flesh; priests commonly kept concubines and raised families to provide care in sickness and old age.[12]

Catholicism is the source of many cultural values in Brazil today, even when these values are no longer tied to religion. From Catholicism came Brazil's strong emphases on the male-dominated family, on procreation, and on community. Today, however, religions other than Catholicism have made significant gains, particularly those appealing to emotion, such as the burgeoning Pentecostal movement. In 1997, Eakin wrote, some 10 percent of Brazilians were Protestants,[13] and the percentage today has increased.

Page relates that the slaves in Brazil merged African *orixás* with Catholic saints and incorporated superficial elements of Catholicism into their fundamental beliefs. In turn, the Portuguese incorporated African religious elements into their own beliefs and practices.[14] Gilberto Freyre writes that African Brazilian religions focus on joy and celebration, whereas Anglo-American Protestantism and Spanish American Catholicism emphasize suffering and asceticism.[15]

Widespread in Brazil is the worship of the saintly black entity, Iemanjá, who represents well the synthesis of African and Catholic beliefs. *Cariocas* celebrate her on December 31 in Rio de Janeiro. Ribeiro writes that she has replaced the ridiculous old European figure of Santa Claus and that she is "the first saint since Greece who has sex." One does not petition Iemanjá to cure an illness but for an affectionate lover, or for a husband not to beat one so much.[16] To Brazil's religious mix, Amerindians added their beliefs in spirits and in powerful intermediaries who can heal the ill, communicate with the dead, and tell the future. This indigenous heritage gives Brazilians a deep-rooted affinity for the supernatural.[17]

Brazilians are deeply religious. Their beliefs emphasize the relationship between this world and "the other world." In the same way that Brazilians have parents, friends, and patrons, they have intermediaries to communicate with the other world—whether through a favorite saint or an *orixá*, or several of both. Rituals add strength to petitions. DaMatta writes that what appears to the Calvinist North Americans, the Puritan English, or the Catholic French to be superstition or cynicism or ignorance, for a Brazilian just broadens the possibilities of gaining protection or success.[18] The anthropologist Nancy Scheper-Hughes describes the pragmatic folk Catholicism that rural workers practice. They "work" the spirit world using the familiar, everyday tactics of barter, blackmail, debt, and shifting loyalties. "An ineffective patron saint is of no more use than a drunken, unemployed husband, and he or she is just as easily dismissed or exchanged for another."[19]

That's a lot of candle for such a small saint. [Muita vela para pouco santo.]

Jeito as Worldview

The only thing that jeito *doesn't work for is death.*[20]

The most significant, pervasive, and typical national filter through which the Brazilians see the world is that of *jeito* or *jeitinho*—the concept of finding a way.[21] The diminutive *jeitinho* connotes acceptance of this attitude and practice; it indicates that the use of *jeitinho* to resolve a problem is not a serious transgression or troubling accommodation.[22] For Brazilians, there is always a way, some way, any way, to accomplish what one needs or wants to accomplish.[23] Scheper-Hughes refers to *jeito* or *jeitinho* as a quick solution to a problem or a way out of a dilemma. She writes:

> *Jeitos* entail all the mundane tricks for getting by and making do within the linear, time-constrained, everyday, uphill struggle along the suffering *caminho* [road]. The Brazilian *jeitoso* is an ideal personality type connoting one who is attractive, cunning, deft, handy, and smooth. When the word *jeito* is invoked to imply a "getting

away with murder" or a "taking advantage" of a situation at someone else's expense, it is closely related to *malandragem*, a term
without an English equivalent, although "swindling" comes close.
Malandragem is the art of the scoundrel and the rascal: a "badness"
that entails an enviable display of strength, charm, sexual allure,
charisma, street smarts, and wit.

The *malandro* (rake) and the *jeitosa* (one who operates around
and outside the law and who lives by her wits) are products of
the clash of competing realities and social ethics in contemporary
Brazil. As social personalities and distinct interactional styles, they
are culturally derived defenses against the rigidity of the race-class
system, the complexity of Brazilian laws, and the absurdity of an
unwieldy, inflated, and corrupt state bureaucracy.[24]

*Lívia Barbosa describes jeito as the art of getting more equality than
anyone else.*[25]

Jeito is a term that is difficult to translate. Page quotes a French
scholar who describes it as "an ingenious maneuver that renders the impossible possible; the unjust just; and the illegal legal."[26] It is a rapidly
improvised and creative response to a law, rule, or custom that gets in
someone's way.

Jeito is such an important and thoroughly entrenched way of life in
Brazil, with both positive and negative characteristics, that in 2000 a São
Paulo theologian, Lourenço Stélio Rega, published a book with the revealing title, *Finding a Way to Find a Way: How to Be Ethical without
Giving Up Being Brazilian* (Dando um jeito no jeitinho: Como ser ético
sem deixar de ser brasileiro). Rega sees *jeito* as both creating and in-
hibiting Brazilian attitudes and behavior. He says that jeito "influences
our decisions and becomes an internal rule that governs our choices."[27]

*"We [Brazilians] are the most malleable people in the world. . . . [W]e
can find a way [um jeito] for everything."*[28]

Employing *jeito* is not always innocent. It is used to get rid of a problem, to make things go the way one wants them to, to close one's eyes
to a situation that will hurt another individual, to bend or circumvent
rules, to take advantage of a situation. To use *jeito*, in sum, is to find a
way to make things go the way that you want them to, even at someone
else's expense. According to DaMatta, the greatest sin of the Brazilian is
that every individual expects preferential treatment (*levar vantagem*)
in everything. The common attitude in Brazil, "Do you know whom you

are speaking to?" is that of the person who imposes himself or herself on others, who disregards rules, who takes advantage of his or her status to be above the law, and who escapes punishment.[29] Anne-Marie Guérin, a Frenchwoman with an MBA from a U.S. university who lives and works in São Paulo, commented that *jeito* frequently crosses the boundaries of expediency into the realm of corruption, and in this form it poses problems for doing business.

Caldeira writes that orderly traffic is a strong indicator of the quality of public life. In Brazil driving behavior is only the most obvious example of the public's routine disrespect for the law. Traffic police disregard some violations simply because they are the norm. They also try to avoid confronting upper-class people, who do not hesitate to challenge their authority. Sometimes when the signs of a person's class are ignored or misunderstood, drivers resort to violence. Some parking wardens have been beaten up when they refused to void tickets, and one ended up in the hospital after an enraged motorist ran his car over her. "These behaviors indicate how violent people can become when they are asked to conform to the law and cannot use their class position as a source of privilege, that is, to evade the law."[30]

But Brazilians also use *jeito* to survive and to extricate themselves from dilemmas not always of their making. An automatic fine may be imposed on them for missing a deadline, even when this deadline was not made known to them. Or the government may institute an unfair and abusive tax without proper process. Brazilians tend to think that citizens of other countries obey their laws because they are disciplined and that, by implication, Brazilians are not. But DaMatta asserts that the difference exists because in countries such as the United States, France, and England the laws reflect social reality and are not intended to exploit or subjugate the citizen. There is consistency between the daily practices of people and the constitutional and legal world. That is why people will stop at a stop sign, which appears absurd to Brazilians. DaMatta points out that the law makes society in the United States, France, and England work well—which he lauds as an enormous accomplishment.[31]

Because of the difficulty in Brazil of reconciling the law with daily social reality, the *despachante* has appeared to fill the gap. The *despachante* has great sociological importance. He or she serves as a broker, a professional of *jeito* who guides his or her clients through the narrow, perilous corridors of official departments, to help them "comply" with requirements that are sometimes absurd or impossible.[32] The legal system in Brazil is complex and difficult to work with, but this *jeito* professional knows every minute change in the law and cultivates friends in all areas. He or she therefore has the key to almost any door and is the high priest of mediation between the feared authorities and defenseless citizens.[33]

Jeito seeks both practical and self-serving solutions. Brazilians tend to view legal requirements as desirable goals, or as inconveniences that one circumvents with a little *jeito* by using the right connections. They are unlikely to treat World Bank loan stipulations intended to protect the environment any more seriously than their own environmental laws.[34] A legislator, a judge, or a governor may resort to the use of *jeito* when it provides a means to compensate for deficiencies of the law. In these instances, *jeito* reveals the weaknesses of legal institutions.[35]

Rega observes that since Christian and ethical people in his country are still Brazilians, they have to use *jeito* if they are to survive, because there is practically no other alternative to meeting the practical needs of daily life in Brazil. Car watchers are a good example. Although they infringe on the rights of others to freely park their cars, they themselves are employing *jeito* to survive chronic economic ills. Brazilians are constant and creative inventors of services—car watchers, sellers of places in lines, and package carriers at street fairs, anything that will provide some meager income.[36]

The need to find a way has sharpened a quick intelligence in the Brazilian. People find surprising ways out of seemingly impossible situations. Daily circumstances encourage adaptability and flexibility because at any moment the necessity or opportunity to use *jeito* may arise.[37] This positive side to *jeito* led an advertising expert to note that since the Brazilian is always alert for clever angles, he or she is very intuitive about new market opportunities and the needs of consumers.[38]

Jeito also has a humanitarian side, such as when a driver lends his spare tire to a stranger on the highway. *Jeito* can also be a conciliatory force. According to DaMatta, it is often a pleasant way of relating the impersonal to the personal, a peaceful and even legitimate way of resolving problems such as tardiness, lack of money, ignorance of the law, legal confusion, or even the injustice of a law that was enacted for a specific situation but no longer applies to current conditions.[39]

Jeito cannot be understood simply as dishonesty, as evidenced by an experiment conducted by *Marie Claire* magazine. A self-service magazine stand with no attendants was set up in Pinheiros, São Paulo. People were to deposit their money and take a magazine. The test was monitored discreetly from a distance. At the end of the day, it was found that all magazines taken were paid for; there was no shortfall in moneys received.[40] And recall the taxi driver who made a twenty-minute trip to return expensive binoculars that had been left in his cab by a foreign visitor.

Jeito is a product of an intelligent, inventive, free, and creative attitude that one should take the initiative of acting in opposition to rules.
The Brazilian opens a new path that is not provided for in any code. But
Rega sees as a result the creation of an ethical abyss that lies between an
ideal of good ethics (*ético divino*) and the moral reality in which people
must live in Brazil. But he also sees an acceptable compromise. He refers
to using a *jeito* that is a "temporal ascendant ethic" (*ética temporal as-
cendente*). He well understands that the Brazilian needs to survive. As
an example of an acceptable compromise, he suggests that one can open
a small business and not pay taxes if it is not possible do so initially; one
should then commence paying taxes as soon as the business can afford
them. This proposed temporal ascendant ethic is not intended to promote compromise but rather to remove the "take advantage of" element
out of *jeito*—the selfish, uncaring, self-centered element that goes beyond what is needed to survive in Brazil's real world.[41]

The use of *jeito* in Brazil is so extensive that it is virtually impossible
to break the vicious cycle and the upward spiral of irresponsibility using
ordinary political and social mechanisms. Recent efforts to eliminate
corruption in Brazil proved this, since many of those directing the effort
and those reporting directly to them themselves ended up being exposed
for committing fraud.[42]

Rega approaches the problems that *jeito* brings to Brazilian society
from a Christian religious perspective. He propounds that decisive action to change men radically from the inside is the only way to break the
negative aspects of the vicious *jeito* circle.[43]

CLEARLY, THE HISTORY, experiences, and current circumstances of living in Brazil color the filters through which Brazilians view their world.
The resulting perceptions, attitudes, behavior, and values directly affect
communication.

CHAPTER TWELVE

Values and Identity

Brazilians are unfailing optimists and are happy even when circumstances do not seem to warrant it.

Values

Values are the set of rules that we learn from our culture and draw on to make choices and resolve conflicts.[1] Values regarding such things as money, work, and success manifest themselves in living patterns and outlook.[2]

Althen explains that North Americans have been taught to value hard work, and they believe that this will result in material success. Therefore, they are likely to measure one's success by the standard of material wealth. Because there is usually a close correlation between a person's job and income, North Americans are quick to ask "What do you do?" to classify persons they meet.[3] It is in vogue to criticize North Americans for being overly materialistic, but many intellectuals around the world concede that in spite of the faults they find with the United States, it is indisputably a place where ordinary people live well.[4]

In Brazil, one's family background, education, and social polish often define one more than does job or profession. Nonetheless, according to Page, Brazilians across the political spectrum believe that Brazil's future depends on economic growth and share a pragmatic passion for development. This focus may derive from the practical Portuguese and sets Brazil apart from the Hispanic countries of the Americas. It may also explain in part why many Brazilians feel an affinity for the United States.[5]

But despite Brazilians' passion for development, Page points out, throughout the country, paradoxically, manual labor is perceived as demeaning. The elitist Portuguese empire used slaves for most physical work for almost a century before Brazil was colonized. Today upper- and middle-class Brazilian families commonly rely on domestic servants to perform all manual work.[6] However, like other aspects of Brazilian society, attitudes toward labor are beginning to change.

The North American attitude toward manual labor is quite different. In the United States people from all levels of society engage in manual labor, to which they attach no stigma. Witness the weekend do-it-yourself shoppers at Home Depots who may be blue-collar workers or attorneys. It is not uncommon for a professional in the United States to work on a home project such as painting a room or building a deck. In Brazil it is not common to see professionals similarly engage in manual labor.

The Cordial Brazilian

Brazilians charm; they radiate pleasantness, gentleness, and sweetness; they extend abundant hospitality, especially to foreigners.[7]

Jack Harding, in his 1941 travel book, I Like Brazil, *noted that people who do not get along with amiable Brazilians must surely be the ones at fault and should take a close look at themselves.*[8]

Claudina, an attorney who is a member of Servas, an international organization whose members host foreign members in their homes, recounted a problem that surfaced in a committee that oversees Servas affairs in South America. The Argentine representatives of Servas complained about the behavior of North American guests. They wanted to exclude all North Americans from visits to host homes in Argentina. Although the Brazilians agreed with some of the Argentines' complaints, with their usual good nature they shrugged and observed that Servas regulations limit guests to a stay of two nights, so if there was a problem, it would not last long. They did not want to say no to anyone.

In a conversation with Annie Nimos, Claudina, the same confident Porto Alegre attorney, commented that she never uses a harsh or combative style. Annie observed that although Claudina has strong opinions, she is not argumentative but uses a "sweet" style and wears people down with courteous persistence. This behavior is typical of Brazilian professionals; it is rare for them to resort to the sort of posturing and flexing of muscle that is common in business negotiations in the United States.

Roberto DaMatta relates that Brazilian culture is inimical to conflict. Conflict exists, but rather than confront crises and make corrections,

Brazilians see conflicts as omens of doom and failure. They prefer to emphasize solidarity and universalism and avoid a penetrating look at the country's problems.[9]

Noêmia Kobeh Ferreira told Annie Nimos,"Brazilians are too nice. They do not react when they should and stand up for their rights. Brazilians will buy something in a grocery store and when they get home discover that the item is spoiled. They look at it and say, 'Oh, that's too bad,' instead of taking it back to the store for a refund or exchange."

Brazilians recount stories about their people's inherent humanity even in criminal encounters. An engineer in Rio de Janeiro told about being robbed at gunpoint on his way home in the early morning hours. He threw up his hands and exclaimed, "But how will I get home? I at least need money for a taxi!" The thief handed him back enough money to take a taxi home. The same engineer's brother had car trouble when driving in the hills outside Rio and was stranded on the side of the highway. The dreaded inevitable occurred when a thief appeared on the scene. With apologies, he robbed the motorist, explaining that he had to feed his family. The thief then helped his victim tinker with his engine to get his car started again, so that he could drive home. Of course, many similar incidents end in tragedy, but Brazilians say that in general in Brazil people commit crimes of hunger, whereas in the United States they commit acts of senseless violence.

In Brazil it is considered a serious social transgression to be aggressive in personal interactions. Conflicts that arise are resolved and forgotten: "That's all right," "No problem," "Don't worry about it" (*Tudo bem, Numa boa, Deixa prá la*). Any open conflict is threatening.[10] But there is a dichotomy in the concept of the Brazilian operating as the quintessential cordial person (*o homem cordial*) in the safe world of personal relationships that exists in the house and how the Brazilian may function in the uncivilized world of the street.

In the United States there is more abrasiveness in personal interactions. Even so, after living in the United States, a number of Brazilians have commented on their appreciation of an underlying and more equitable respect of persons and human rights in society overall than they enjoy in their own country.[11]

Brazilians value gentleness, which, Page points out, permeates the songs of the contemporary singer Caetano Veloso, who is worshiped as a national hero. Even President Getúlio Vargas, who brought the country to the brink of fascism, was a benevolent figure who could not have been more different in manner from his contemporaries, Adolf Hitler and Benito Mussolini.[12]

John F. Santos states that Brazilians characteristically make quick, natural, and easy promises, which are often forgotten just as quickly, naturally, and easily. The gesture, however, is neither meaningless nor insincere. The personal involvement, warmth, and friendliness of the encounter bring joy and satisfaction to both parties. To focus on the details of what is being said and then to project these details into the future puts the emphasis in the wrong place and detracts from an appreciation of the interaction here and now. Making promises also saves one from the embarrassment of not being able or willing to help and thus protects oneself and the other person by preserving the cordiality of the encounter. But, Santos maintains, since Brazilians are consistently unpredictable, a promise may just as well be kept as not.[13]

Grandiosity

Brazilians have an affinity for grandeur, and perhaps the most original feature of Brazilian culture is that cordiality and grandiosity coexist harmoniously.[14] Underneath Brazilians' grandiosity lies an inferiority complex. Brazilians are prone to ignore their virtues and focus on their shortcomings. Many Brazilians used to deprecate their own culture and try to imitate Europe and the United States. They believed that goods produced at home could not equal those imported from abroad, and this attitude slowed the process of industrialization.

Annie Nimos discussed North American and Brazilian cultural characteristics as they relate to hiring practices with a Dell Computer Corporation executive. The conversation centered on hiring people with MBAs. Juan Mario, born in Mexico and educated in the United States, said that he would hire a North American MBA in a junior executive position right out of school, because she or he would be willing to implement company decisions and policies and to bide her or his time to become a creative problem solver for the company. In contrast, he said, the Brazilian MBA wants to be more grand and creative immediately, which is not possible in a North American company. Given the disparity in expectations, hiring the Brazilian would not be fair to the employee or to the employer. However, he explained, for a position requiring the person to work in Brazil rather than in the United States, he would hire the Brazilian, because a young North American would be totally out of his or her element in the Brazilian business and cultural world. A Brazilian could more quickly learn North American ways than a North American could adapt to the Brazilian environment.

Violence

Page writes that under the cordial surface of Brazilian culture lies the capacity for extreme violence. He cites as examples the extermination of Amerindians, the suppression of slave revolts, the slaughter of peasants challenging the rural landholding system, the class warfare waged by the poor against the rich in the contemporary urban crime wave, the "death lottery" as a protest by inmates of overcrowded prisons, the systematic assassination of street children, and the endemic neglect of the poor.[15] A statistic that brings home the magnitude of contemporary urban violence is that the São Paulo police in 1992 summarily killed 8.5 times more people than South Africa's apartheid regime in its worst year (South Africa carries out half of all the judicial executions in the world).[16]

Santos points out that Brazilians have immense tolerance for the frustrations of their social system but that this tolerance has limits. He suggests that the frustration is often vented in such acts as aggressive driving, surfing on top of moving buses, and the orgies of Carnival and soccer.[17] Page finds that Brazilians place low value on human life and often exhibit indifference to and even a preference for physical risk.[18]

Brazil's undercurrent of violence contrasts sharply with stories of the kindness expressed by robbers to their victims. The violence that takes place in DaMatta's impersonal street may be suspended when a personal connection is sparked between predator and prey.

Rules

From cultural values evolve rules, and the rules themselves create and re-create values. Every culture has its rules, some expressed, some implicit. Cultural rules are learned and mostly subconscious. They cover customs, manners, courtesy, etiquette, and rituals and regulate such behavior as bribery, nepotism, table etiquette, touching people, use of time, and social relationships.[19] They govern formality and what types of interaction take place when and where.[20] There is not much flexibility in customs, such as "white tie with tails,"[21] or whether and how to kiss a woman's hand. It is essential to learn these rules to successfully communicate with a target culture.[22]

North American rules require more numerous verbal expressions of courtesy, such as "please," "thank you," and "excuse me," than are used by Brazilians. Brazilians notice and admire this, but their culture has strict nonverbal rules such as personal greeting and leave-taking rituals that are punctuated physically with touch. The failure to comply with these rules is conspicuous to Brazilians.

Knowing the rules is not always easy. One writer provides humorous counsel for a North American man going on a date with a Brazilian woman in Rio de Janeiro. She cautions that the following rules are imperative for anyone wanting to get the evening off to a good start in similar circumstances.[23]

Steve should plan to pick up Yara, the lovely Brazilian siren whom he met on Copacabana beach, at 8:30 P.M. At 8:45 Steve should call Yara to confirm that he does indeed have a date on that day and for 8:30. He should arrive around 9:30. As a greeting, Steve should go around and kiss Yara's mother, aunts, sisters, and grandmother on both cheeks; he should warmly and enthusiastically shake hands with her father, uncles, brothers, and grandfather with one hand, accompanied by affectionate pats on the back with the other. It is important that Steve greet the maid, Graciela, and make friends with her, because she probably is the one who will make the decision, after lengthy discussion and analysis with Yara and the family, as to whether this North American suitor is of interest to Yara. Steve should accept the *cafezinho* that is offered, and he should chat for about thirty minutes about weather, crime, inflation, and the last installment of the currently playing *novela* (serial story) on television.[24]

Around 10:00 P.M., when conversation begins to slow down, Steve should begin the leave-taking ritual. He should be sure to kiss Yara's mother, aunts, sisters, and grandmother on both cheeks, shake hands with her father, uncles, brothers, and grandfather, and tell everyone how much he enjoyed meeting and talking with them and that he is looking forward to seeing them again soon. It is imperative that he stop by the kitchen to compliment Graciela on her excellent *cafezinho*. By 10:30 to 10:45 Steve and Yara will be ready to leave and can begin to decide where they are going to eat and what they are going to do.[25]

On a more serious note, Caldeira describes interaction in another venue. She writes that Brazilians tend to be uncomfortable with democratic procedures, such as voting or respect for opposing opinions. For example, all *paulista* condominiums have covenants, usually drafted by the developers and residents. They are constantly reviewed and rewritten. All disputes tend to be treated as private matters among residents, and the justice system is not routinely used as a method of enforcement or solution. Although disputes among condominium residents are quite common in the United States as well, there they tend to be dealt with legally rather than privately.[26]

Caldeira observed that condominium meetings are often arenas of conflict and that people may be nasty and disrespectful if they fail to impose their will. Residents stand up and shout at each other, pound on tables, make verbal threats and insults, and use derogatory language. Although all decisions are supposed to be made by vote, discussions might last four or five hours before a vote is taken. Meeting participants prefer trying to convince each other (to reach consensus), or to have their own views prevail, over voting.[27] The Brazilian rule of cordiality may ultimately break down in this venue because the participants do not view themselves as belonging to the same collective in-group, the house. They may see the meeting as the street, bringing together representatives from a number of opposing out-groups, and therefore the rule of using *jeito* and trying to impose rank prevails.

Identity

To create a model of national character, a basic identity shared by some 170 million individuals, is complex and difficult. Rega sees Brazilians' identity as residing in Brazil's laws, politics, and economics, in the food they eat, in the houses in which they live, in how they love, and in the rules that govern their friendships and family relations. He goes on to list some of the specific characteristics that comprise Brazilian culture. He sees these as fatalism, a disregard for commitments and promises (*descompromisso*), paternalism, racism, rationalization, religious syncretism, and a focus on humanist rather than technical education.[28] From Page's enumeration of characteristics of Brazilianness, one can add to the Brazilian model tropical languor and the traditional habit of indulging in excessive rhetoric and display.[29]

Brazilians are also hospitable, enthusiastic, expansive, warm, flexible, and curious. They need close physical contact with people and emotionally close family relationships and friendships. This physical and emotional closeness can overwhelm people from more reserved and formal cultures.

Lauro Moreira, a Brazilian career diplomat, compares the psychology of the Brazilian people to that of a developing adolescent. They retain, he writes, traits from their colonial childhood, mixed with elements of current maturity. The Brazilian does not consider himself tied to any past. In Brazil yesterday seems like the last century, whereas in some countries the past century seems like yesterday. The Brazilian does not focus on the past or the future. He lives in the present. Moreira calls the Brazilian naive in dreaming of a brilliant and important future, without comprehending the effort required to become, for example, a famous astronaut or surgeon.[30]

Moreira goes on to describe his Brazilian compatriots as undisciplined and rebellious against arbitrary order and systems. However, if one appeals to their reason—and especially to their emotions—they are docile and tractable. The Brazilian is psychologically mercurial, alternating easily between euphoria and depression. This is neither good nor bad. It is Brazilian. Although the Brazilian may have momentary outbursts of anger, lasting hatred is not part of the Brazilian psyche. Moreira states that the Brazilian is very hard to rouse to fanaticism, which he thinks one of the most important aspects of the Brazilian psyche. Brazil could never be, in his opinion, a communist or socialist country. That Brazilians will never allow themselves to be treated like sheep he considers a Portuguese rather than Spanish trait. The Spaniard can more easily be aroused to fanaticism. "We do not have this in common with our Latin American brothers," Moreira writes.[31]

Although Brazilians appear to be extroverts, they are self-critical and lack confidence. Moreira describes North Americans as the opposite—self-confident, secure, and tranquil.[32] However, after nearly a decade of economic openness and stability, Brazil is embracing aspects of its own culture that were once considered marginal, and even exporting them. *Cachaça,* a powerful sugarcane liquor that used to be the poor man's drink, is served in trendy bars and fine homes in *caipirinhas,* made with lime, crushed ice, and sugar. The *capoeira,* an African martial arts form with the grace and flexibility of dance, has become popular among the middle class. Milton Nascimento, Gilberto Gil, Caetano Veloso, and João Gilberto, who won Grammy awards for World Music four years in a row, have regained popularity at home.[33]

Page describes Carnival as the national allegory of Brazil. It manifests their love of spontaneity, disorder, glitz, excitement, pleasure, and pathos.[34] Many Brazilians disclose who they really are by what they wear during Carnival; the masked faces of Carnival may represent the real countenance of Brazil.[35]

The Rogue

Page describes the *malandro* (the rogue or rake) as an important national figure in Brazilian culture. The *malandro* survives by his wits in a struggle against poverty and the injustice of a society where social mobility is almost impossible. The *malandro* creatively operates between the legal and the illegal, with a paradoxical playful mien.[36]

Dias proposes that the national hero of the Brazilian people is the legendary rogue Macunaíma, created by the writer Mario de Andrade.[37] Macunaíma is a hypodigm, an imaginary person who has all the characteristics ever encountered in a Brazilian, and he has his roots in Brazilian folklore. A model of dis-virtues, he symbolizes the ordinary Brazilian. Macunaíma has many personalities, some good, some bad, and some ingenuous.[38] He lives his misadventures without learning anything from them. Dias describes Macunaíma as an antihero, without character, good and bad, sentimental and insensitive, diligent and lazy, Indian, black, and white—"just like us."[39]

Humor

Brazilian humor is often self-deprecating. Brazilians poke fun at themselves in a manner that is rarely barbed or offensive to others. One Brazilian travel writer declares, with characteristic national humor, that the most beautiful, sweet, sonorous, poetic, evocative sound in Brazilian Portuguese—and the most revealing of Brazilian heart and soul— is the word for "long vacation" (feriadão). Fortunately, he explains, this yellow-green (i.e., Brazilian) neologism compensates for the horrible words Brazilians have had to import from English, such as "reengineering," "downsizing," and "workaholic." Long vacations ennoble man, he quips, but, unfortunately, they also make him poor (enobrecem e empobrecem).[40]

DAMATTA PROPOSES that a nation's identity can be defined in two ways. One can use precise statistical data such as gross national product, per capita income, and inflation per year. These impersonal, hard data scare Brazilians. They see these statistics as confirmation that their country is not all they want it to be rather than as a definition of what it is and all that it offers in the present. They note with surprise that some countries, such as England, France, Germany, and especially the United States, almost exclusively define themselves by this classification system, which they themselves invented. Judged by such quantitative data, Brazil and other "third world" countries always appear to leave much to be desired.[41]

The other way in which one constructs national identity is by means of qualitative data. In applying this method to Brazil, one focuses on its richness: delicious food, enchanting music, the saudade (yearning) that humanizes time and death, and friends with whom one can survive all the hardships of life.[42]

CHAPTER THIRTEEN

Sex and Food

Brazilians know they are good at food and women—and at soccer.[1]

Sexuality

The physical environment of Brazil shapes important Brazilian characteristics.[2] It is tropical and lush, nurturing a ripe sensuality in every level of society.

In 1981 Freyre published his renowned sociological study of Brazil, *The Masters and the Slaves,* in comic-book format under the title *Casa grande e senzala em quadrinhos.* The stated objective of the book is to be educational and helpful "even to adults." The illustrations represent Amerindians and Africans as physically attractive and the women especially as voluptuous and sexually provocative. The whole image of the era is physical and sensuous, as is Brazilian society today.[3]

Gambini comments that at the time Freyre published his work, the tropics were seen as generating unbridled lasciviousness, laziness, and the abandonment of the body to immediate pleasure. Of course, Gambini observes, a tropical beach stimulates the senses more than does the European winter, where the act of love has to take place under the weight of heavy blankets—or in front of a fireplace, unless that happens only in movies. Gambini believes that Brazilians are a people blessed by their eroticism.[4]

According to Verónica Ribeiro, a university professor, Brazilians are very sexual and very explicit about sex, and sex is an important factor in Brazil's culture. Girls as young as five—or younger—are encouraged to imitate television personalities and act sexy. There is, she says, a fine line between sensuality and pornography. Ribeiro's local newspaper has started a supplement that she describes as all buttocks (*bundas*) and sensationalism. Looks are what count most for women in a relationship. In public, men look women over from head to toe, and this overt inspection is acceptable. Plastic surgery is very popular to maintain one's youthful appearance. People also pay attention to what a woman wears. Ribeiro commented, "Brazilian women feel 'not as pretty' when they are abroad, for men do not turn their heads to watch them walk by and do not give unsolicited compliments on their looks."

Claudina Junker explained that Brazilians are as crazy about *bundas* as North Americans are about breasts. Brazilians do not appreciate "giant" breasts. In comparing television programs, provocative photos, advertisements, and the gamut of periodicals, from "girlie" to fashion magazines, one can see that the majority of "sexy" female shots targeting a North American public in the United States show front views and emphasize the chest, whereas those intended for public consumption in Brazil display a preponderance of rear shots, emphasizing the buttocks.

A paradox of Brazilian culture is that the comfortable attitude toward sexuality coexists with a patriarchal, repressive social structure that exalts both virility and virginity.[5] Junker related that although Brazilians are very sensual, they are also predominantly Catholic, and the Catholic church and Brazil's patriarchal culture insist on women's virginity at marriage. The result is that many girls who marry have had extensive sexual experience, with the exception of vaginal penetration and loss of the hymen. Junker explained matter-of-factly that anal sex is common and generally accepted, particularly among less sophisticated young women before they marry. Physicians routinely counsel women on the necessity of prophylactic measures for anal intercourse.

Lucy Dias writes that there is a culture of masculinity linked to violence and power in the psyche of the Brazilian male. This culture began in the master's house on sugar plantations (*fazendas*), where the patriarch had ongoing sexual relations with wife, mistresses, and concubines. *Fazendas* had the atmosphere of a harem. Wives and daughters were confined to the house under layers of locks and keys. Sons were encouraged to impregnate female slaves to increase the stock of labor. A legacy of this *machismo* can be seen in research conducted among married women who have been infected with HIV by their husbands, who have multiple sexual partners. It is not conceivable that a woman can ask her macho husband (*marido machão*), the father of her children, to use the "little shirt" (*camisinha*), and so she submits without the protection of a condom. Statistics scream, Dias writes, women continue to be completely passive, and the modern "master of the plantation" continues the same practices.[6] Nonetheless, there is wide acceptance of homosexuality and bisexuality among men in this macho culture.

The wife of a judge commented to Annie Nimos that she thinks former U.S. President Bill Clinton's sexual forays were his personal business, a matter to be dealt with between Clinton and his wife. "A man's sexual infidelities are hardly news," she said. Although these matters were covered in the North American press ad nauseum, Brazilians seem hardly aware of this aspect of the Clinton administration. In their view, there wasn't much for North Americans to complain about because the economy was strong. In Junker's words, "Clinton's sex life was not detrimental to the United States. By comparison, look at how [former Brazilian President] Collor robbed Brazil." She went on to say that Clinton should be penalized according to the laws covering perjury, but a sexual offense was not serious enough to warrant removal from office.

On a lighter note, one *carioca* quipped that if you think motels are hotels for tired drivers, you are in the wrong country. Motels in Brazil are for *sex*.[7] Junker explained that if you want to sleep, you should go to a hotel. On one driving trip to the Uruguay frontier on a holiday weekend, she and her husband had no choice but to spend a night in a motel because no other rooms were available. They were reading and talking and then realized that their talkative seven-year-old daughter, Bettina, was unusually quiet. They found her in front of the television in the bedroom engrossed in the establishment's porno movies.

Page writes that near-nudity and steamy romance are staples of Brazilian *telenovelas*. Even commercials on Brazilian television display performers in advanced stages of undress. These images reflect the carefree sexuality of Brazilian society, at least on the surface and in urban environments.[8] One evening Annie Nimos was visiting with Claudina Junker and her family. The television was on, and the serial *Laços de Família* (Family Ties) was showing an episode that took place during Carnival. Prime-time television aired in family living rooms across the country displayed firm bare breasts and ripe round bottoms clad only in a "T" (*tanga*). The scene then switched to three middle-class wives and mothers eating at a table in a home. One recounted to the others that she had had her first erotic dream that resulted in orgasm. Between bites she confided that if you dream of the right person, such an orgasm is even better than a real one.

Annie and Claudina discussed the fact that naked breasts and buttocks and the discussion of erotic dreams and orgasms would not be featured on a prime-time family television show in the United States, which prohibits exposing children to such material. This type of content would be played on certain channels only, or at later hours, or rated X. Claudina mused out loud to Annie, "I wonder why this is? Don't North Americans have erotic dreams and orgasms? And buttocks and breasts?" Claudina shrugged.

A well-informed, incisive woman, Junker did not understand why such content would be an issue and why it would not be aired freely in the United States. It seemed no less representative of mainstream life than people having a picnic in shorts or discussing a dream about a traffic incident. Claudina's daughter, Bettina, ten years old at the time, paid no attention to the dialogue or images and never missed a bite of her *maracujá* mousse.

Page writes that Xuxa (Shoo-shah), a tall, sensuous blond known to millions of fans in Brazil and South America, targets Brazil's preteens on the televised weekday *Xou de Xuxa* (Xuxa Show). Young girls emulate her eroticism. Xuxa launched a syndicated television program for children in the United States in 1993, but since the more puritanical attitude of North American society forced her to tone down her sex appeal, she was unable to capitalize on the primary ingredient of her huge success in Brazil.[9]

Visiting a beach in Rio, one cannot help but wonder at the variations in the minuscule bikinis designed to reveal the golden bodies of the women from Ipanema. One has to be innovative when working with so little fabric. It seems that no woman is too old or too chunky to wear a bikini. Middle-aged mothers, pregnant women with round bellies, wrinkled old ladies, and lithe goddesses tan, exercise, and socialize virtually unclad. Maria Brasil claims to have done scientific research in the United States, armed with a Brazilian bikini and a measuring tape. She reports that Brazilian bikinis measure two to three inches smaller in every direction than their North American counterparts. Brazilian women complain that even panties in the United States are too high in back and the leg openings too low.[10]

Brazilians are very comfortable with the human body. They both expose and appreciate them. While Annie Nimos and Claudina Junker were sitting and talking in front of the television set in Claudina's home, a public health program about breast cancer aired. A physician explained to a woman seated facing the camera that mammogram screening was very important, as were regular self-examinations of the breasts. The woman then lifted her blouse and demonstrated how to palpate her bare breasts. A cover of a magazine for expectant mothers called *Mãe* (Mother) displayed a smiling young woman with a bandeau top, happily clasping her hands over her rotund and pregnant belly that was totally exposed.[11] Pregnancy is natural and enjoyed. In winter in temperate Porto Alegre, almost without exception, neatly dressed and well-groomed pregnant women revealed at least the lower parts of their bellies as they walked around. They slung their pants conveniently under the protuberance, their snug sweaters and knit tops exposing some four or five inches of belly that was too large to fit inside their regular clothing. A practical side of this is that a woman does not have to invest in a great deal of special clothing for pregnancy.

All this demonstrates that attitudes about gender and sex are very different in Brazil and in the United States. Lourenço Juvenal, who has worked for three multinational corporations, stated that North Americans are paranoid about sex. It is ridiculous, he maintained, to be charged with sexual harassment in the workplace for inviting a woman out to dinner, because "inviting a woman out is a civilized thing to do."

Flirting in Brazil is akin to a national sport, and many Brazilians consider sensuality part of the national character. The Brazilian television personality Monique Evans, when interviewed about pending sexual harassment legislation, said that for years her career did not advance because she would not sleep with producers and directors. Although she knows that sexual harassment is a serious problem, she feels that there are more important issues that need to be addressed through legislation. She stated that sexual harassment is part of Brazilian culture and that "there are thousands of laws in Brazil that people ignore." A sexual harassment law would just be one more. There are, of course, women's organizations that support legal protection from sexual harassment.[12] Regarding passage of the new legislation in 2001, university professor Verónica Ribeiro told Annie Nimos, "I do think the legislation should be able to help women. However, as in Brazil laws are relative, and most of the time they are there just for the sake of it, I doubt it will be applied effectively."

It is not surprising that such different cultural attitudes about the body and sex vest beauty in the eye of the beholder. Marina is a petite, trim, attractive Brazilian woman in her thirties. She was taking courses at Brandeis University where her husband was doing postdoctoral work in physics. On one occasion, she went to sun on a beach north of Boston. She stretched out in the sun in her Brazilian bikini. She could hear a family of obese persons next to her making comments about how "scandalous" someone was and how awful the person looked. Marina looked around to see who they were criticizing and finally realized they were talking about her. She was surprised. "You know," she said, "those people did not look so good in bathing suits."

Food

Rega points out that there are two important aspects of nourishment in Brazil. For a Brazilian, *alimento* (food) is everything that can be ingested to sustain life; *comida* (a meal) is everything that one eats with pleasure, that should be savored, and that is aesthetically pleasing. To properly appreciate *comida*, one needs to partake of it as a social activity. North Americans invented fast food, and Brazilians note that they eat standing or sitting, or with strangers or friends or alone. It seems to Brazilians that North Americans eat more to sustain life than to participate in the social activity that is inextricably entwined with the ritual of eating in Brazil. Eating is rarely a solitary act for a Brazilian.[13]

Brazilians may have a self-deprecating attitude about some aspects of their society, but this does not extend to food.[14] Whether at home or in a restaurant, meals are sacred. This is not only a time to eat but also a time to enjoy family and friends. Brazilian expatriates miss this practice enormously. Maria Brasil said that she constantly asks her North American husband what is his big hurry when they eat. One of the things she looks forward to when she goes to Brazil is the savory, lengthy, and sociable family meal.[15] Gisela, an engineer from southern Brazil, commented that adult children do not often move far from their families and may live only a few blocks away. Even when married, working, and living in their own houses or apartments, they regularly eat lunch, the main meal of the day, at their parents' homes. The meal constitutes an important link in family interaction.

The staple food of Brazil is rice and beans, the equivalent of "meat and potatoes" in the United States. "Rice and beans" is even an expression used to mean one's daily routine—the *feijão com arroz* of everyday life. Brazilians cook rice and beans separately but eat them together, mixing them on their plate. DaMatta points out that, in Brazilian fashion, the black is no longer black alone and the white is no longer white alone but a mixture, like Brazilian culture and people.[16]

Breakfast is usually a simple meal in Brazil, consisting of coffee, milk, bread, and jam. It is sometimes served with cheese and ham and fresh fruit, a *café colonial.* Papaya is often served at breakfast. It is delicious, digestible, and rich in vitamins A and C. In Brazil's Northeast, visitors are regaled with the panoply of exotic fruits that hotels routinely include in their breakfasts.

Because lunch is usually the principal meal of the day, it is more substantial than the typical lunch in the United States. Brazilians joke that in the United States, if you see people sitting around a table for lunch for longer than half an hour, it must be a business lunch. They consider it uncivilized to sit at a desk or in a cubicle to eat lunch. Eating lunch while you work is incomprehensible to most Brazilians, who leave their offices to eat with colleagues and friends in restaurants and cafés.[17]

In Brazil dinner is eaten much later than is typical in the United States. In large cities Brazilians take their children out to dinner at all hours, so it is common to see children in a restaurant at night. For many Brazilians, dinner is a light meal of café au lait, bread, cheese, and cold cuts. North Americans can expect either type of meal, a substantial dinner or a lighter repast.[18]

Brazilians cook and serve abundant amounts of food to their family and friends. In the United States it is typical to ask each person how much he or she will eat—how many ears of corn or how many sausages. The person cooking then prepares that number, plus one or two "for the pot." This concept is foreign to Brazilians. Their response is, "How do I know how many I will eat? Maybe I will eat one, and be full. Or maybe one will taste so good I will want another. You cook as many ears of corn or sausages as you have, people eat as much as they want, and you have what is left over at the next meal."

The food served at birthday parties is a real treat. Usually there are small savory pastries and appetizers called *salgadinhos* and small sweets called *docinhos* and, of course, a cake with candles. Frequently, creamy coconut candies in colorful wrappers decorate the table. These can be ordered from specialty stores called *doceiras*, and in smaller towns women specialize in making these *doces* and *salgados* for parties.[19] For children's birthdays, family and friends, from children to adults, all gather to enjoy the festivities and food. As a child, Annie Nimos always particularly enjoyed miniature pies (*empadinhas*) of cod, shrimp, and olives, or the inimitable Brazilian *pastéis*, pastry dough filled with well-seasoned meat or cheese and deep-fried until they become crisp and light. If a Brazilian living overseas is suffering from *saudades*, that national nostalgic yearning, just feed the person some *pastéis* as a remedy and he or she most likely will quickly recover.

Cafezinho is the Brazilian version of espresso, but it is not quite as strong. It is served as a demitasse of dark roast black coffee sweetened with a generous amount of sugar. In homes and in most Brazilian government offices and businesses, coffee will be offered to you when you arrive. It is served on a tray with a sugar bowl and tiny spoons or is sometimes already sweetened. Brazilians drink *cafezinho* several times a day.[20]

Brazilians say that Brazil possesses the greatest variety of fruit in the world, and, indeed, the variety seems infinite. Brazilian mangoes and avocados are delicious. Avocados are usually eaten creamed, with sugar and a little lemon juice. They are also liquefied into a light green, sweetened "smoothie" drink, which in Brazil is called a *vitamina*. And a number of the many vegetables that are commonly eaten may be unfamiliar to North Americans: *xuxú, maxixe, jiló,* fresh hearts of palm, and manioc root (called *mandioca* or *aipim*).[21]

Brazilians like freshly baked breads. Families buy bread early in the morning and again in the evening from the nearest bakery (*padaria*). Big cities in Brazil have good supermarkets, and shopping seems to be family recreation. Since it will take more time to shop in Brazil than in the United States, a visitor fares best if he or she just relaxes and enjoys it.[22]

Many restaurants in Brazil have a practical way to sell food. The food is set out as a buffet, and customers help themselves. The standard-size plates of food are then weighed, and patrons pay for the quantity of food taken. On this system, it seems that people serve themselves portions of a reasonable size and overeat less. It is also an equitable way to price food, because those who are especially hungry or require more food pay more and those who eat less pay less. Desserts may be on the same buffet, but if there is a wide selection they are usually sold from a separate dessert buffet, also by weight. Even ice cream is commonly sold by weight.

Brazilians often stop at a *lanchonete* (snack bar) or *loja de sucos* (juice bar) for juice, a snack, or a light meal. They eat and drink at the counter. Brazilians do not eat walking down the street, nor do they consume coffee and beverages in their cars. Eating is an activity that is generally confined to spaces formally designated by the culture for that purpose. There are, of course, some exceptions. One is the ubiquitous *mate* tea with gourd and thermos of hot water that people carry and consume while sitting in public in Rio Grande do Sul. Another exception is that Brazilians eat small bags of popcorn at the movies (they are surprised at the quantities of food and drink that people consume at the cinema in the United States). An additional exception is sharing a snack or drink with friends in the city park. Brazilians do not eat in front of others without sharing.

Compared to Europe in the Old World and to Mexico in the New World, Brazilian culture is somewhat less formal. However, Brazilians are both different and more formal than North Americans in the norm for table manners. They will usually use a fork and knife for pizza, open sandwiches, and even chicken. They are surprised at how North Americans eat many foods with their fingers. Brazilians, like Europeans, hold the fork in the left hand and the knife in the right, rather than constantly switching the utensils from one hand to the other. Brazilian children are taught good table manners and etiquette at an early age, at the Sunday lunches that are traditional in many families, and when they eat out in restaurants.[23]

But despite the cultural emphasis on socializing and eating, Brazilians who can afford all the food they want generally eat smaller quantities and are not as fat as most North Americans. Brazilians eat more fresh vegetables and fruits. They are body conscious, and they work out. The result is a panoply of lean and muscled bodies to appreciate while ambling down the street. The shapely *bumbuns* of Brazilian women look particularly good as they undulate gracefully along in tight pants and heels. Not only the very young look good. For example, one professional couple who work in São Paulo has three daughters in their twen ties. When the parents go out to lunch, they usually split a meal, and they regularly work out in a gym after work. They are tanned and healthy and make sure that they look great in their skimpy bikinis. Like so many Brazilians, they are in love with the beach, and they spend every possible weekend, holiday, and vacation at their apartment on the coast.

Their daughter, Joana, is a chemical engineer. When in training with Schlumberger in the Houston area, after observing people in supermarkets and shopping malls, Joana asked Annie Nimos if food in the United States is genetically altered. She said she kept trying to explain to herself why the general population is so fat. She had never before seen so many huge people. "They are not just round, they have enormous amounts of flesh," she said. Annie replied that this physical profile is explained simply by a diet consisting of large quantities of starch, fats, and sugar in processed foods and few fresh fruits and vegetables. On one trip of several months to southeastern and southern Brazil, Annie noted that she saw only three truly obese persons during her entire sojourn.

Annie Nimos talked with Bill Stevens, a representative for a U.S. gaming machine company who was in Brazil to provide technical services to customers. Bill had worked and traveled in Canada and Mexico, but this was his first trip to Brazil. He told Annie that the most salient cultural difference he noticed was the time Brazilians take for meals and for their families. He was working with a colleague named Ademar, and they were visiting the various sites where Ademar's company had machines. In the United States, under similar circumstances, two men trying to visit a large number of locations and share as much information as possible in a short time would just grab lunch on the go. But Bill remarked that Ademar always stopped for lunch, and the two men would sit down and eat a complete meal and talk. When they met for breakfast, Ademar also ate and drank without haste and conversed with Bill. Bill also noted that frequently Ademar spent time with his children in the morning before they went to school, so he did not begin working as early as Bill would have liked.

BRAZILIANS CONSCIOUSLY and openly enjoy and explore sensuality, and the sexual dimension of male-female relationships in communication is generally more overt than is acceptable in the United States. In addition, the savoring of food and socializing at a meal is a cultural ritual that is extremely important in relating to others on a daily basis. To understand and to communicate more effectively, foreigners need to be aware of these dimensions of personal interaction in Brazil and to understand that these behaviors are a significant and valued part of Brazilian culture.

CHAPTER FOURTEEN

Thought Patterns and Directness

Brazilians abhor disciplined thinking. Their actions are improvised, not premeditated. This has a positive as well as a negative side. Although the ideal may be to plan ahead, Brazilians use their improvisational abilities to overcome the difficulties of daily life.[1]

The Facts

People in different cultures arrive at their concepts of reality in different ways. They may perceive reality through faith or belief, independent of fact. They may base their perception on fact supported by evidence. Or they may perceive reality primarily through feelings or instinct, the most common means of constructing reality.[2] Different cultures teach different ways of gathering and evaluating evidence, presenting viewpoints, and reaching conclusions. These differences are evident in discussions, speeches, and writing.[3]

To communicate effectively across cultures, one must understand that different thinking patterns often produce different strategies for performing the same communicative task—conversing, persuading, or negotiating. People can perceive differently, for example, the appropriate or most effective way to make a point.[4]

North Americans rely on the presentation of what they perceive as the facts to persuade and make points. They seek specific quantities, percentages, rates, and rankings.[5] Along with North Americans' trust in facts goes a distrust of emotions. Conversely, Brazilians have a tradition of eloquent, emotion-filled speech. They seek to move and persuade their audiences through shared feelings as well as facts. A Brazilian graduate student who was having difficulty writing papers in English explained that it was not just a matter of grammar or vocabulary. A professor told him he was too subjective and emotional in making and supporting his points.[6]

Moreover, the United States is a pragmatic culture that prefers to focus on facts rather than theory, if the facts are available, whereas Brazilians focus on theory. Christophe Duval works for the Canadian telecommunications company Telet in Brazil. He noted that when North American and Canadian companies hire employees directly out of school, they often assign them specific responsibilities and require immediate, measurable results. When Brazilian companies hire recruits out of school, they are given lengthy training programs. The new employees like the training programs because they are theoretical and entail no responsibility: "It's like a party." He found that, in general, Brazilians list all the training they have received on their résumés, whereas North Americans are more likely to list successful projects they have handled and specific, usually quantifiable results they have achieved for their employers.

Darcy Ribeiro writes on the Brazilian national character. He notes that the historian Sérgio Buarque de Holanda attributes to Brazilians an adventurous spirit, appreciation of loyalty, greater pleasure in leisure than in commerce, and Portuguese laxness and plasticity combined with Hispanic arrogance. From this mixture probably come anarchy, lack of cohesion, disorder, indiscipline, and indolence. A tendency toward despotism, authoritarianism, and tyranny also probably derives from it. These all seem to be defects, but he affirms that the opposite—servility, humility, rigidity, a spirit of order, a sense of duty, a liking for routine, gravity, and circumspection—would be worse. The latter would take away the creativity of the Brazilian adventurer, the adaptability of someone who is flexible rather than rigid, the vitality of the person who faces fate with daring, and the originality of an undisciplined people.[7]

Specific and Ritual Verbal Content

Most North Americans become impatient with people who talk at great length. They admire conciseness and will often say bluntly, both in business and in personal conversations "Get to the point" to cut off lengthy explanations or chitchat. This brusqueness that so shocks Brazilians stems from the North American concepts of time and efficiency, their lesser need for personal involvement, and the fact that they seek specific information content in communication. Without some mitigation of style, North Americans may be too direct for comfortable interaction in Brazilian culture, where indirectness is the norm.

In Brazil, to get to the heart of the matter is to get to the liver of it: "Vai ao fígado da coisa." It is just a matter of perspective.

Getting straight to the point is something Brazilians find offensive. Even in important negotiations, Brazilians engage in what North Americans might think of as unnecessary preliminary socializing. North Americans would do well to remember that more personal interaction is required to do business in Brazil than in the United States. Protocol requires that people become acquainted and comfortable with each other before settling down to address business.

Based on a summary prepared by a Brazilian business professor, one can define the differences in style for cross-cultural negotiations between Brazilians and North Americans. Brazilians first establish rapport; the personal relationship is everything. The presentation of information requires frequent feedback from the listener. Persuasion is seductive, avoids confrontation, and includes no direct pressure. Agreement depends on the establishment of rapport; people come before money. The time North Americans allocate to establishing rapport is minimal. The presentation of information is short and direct. Persuasion is aggressive. Progress toward agreement is made sequentially and ends with a definite outcome.[8]

North Americans should mitigate their directness to communicate successfully with Brazilians. Even for something as simple as a telephone call, North Americans should "chat" first and only then proceed to the reason for the call or to the discussion of business. After more than twenty years in the United States, Maria Brasil is still startled and upset when people launch directly into their reason for calling her. She said she expects a few minutes of general conversation to break the ice and to show that the caller cares for her as a person. A person who uses an abrupt, blunt approach will never get her business, nor will an acquaintance build a good personal relationship with her by using that style of communication.[9] Because of Brazil's telephone protocol and people's desire to cultivate personal relationships, telemarketing has not been the nuisance it is in the United States. Gisela Hauptman observed, though, that since Brazilians emulate so much that comes from the United States, credit card companies have recently tried cold calling in Brazil to sell their services.

Brazilians find impersonal treatment cold, distant, and unsatisfying. North Americans do not like to be treated impersonally either, but what they consider impersonal and unacceptable and what they require to feel that they are experiencing satisfactory personal interaction is quite different from what is needed to satisfy Brazilian requirements.

On meeting, Brazilians will typically exchange greetings and information about the health and well-being of each other's family members at some length. North Americans might inquire perfunctorily, "How is your wife?" or "How are the kids?" but politeness in brief and casual encounters does not require dwelling on these personal inquiries. Obviously, North Americans do engage in brief ritual interaction, such as "Hi, how are you?" "Fine, thanks," "Nice to meet you," and "Hope to see you again." These queries and responses are concerned more with form than with content and have little to do with what people think or how they actually feel. Many North Americans become impatient with long, ritual interchanges about a person's well-being and family members' health.[10] They prefer verbal communication that contains specific information.

Cariocas embody the ritual Brazilian communication style. They are effusive, open, and friendly. In an amusing account of local interaction ritual, one Rio resident writes that since "Good-bye" would sound too curt, *cariocas* will say "I'll see you," or "I'll call you," or "Drop by the house." But one must understand that this means "I probably won't see you very soon," "Don't hold your breath for me to call," and "Don't be dumb enough to just drop by." In her glossary of *carioca* expressions, she defines "I'll call you" as the preferred phrase for ending an encounter, and its meaning is "I *won't* call you."[11] These utterances are clearly not information-specific and will disappoint, anger, or frustrate the foreigner who takes them literally. In the United States, southern culture encompasses similar "courteous" language usage that is not information-specific in content.

The owner of a company that provides assistance to business executives and families that have been transferred to Porto Alegre talked about the difficulty many foreigners have distinguishing language specificity from language that is nonspecific or ritualistic. The people she counsels express frustration, disappointment, and even anger when Brazilians do not call when they say they will or do not "keep their word." A Brazilian business professor observed that the Brazilian talks a lot but may not really say much; conversely, the North American talks less, but when he does decide to speak he is direct and his words are specific.

Personal Style

Brazilians' very personal style can benefit them in the business world. In 2000 the Brazilian firm Embraer was on the verge of displacing Canada's Bombardier as the world's third largest manufacturer of commercial aircraft and had American Eagle and Continental Express as its two largest customers in the United States. Thomas Bacon, senior vice president for marketing and planning at American Eagle, commented, "We had no way of anticipating the kind of customer service support that we have had from Embraer," which "bent over backwards" to accommodate American Eagle's requests. Embraer personalized service even to the extent of agreeing to make customized changes on planes that were already in production.[12]

Mauricio Botelho, a fifty-eight-year-old Brazilian mechanical engineer, was brought in to run Embraer in 1995. He not only instituted policies that value the human element, but he had a reputation for being more of a long-term strategic thinker than the average Brazilian executive. The daily *Jornal do Brasil* described him as "methodical and thoughtful." It would appear that Botelho not only embodies the Brazilian emphasis on personalizing communication, but, rather than abhor disciplined thinking, puts it to very good use.[13]

Indirectness

To say that Brazilians never say "no" is only a slight exaggeration. They find all sorts of indirect ways to avoid the unpleasantness of saying "no" to any request, especially from family or friends.

Mary Wheeler spent two months in Porto Alegre compiling statistical data for her company, where she met Iracy and Cláudio Saldanha. The couple invited Mary to a party. In return, on a Monday, Mary called to invite Iracy and Cláudio out to dinner on Friday or Saturday, to meet Mary's husband, Bill, who had just arrived for a week's stay. Iracy told Mary she already had a commitment for those nights but would call the next day to let Mary know if they were available Sunday or the following week.

Iracy did not call back. Mary waited several days and called again and left a message. The following week, Mary called Iracy again, because she felt it proper to follow up on the dinner invitation she had issued. This time she left a message with Iracy's son, who had just graduated from medical school. Unfortunately, Iracy did not call back before Mary and Bill left Brazil.

Mary was disappointed and perplexed. It was possible that Iracy did not want to go to dinner or even that she did not like Mary. Mary knew Iracy was very busy with the demands of her medical practice and planning a big celebration for her son's graduation. In retrospect, Mary realized Iracy's comment that maybe the two couples could get together "on Sunday, or next week," was a ritual softening of "no." Iracy probably knew her schedule was full and never intended to call back—but because of cultural conditioning Iracy could not say "no" directly.

Mary Wheeler had corresponded with and stayed a few days with Claudina on arriving in Porto Alegre. Claudina had been most helpful. She told Mary that a mutual friend, Circe, was organizing a party for Friday of the following week and that Circe would call Mary to invite her.

Circe never called, and Mary thought perhaps Claudina was mistaken that she was to be invited to Circe's party. Mary wondered if she should make other plans, since she was trying to fit in so many things during her stay. But the Thursday before the party, Claudina called to say that Circe would pick Mary up on Friday, because the party was at a house some distance away and might be difficult to find. Fortunately, Mary had not scheduled anything else for that evening in the meantime. It was obvious that a fair amount of coordinating had gone into picking Mary up, because Circe was accompanied by several friends.

It seemed strange to Mary that all of this care and planning to include her in the party had gone on around her but that what seemed to her the key ingredient was missing—an invitation to the party. That the party would take place and that Mary was indeed invited was never confirmed. Circe may have assumed Mary was planning on the event, knowing that Claudina had "mentioned" it to Mary.

Claudina and Circe also organized a going-away party for Mary and Bill, scheduled for four days before the couple left, but they did not tell Mary about it until two days before it was to take place, and Mary and Bill had committed to dinner at the home of a representative from a trade association on that evening. Claudina said to Mary, "Well, just invite him to the party instead of going to his dinner," but Mary did not feel comfortable canceling her host's dinner invitation and substituting another activity, even if it included him. She still wonders if that is what she should have done.

When Annie Nimos was discussing Brazilian cultural characteristics with a *paulistano* friend, the friend observed that Brazilians in the Northeast use an even softer style of communication. If you ask someone a simple question such as "Do you have a real?" the response will be, "Tenho, não" (I have, no), probably because the directness of beginning the response with the word "no" seems too harsh. Communicating meaning indirectly can become a complex process requiring subtleties of interpretation. As Claudina Junker pointed out, if a person says something and you do not respond, a Brazilian takes that as agreement. Nonagreement is frequently signaled by side-stepping rituals—"I'll see if I can do it"—or postponement—"I'll look into it. Check back with me next week."

North American thinking patterns sort primarily into black or white categories, seeking specificity and "yes" or "no" answers. Brazilians, in contrast, see shades of gray.

Brazilians observe that North Americans take their laws very seriously. Several attorneys who work with both codified and common law state that Brazilian codified law allows for more interpretation, whereas North American common law provides specific examples in black and white. Even individuals in the United States have been legally classified as either black or white.

North Americans' direct communication style holds especially true in a business environment. Lourenço Juvenal observed that North American executives do not like surprises. It is understandable that a corporation wants accurate financial projections. However, Lourenço goes on to explain, he has found that even good surprises are unwelcome, because it means that projections did not give black and white quantifiable information that matched results. This outcome signifies that one is not in control. In his view, North American solutions are less creative than Brazilian solutions. His perception is that North Americans want to "go to a report, look on page 7, and find paragraph 4.b for a specific answer to a problem." A Brazilian business professor who teaches in a North American university confirms that the communication style in North American businesses is direct and information-specific and that Brazilians are indirect and less specific. In addition, because Brazilians are incurable optimists, their forecasts tend to be more favorable than reality would support.

Santos writes that Brazilians are more adept at coping with certain types of problems, such as those requiring quick innovation, whereas North Americans deal more successfully with others, such as those requiring methodical analysis and planning. A partial explanation for this is that each culture has its own perceptual and cognitive styles affecting attitudes, beliefs, and coping responses. The realities of Brazilian life do not inspire confidence, Santos observes; they seem more likely to instill a sense of helplessness. Mountains, jungles, and vast distances are responsible for a cosmic terror that has been passed down through generations. In addition, Brazilians must cope with the frustration and ambiguities of their social system. The cultivation of *jeito* is probably a legacy of skills to adapt first to Brazil's physical environment and then to the intricacies of its social system.[14] One of Caetano Veloso's recordings includes a spoken comment that one should never be certain about anything, because things may change.

Hal Brandon observed that Santos underestimates the amount of real-time innovation that takes place in North American transactions. He found that North Americans are adept at "thinking on their feet." Perhaps the difference is one of degree: Brazilians have had to perfect improvisation to a fine art as a survival skill. In the Dell plant and offices in Rio Grande do Sul, one never knows whether electrical power will be available continuously throughout the day. The North American reaction is, "Who ever heard of having such problems? We have enough to contend with under 'normal' [i.e., U.S.] production conditions!"

In explaining Brazilian indirectness and North American directness, yet another paradox becomes evident. A number of Brazilians who have lived and worked in the United States insist that Brazilians are direct and that North Americans are indirect. For example, Gerardo Bernard maintained that although Brazilian culture is socially structured in a steep hierarchy, Brazilians are open and direct with each other. Since Brazilians know where they stand, he stated, they can be direct in their communication style even between classes. The prescribed behavior in the United States for dealing with others may give the appearance of a just, sophisticated, and egalitarian society, but he feels that it masks a degree of hierarchy and, most of all, that it makes North American communication indirect.

What emerges from numerous conversations and interviews is that when Brazilians say they find Brazilian communication more direct than that of North Americans, they are referring to an emotional connection and a communication of *feelings*. Brazilians want and need to connect to people on this personal level, which they can rarely do in their dealings with North Americans. One can explain the assessment of Bernard and others in this way: Brazilians are *emotionally* direct, whereas North Americans tend to mask their emotions and feelings. When Brazilians cannot read a North American's feelings, "what they really think," they feel that North Americans are not communicating directly and openly. In turn, North Americans sometimes react to Brazilian emotional expression as insincere.

Althen writes that North Americans regard their feelings and their opinions about controversial matters as private and reveal little that is personal about themselves except to close friends over time.[15] Brazilians, who are accustomed to more self-disclosure, often are frustrated in their efforts to get to know North Americans. The perception of "directness" is a two-way problem in communication between Brazilians and North Americans.

I wrote to Michael Dell to request that he facilitate interviews with Dell executives in the United States and Brazil. I received a "direct" response at "the speed of Dell," and a Dell executive immediately arranged for the interviews. Michael Dell's communication style epitomizes the best of North American cultural emphasis on direct communication and time efficiency, in keeping with Dell's innovative marketing slogan, "Be Direct."

My letter is an example of direct communication in the flat hierarchy, low-context, monochronic, direct culture of the U.S. business world. Features of my letter that constitute direct communication style are

- Address the highest-ranking decision maker directly.
- Use the fewest possible words, in a single page.
- Begin by stating the purpose directly.
- Be clear about what is being requested.
- Give a reason for the recipient to comply.
- Address anticipated objections.
- Remember that there is never a second chance to make a first impression.

This is the polar opposite of Brazilian communication style. A person normally gains access to a key decision maker through an introduction to pave the way in the steep hierarchy of Brazil's polychronic, high-context culture. More time is devoted to allowing the parties to get to know one another, even on paper. Requests are usually made in an indirect manner. Persuasion style commonly provides more background information about the request and the writer. More titles, formal forms of address, and opening and closing rituals are observed in letter writing.

Making a Point: Brazilian versus U.S. Negotiation Style

One's communication style is a combination of features learned from one's culture and features that are idiosyncratically developed, so that communication style is culturally shared and personally differentiated.[16]

On four consecutive days, Pedro de Moraes Garcez of the state of Rio Grande do Sul videotaped negotiations between two representatives of a Brazilian leather goods manufacturer and two representatives of a North American importer. True to Brazilian cultural norms, Garcez gained access to the negotiations through personal introductions.

Garcez has done innovative work on "point making" in communication. The following interpretation is based on Garcez's insightful analysis of the negotiations he videotaped.[17] In this scenario, I refer to the Brazilian company as CouroFab and its representatives as Rolando and Egídio and to the North American Company as ImporCorp and its representatives as Henry and George. At the time of these negotiations, Rio Grande do Sul supplied 80 percent of the shoes exported from Brazil, and 75 percent to 80 percent of Brazil's shoe exports were being shipped to the United States. The four participants in the negotiations knew and liked each other. Even so, their point-making styles interfered with their communication.

People make points in two common ways. They state their point and then back it up with supportive information (point > information), or they present the supporting information first as background and then state their point (information > point).

Brazilians commonly begin by presenting a series of observations or information intended to support their point and subsequently make the point (information > point). Presenting supporting information first relies heavily on high conversational involvement on the part of the listener. It is typical of collective and polychronic cultures. The speaker expects the listener to be posing questions mentally and to participate orally with queries such as "So?" "Why?" "What for?" "Then what?" in increasing order of importance. Together the participants build up to stating the point. If the listener participates as expected, the supporting information makes sense. The point may even become so self-evident that it does not need to be stated explicitly.

In contrast, North Americans focus on "the point" itself. Frequently, they signal it verbally: "Let's get right to the point"; "My point is . . ." They expect speakers and writers to explicitly express the main idea or piece of information they wish to convey.[18] North Americans are culturally trained in a thought process that first makes the point (point > information) and then moves to support the point with only as much information as seems necessary. Further, they will cut short their presentation of supporting information if the other person no longer appears to require it.

We listen in the same format that we present, because this is how we organize and make sense of the information that we hear. Brazilians therefore commonly expect to hear supporting background information first. If North Americans state the point at the beginning of a presentation and do not signal it by a statement such as "My point is this . . . ," it can slip by as background information and the Brazilian might wait for a point that never comes.

North Americans expect to hear the point first, because this is how they organize their own presentation of information. They frequently get lost in the information > point style because they mistake successive bits of supporting information for the point, which then do not make sense. In frustration, they typically interject premature or erroneous points, or they become frustrated and demand, "Get to the point," which breaches Brazilian etiquette.

Carl Nimos is a North American who began his career with Citibank by working in various countries. In considering this explanation of opposing point-making styles, Carl commented that in negotiations in Africa, the Middle East, and Latin America, instinct told him to slow down, wait patiently, and allow the other person to speak as long as he wanted about whatever he wanted. Carl attributed his attitude to common sense and respect for foreign customs and rules of courtesy, but in retrospect he could see that what was taking place was clearly presentation in an information > point style. He affirmed that it would have greatly helped his cross-cultural communication skills to have consciously understood from the beginning of his first assignment these different point-making styles. He could have listened and mentally organized the information he was hearing more constructively.

Lúcio Lara also confirmed in retrospect the difference in how North Americans and Brazilians make their points. He recounted making a report to a Dell manager in Austin. Lúcio had analyzed a production process and organized his findings and conclusions into a Powerpoint presentation of twenty-five slides. After the first three slides, his manager queried, "But what's your point?" Lúcio was presenting supporting facts first, planning to end with conclusions, as he was accustomed to doing in Brazil. He thought, "Oh, I can fix that." He immediately went to slide 25 and made his presentation backward. The reverse order made total sense to the manager.

In the CouroFab–ImporCorp negotiations, the Brazilians did not have as much difficulty understanding the North Americans' direct style of point making as the North Americans had with the Brazilians' indirect point making. There are a number of reasons for this. First, the North Americans often signaled their points lexically, for example, "This is my proposal" or "Here is my final offer." Second, Brazilians are familiar with the point > information style both from interacting with North Americans and from reading educational texts. In addition, the Brazilians were negotiating in English, their second language, with individuals from a more powerful nation (i.e., the power factor); they were negotiating as younger and less experienced learners in this business transaction (i.e., the hierarchical factor); and they may have needed to sell more than the North Americans needed to buy (i.e., the motivation factor). All of these factors usually make participants in conversations and negotiations more flexible and open. Henry and George, in contrast, only expected to hear their own conversational style. Fortunately, because the team on one side of the negotiations was more adaptable and because the discussions opened with goodwill on both sides, the differences in style did not always cause communication problems. However, in these negotiations, the point was not always successfully communicated and was sometimes misinterpreted. Misinterpretation, that is, misunderstanding, caused the most serious breakdown in communication.

In the CouroFab–ImporCorp negotiations, four types of problems arose because of the difference in point-making style.

1. ATTEMPT TO PREMATURELY IDENTIFY THE POINT.

To follow and understand a conversation, persons accustomed to point > information style tend to expressly or mentally supply a point if it is not provided when expected. In the ImporCorp–CouroFab negotiations, Henry and George would listen to bits of information that seemed unrelated based on their own point > information style. To make sense of what they were hearing, they would interject "the point" they thought CouroFab was trying to make before Rolando and Egídio finished their speaking "turn."

Hypothetically, and to involve ImporCorp by first presenting background information, CouroFab began to explain that CouroFab could not produce an order to ship on time if they ordered leather from Argentina when they received a firm order from ImporCorp. ImporCorp understood from this explanation that the Brazilians would only order the leather after they received the ImporCorp order. This sounded unreasonable, so they interrupted: "But you need to order the leather in advance."

After further explanation, ImporCorp got the point that the Brazilians were saying they needed an advance idea of quantity to schedule large shipments of leather from Argentina to be able to fill specific orders on time.

Henry interrupted, "OK, then just give us the ground rules of how you want us to place our orders," just as Rolando began to explain the notice and quantity estimates he needed. Henry and George looked down and began to write, no longer paying attention, and Rolando felt as if he were talking to himself.

While this caused frustration, it was not the most disruptive type of communication problem, because Rolando's intent was eventually communicated. If Henry and George had been aware of the information > point style they would have been less confused and they would have allowed Rolando to present his background information and then make his point. If Rolando had understood the North Americans' thought process and listening style, he could have stated explicitly that his opening information was hypothetical. Time, energy, and face could have been saved.

2. THE POINT WAS NOT COMMUNICATED.

Rolando and Egídio wanted to use less expensive Argentine leather rather than more expensive Brazilian leather to manufacture the Impor-Corp items. But they had never dealt with the Argentine tannery and did not know if they could rely on supply and prices. To be fair, they wanted to quote two prices for each item to ImporCorp, in case they could not get the Argentine leather. They began by explaining that there was a source of Argentine leather that was less expensive than Brazilian leather but that they had not dealt with this source before. Henry and George showed annoyance at receiving information that seemed irrelevant and bobbed their heads impatiently. George stated that he did not care where CouroFab got their leather, as long as the price to Impor-Corp was right. ImporCorp did not recognize that CouroFab was giving them information to support why they were going to quote two prices per item.

When Rolando proceeded to quote two prices per item, based on their two possible leather sources, this seemed absurd to Henry and George. George asked why CouroFab was quoting two prices on every item. Henry asked why he should even contemplate buying at the higher price if the quality was the same. Rolando had thought that Henry's and George's nods had indicated understanding of CouroFab's dilemma and expressed his embarrassment and frustration nonverbally with head down and drooping shoulders.

Henry began a Socratic style of interrogation, asking if someone quotes you $33.10 from Argentina and $36.10 from Brazil for Y, for the same quality, which would you buy?

Rolando responded, "Argentina."

"So why would I consider Brazil?"

This caused loss of face for the Brazilians, and the subject was abruptly dropped.

3. INTERRUPTION OF THE PRESENTATION
OF SUPPORTING INFORMATION.

This results in a poorly supported point. CouroFab wanted first to explain how they arrived at a price and began by presenting information about leather supply and the labor involved in producing certain items. CouroFab also wanted to discuss exchange rates as part of the supporting information for arriving at a price. ImporCorp directly refused this style of presentation.

Henry interrupted, "I don't have the patience for this." "Get to the point," George interjected. "Get to the point" is typical of North American communication style, and North Americans frequently use this phrase in discussions among themselves. When ImporCorp interrupted CouroFab to demand "the point," Rolando and Egídio had to stop their buildup to point disclosure in order to respond, which slowed down the discussions and frustrated CouroFab. Because of constant interruptions, CouroFab ended up delivering most of their supporting information in fragmented fashion. This fragmentation made their arguments appear weak even though they were not. When this type of breakdown in the talks occurred, the Brazilians were as sure they were right in their reasons for arriving at price as the North Americans were sure they were wrong. The interruptions affected the Brazilians more negatively than it did the North Americans, and it made the Brazilians seem incoherent and unreasonable. ImporCorp stated that they thought CouroFab's prices were unsubstantiated. The negotiators arrived at an impasse, and a series of intense arguments ensued.

Despite all of the problems with this communication style, CouroFab quoted all prices in the same manner. Henry interrupted many times to demand that the price be quoted before there was any discussion of whether it was right or wrong. For a number of reasons, the Brazilians had not pinned down a price on a briefcase that ImporCorp wanted, and they maintained that discussing how they would arrive at the price was particularly important. Henry again demanded the price first, but Rolando made it clear the price was not yet available. In this instance, CouroFab succeeded in obtaining a compromise from ImporCorp on presentation style, and CouroFab was able to discuss costs and labor before quoting a price. George did what Egídio had been wanting him to do. George followed the development of background information, asking for clarification, until Egídio was able to make his point. Henry and George agreed that this item was more labor-intensive than a style from Czechoslovakia they were comparing it with, and they both finally saw that there were production problems of which they had not been aware. Sufficient discussion time probably was dedicated to successfully communicate on this item because it was of particular interest to the importers.

Although the negotiators communicated successfully regarding the briefcase, the arguments that had taken place over pricing left them with a residual unpleasant feeling. Since they were unaware that this feeling stemmed from a problem of communication *style*, each side blamed the others' personalities or the quality of their relationship, and what had been a communication difference turned into attributions of personal identity.

4. MISUNDERSTANDING THE POINT OR THE INTENT.

The three preceding problems caused lack of communication, frustration, and unease. Although the problems ultimately were resolved to some degree, *misunderstanding* the point was the most detrimental to the course of the negotiations.

CouroFab wanted to propose importing some items from Rumania through ImporCorp at a discount to be offset by discounts from Couro-Fab to ImporCorp. Egídio approached this subject by asking Henry if he couldn't get a better price than those Henry had quoted for the Rumanian items. Henry took offense. He interpreted Egídio's opening request for background information as questioning his honesty regarding price quotations.

He retorted, "What? Are you some kind of smartaleck?"

Egídio understood that his question had been misinterpreted and responded, "No, I'm thinking something else." He was ready to drop the subject. But Henry continued to react to his misunderstanding of the question. He pulled some papers out of his briefcase and stated that he was going to *show* Egídio Rumania's prices, even though Egídio protested that he did not need to see them. Because ImporCorp took offense, ultimately the parties abandoned discussion of a business arrangement that might have been mutually beneficial.

Frequently, people will just drop the subject when their point is not understood, because further communication does not seem worth the effort or because offense has been taken. But when an important outcome depends on the point being understood in business negotiations, dropping the point because of misunderstanding can result in material loss.

THE TOTAL EXPERIENCE of living in a culture colors our perceptions of the world and affects our thought patterns, both of which are expressed in our communicative behavioral processes. Being aware of transnational differences in perception of "facts," in specificity of use of verbal language, in directness (or indirectness) of style, in needs for personal connection, and in how points are made will help to bridge the communication gap between cultures.

PART III

Processes of Communication

CHAPTER FIFTEEN

Verbal and Nonverbal Messages

We must learn to speak a foreign culture in the same way that we must learn to speak a foreign language.[1]

Verbal Language

Although this book is about speaking culture, rather than about speaking a language, a few observations about language are in order. Brazilians speak Portuguese. The difference between Brazilian Portuguese and that of Portugal is somewhat greater than the difference between North American English and British English. There are differences in common vocabulary preferences, spelling, and accent. The accent of Portugal is somewhat harsh, whereas Brazilian Portuguese is soft and mellifluous.

The Portuguese language is not "almost" the same as Spanish, any more than Italian is almost the same. A Spanish speaker does not readily understand spoken Portuguese, although there are words in common and both languages derive from Latin. A Portuguese speaker can more easily understand spoken Spanish. Spanish speakers usually enunciate the sounds and syllables of a word more clearly than do Brazilians. There are complex vowel sounds and nasalities in Portuguese that do not exist in Spanish. Due largely to the unwritten conventions of living language, the pronunciation of Brazilian Portuguese does not always correspond to the written word. Many words are therefore not recognizable until a person has been initiated into these conventions. The written *o* of Spanish is pronounced like "oh," but in Brazilian Portuguese the written final *o* is pronounced like *oo* in "choose," as is the final letter *l. Sal* (salt) sounds more like "sah-oo" and rhymes with cow. The final *-te* is pronounced "chee" or "jee" in many regions of Brazil. And *r* and *rr* are pronounced as an aspirated *h* in many positions in a word. In addition, Brazilian Portuguese has a very heavy tonic accent, and the heavily accented syllable of a word tends to drown out the others.

During the evolution of Portuguese and Spanish on the Iberian Peninsula, Portuguese ended up with fewer syllables than Spanish in many similar words. This makes it harder for a Spanish speaker to recognize a word in Portuguese that has the same root as the Spanish word, because there is less of the word to work with. It is easier for a Portuguese speaker to recognize a word in Spanish that has the same root as the Portuguese word, simply because there are often more syllables to spark recognition. Add to this the fact that Brazilians are generally curious, malleable, and adaptable as a people. Some examples of words follow.

Portuguese	Spanish	English
empada	empanada	small savory pie
côr	color	color
dor	dolor	pain
geral	general	general

A North American executive of a high-tech company in Brazil who is well traveled and fluent in Spanish, said that it does not seem worth the effort to learn Portuguese because he will never work in Portugal and probably will be transferred out of Brazil back to Spanish-speaking countries in the Americas. For him, Portuguese has more limited use than Spanish, and he said that he finds learning a new language more difficult than it once was. He has learned many courtesy words and phrases and some basic vocabulary in Portuguese, so he speaks a mixture of "Portunhol" (português-espanhol) in most of his business and social conversations, and amiable Brazilians at all levels indulge him. They seem to appreciate the interest and respect that his efforts at Portuguese convey.

Were he to speak Spanish and assume that Brazilians can or should understand it, he would not meet with much success. Brazilians are proud of their language and protective of its use, and people who do not know that Brazilians speak Portuguese rather than Spanish label themselves as ignorant.

Brazilians frequently use words for effect and not just content. Words are chosen for their pleasant sound and connotation. Page writes that in the nineteenth century Brazil deliberately appeared to comply with British demands to terminate Brazil's slave trade when they did not intend to do so. This popularized an expression commonly used in Brazil today—para inglês ver (for the English to see), which means that something is just a front or done to placate. There has always been a gap between rhetoric and reality in Brazil, and lofty pronouncements can be "for people to see" and not necessarily reflect actual intent or practice.[2]

Solange, who owns and operates a visitor assistance company, stated that foreigners find the Portuguese language difficult. Language difference is an obvious barrier for foreigners arriving in Brazil, whether they are immigrants or sojourners.

George, a North American, and Rodolfo, a Brazilian, were looking at a menu posted outside a small sandwich shop in Brazil. The menu had a vertical list of eight items, all of which began with the word "Xis": Xis Presunto, Xis Tomate, Xis Tocinho, and so on. Although George spoke fair Portuguese, he was stumped. He asked Rodolfo to translate. Rodolfo responded that the menu listed a variety of cheeseburgers. On hearing the word "cheese," George instantly understood. In keeping with Brazilians' adaptability, instead of using the Portuguese word queijo *for "cheese,"* xis *was used as a phonetic approximation of the English. The sandwiches were Ham Cheeseburger, Tomato Cheeseburger, Bacon Cheeseburger . . .*

Literacy and Orality

Brazil is an oral culture. Claudina Junker said, "Brazilians don't read. They want you to tell them things, not to read about them." Oral and visual presentations are important, and comic books, such as Freyre's, are popular. In Brazil, television has a great deal of influence (as it does everywhere in the world), but it carries special weight because of the low literacy rate. One obvious reason for the orality of Brazil is the relative lack of education among the poor and the large number of functionally illiterate persons. César Guardini talked about the importance of oral communication with his employees, whom he has painstakingly trained to do their work. The majority of the people working for his electrical contracting firm average a third-grade education.

The educational level in Brazil, illiteracy, and oral traditions are reflected in the small number of books sold relative to the size of the population. This in turn affects the cost of printing. Although big bookstores and the bookstore-café combination that are common in the United States have recently become popular, books everywhere in Brazil are exorbitantly expensive. The beautiful photography books of the country that are available are offered at astronomical prices.

Names

Although the name used to identify a person is a verbal symbol, the choice of how to address a person and what name to use is a cultural ritual, which is a nonverbal process. The practice of using several surnames reflects collective Brazil's concern with family ties. This custom has evolved because in Brazil a person's identity, influence, and power depend in great part on family connections. In early Brazil's feudal-like society, slaves and the rural poor, like serfs, had no need for surnames. Only in the twentieth century have all Brazilians been dignified with full names.[3]

Verónica Ribeiro, a university professor, observed that in social gatherings, the first question one will ask about a person is her or his family name. As in most countries, there is prestige in being connected to this or that family, but in Brazil it is more important than in the United States, where the principal question is more often what a person "does" to determine who he or she "is."

Many English speakers have learned that Spanish-speaking countries use the father's surname followed by the mother's surname, as in Mariano Vargas García. This gentleman would be called Señor Vargas (by his father's surname) in a country such as Chile or Mexico. In Brazil, the father's surname comes last, as it does in the United States. Therefore, Lúcio Cunha Texeira would be called Senhor Texeira. (Note that in both examples, it is the father's surname that is taken, but the placement changes.)

Brazilians are very imaginative in their selection of children's names. Names ending in -on for men are very popular. Witness Ayrton, Washington, Robson, Denilson, Wilson, Enylton, and Nilton, to list only a few. Annie Nimos had a classmate in Brazil who had three brothers, Gerónimo, Washington, and Napoleão. And no one found it unusual that original Greek names from Sophocles' *Oedipus Rex* were used in the television serial *Mandala*. The modern characters were called Edipo and Jocasta.[4]

Forms of Address

Hierarchy governs forms of address, such as the use of formal or informal pronouns, names, and titles. The recent North American custom of calling everyone by their first names in the workplace is disconcerting to Brazilians, who are accustomed to addressing each other in a way that delineates social status, age, and position. As one Brazilian sees it, calling her employer "Peter" doesn't make her his equal, so she thinks it is preferable to keep her distance linguistically. In Brazil, one does not call someone by his or her first name only, unless invited to do so. When introduced to people in formal or business situations, one is usually given the person's last name, often on a business card. The last name should always be used if it is given. However, the paradox is that the first name may be the only name one is given, in which case the typically Brazilian use of the first name with a title applies, for example, Senhor Pedro (or the oral form, Seu Pedro), much like in the U.S. South.[5] The academic coordinator for the Instituto Cultural Brasil Norte-America in one city remarked that he does not know the last names of most of the people he is acquainted with. The telephone company even lists a person by a single nickname at no extra charge. And until recently in many small cities, telephone books listed people alphabetically by first names.

When addressing someone directly, Portuguese provides for linguistic distance and maintaining hierarchy with formal usage: "o Senhor" (masc.) and "a Senhora" (fem.). "Would you like a *cafezinho*?" becomes "O Senhor [A Senhora] aceita um cafezinho?" (Would the gentleman [the lady] accept a coffee?).[6] In spoken Portuguese, Brazilians transform "Senhor" into "Seu" before the first name for men, and they use "Dona" before the first name for women. These titles should always be used when addressing someone, unless one is told not to. Therefore, a male business associate or employee would be called "Seu Pedro" and a female business associate or employee, "Dona Ana." Male or female counterparts, if they are about the same age and rank as the person they are speaking with, will probably ask to be called by their first names without any title.[7]

It is very common for male employers, managers, executives, and higher-ranking officials or bureaucrats to be addressed as "Doutor" in Brazil. This does not mean that this person is a physician or has a Ph.D. Frequently, the title is honorific. Elementary school teachers, usually women, are often addressed as "Tia" (Aunt).[8]

The choice of pronouns and the use of titles in addressing people convey formality and respect and maintain the hierarchy. Persons of lower social status express respect and indicate awareness of social stratification by using formal pronouns and titles when addressing those of higher status. Persons of higher status addressing those of lower status maintain distance and dictate a reciprocal form of address by the same usage. Social position is not the only determinant. Persons of the same class maintain distance by using formal pronouns and titles. All social classes employ the formal form of address when speaking to an elderly person, respectfully using "o Senhor" and "a Senhora" in deference to the person's age, regardless of social rank.

It is common in casual speech to hear Brazilians use the familiar pronoun *tu* (second-person singular) incorrectly conjugated with the verb form for *você* (third-person singular). Persons who know correct grammar will often use this incorrect grammatical form when speaking informally but speak correctly when they wish to be formal. Following is a list of forms of direct address.

• *Excelência; Vossa Excelência/V.Exa; Sua Excelência/S.Exa.* —High-ranking authorities

- *Vossa Magnificência/V.Mag^a*—Rectors of universities
- *Vossa Santidade/V.S.*—The pope
- *Reverendíssimo/V. Revma.*—Priests and pastors
- *Vossa Majestade/V.M.*—Kings and queens
- *Vossa Alteza/V.A./S.A.*—Princes
- *Vossa Senhoria/V.S.^{a}*—Persons of rank; also used for ceremonial purposes
- *Doutor/Senhor Dr.*—Doctor
- *Senhor/Sr.*—Formal for men
- *Seu*—Used orally in addressing a man by first name
- *Dona*—Used orally in addressing a woman by first name
- *Senhora/Sra.*—Formal for woman
- *Senhorita/Srta.*—Formal for single woman
- *Professor/Prof.*—Teacher at any level, or a specialist, such as a sports coach
- *Você/V.*—Informal for anyone
- *Tu*—Informal for anyone, but used only in Rio Grande do Sul, where *você* is one step more formal.

Context

In verbal communication words are not only used in the context of other words, but in the context of nonverbal behavior, which amplifies, explains, and supplements words, as well as communicating on its own. The preponderance of our communication takes place through nonverbal context. Context includes both our filters of perception and the use of nonverbal communication such as gestures, manner of dress, eye contact, tone of voice, and courtesy rituals. These filters and processes intertwine and interact. In cross-cultural communication, we need to learn to "speak the culture" to correctly interpret its nonverbal context.[9]

Cultures vary in the proportion of nonverbal communication they use relative to verbal communication. Low-context cultures focus relatively more on words, and high-context cultures focus relatively more on nonverbal context. The difference in style is similar to that of reading time to the second on the precise, numeric display of a digital watch versus gauging the time of day by assessing light, shadows, and position of the sun.

North Americans use a low-context communication style and focus on the words in messages, which they amplify and override relatively less than many other cultures by nonverbal context. Since a high-context person is acculturated from birth to send and receive a large proportion of messages through behavioral context, both consciously and unconsciously, he or she often attributes meaning to nonverbal context that is not intended, which results in misunderstanding. Offense may be taken when none was intended. This same high-context person often uses words for their pleasant effect, but a low-context person takes the words literally. Furthermore, a low-context person may not even apprehend, much less understand, much of the contextual nonverbal message transmitted by a high-context person. The low-context person focuses on the words when in fact the context contains the real message.

Brazilians by far prefer the high-context communication, rich in nonverbal cues, that takes place in person. A significant characteristic of high-context communication is that it focuses on maintaining personal relationships.[10]

This does not mean that context is meaningless in low-context cultures. People in most cultures will understand the negative message conveyed when a person throws a report down on a table. The difference between high- and low-context cultures is that they respectively dictate a large variation in the amount of meaning that is transmitted through contextual nonverbal behavior.[11]

Reading the Signs

In accordance with Brazil's high-context communication style, a courteous response such as "Maybe" or "I will try" is clearly understood as "No" to a person familiar with Brazil's culture and contextual ritual. A person from a low-context culture such as the United States, England, or Germany will typically ignore the ritual because he or she is accustomed to focusing on the words. The listener takes the words literally, treats them as being information-specific, and is then disappointed.

Helen Simpson visited a Department of Tourism office in Rio. She inquired for some specific information and statistics and was told that the information was not readily available and might take some time to find. Senhor Gilberto said that he would look into the matter and told Helen to check back in a week. Any Brazilian would have understood that either the information was not available or that Senhor Gilberto was not going to procure it. But Helen listened to the verbal content of what he was saying. She recorded in her Palm Pilot calendar a reminder to follow up with him the following Wednesday at 11:00 A.M.—in exactly one week. When she called at the office a week later, she was irritated that the information had not been obtained. If she had been more familiar with Brazilian culture, she would have understood from her conversation with Senhor Gilberto that there was a greater likelihood that the information would not be available than that it would.

A Brazilian professor who teaches cultural awareness and language and literature in the United States thinks that several factors operate in an instance such as this. Brazilians use an indirect, high-context style of communicating. But they are also amiable and well intentioned. Responding that he would see if he could get the information allowed Senhor Gilberto to avoid the unpleasantness of saying "no," and it also allowed him to feel good about his intentions. The answer that the information could not be obtained then shifted responsibility to circumstances and factors beyond his control. It was not his fault that the information was not available.

Human communication contains two kinds of messages. The first occurs intermittently and conveys new information. The second continuously maintains the relational aspect of interpersonal communication. The conveyance of information is no more important than relational maintenance, because the latter keeps the communication system in operation and regulates the interaction process. Information is most often conveyed by a low-context verbal message, and the relational aspect is most often communicated nonverbally as a contextual metamessage.[12] People often are aware that they are having difficulties in intercultural communication exchanges, but they cannot pinpoint what is causing the problem. Contextual, nonverbal communication most frequently is the culprit.

Time Sense

North Americans live on time. Brazilians live in time.

A fundamental and important aspect of every culture is a people's accepted and shared sense of time, because it affects personal interaction on a daily basis.[13] When people of two different cultures "use" time differently, their interaction can generate misunderstanding, misinterpretation, and ill will. The time cues that people give each other can be intentional or unintentional, are often ambiguous, and, to further complicate matters, frequently evoke strong emotional reactions in persons from monochronic cultures.

People seem to easily understand the differences in formal time between cultures. But the elements with which a culture structures informal time are loosely defined, not explicitly taught, and typically operate outside of conscious thought. They are more difficult to comprehend. Time can be measured formally by symbols on a calendar or clock, or seasons and activities can structure the allocation of time informally. A monochronic or polychronic treatment of time usually dominates in a given culture.

A polychronic concept of time is typical of cultures that have their origins in Mediterranean countries. These cultures typically have a multiple-activity, matrix concept of time that only loosely measures time with the symbols of a formalized system. Business relationships are personalized, based on trust, and take time to establish. It is time to move on to the next activity when the current set of activities is over. An activity in progress is in itself more important than an abstract measure on a clock. Brazil is a predominantly polychronic culture.

In Brazil the celebration of Carnival is an activity that structures time. The country shuts down for four days. And in the Northeast particularly, not much will get done during the weeks before Carnival or during the recovery period afterward. Even if they are offered incentive pay, people who greatly need the income would rather "play" Carnival (brincar carnaval) than work on those days.

Religion also affects Brazilians' sense of time. European Christianity has a linear, historical vision, while African-Brazilian religion views the universe as a cyclical and never-ending struggle between good and evil. Marshall Eakin refers to the mystical and magical sense of time that pervades Brazilian culture.[14]

Cultures that are monochronic have a predominantly linear and sequential approach to time that is rational, suppresses spontaneity, and tends to focus on one activity at a time. People in monochronic cultures value punctuality, efficiency, and get quickly to the point. The United States is a predominantly monochronic culture.

When trying to communicate, northern Europeans and North Americans tend to find multiple, simultaneous activities and conversations chaotic and difficult to follow. They may be overwhelmed when trying to meet with someone in an office in Brazil where people come in and out, the secretary asks a question, the errand runner brings back a part for the car, the phone rings, and several conversations are carried on at once. They find social situations with multiple cross-conversations and people talking loudly all at the same time uncomfortable and confusing. They commonly state that such situations "drive them crazy." Nonetheless, some individuals from predominantly monochronic cultures easily adapt to polychronicity, and there are North American production managers who specialize in coordinating multiple activities. It is also true that North American accountants and North American musicians who live in the same monochronic culture usually conceive of time quite differently from one another.[15]

The biggest adjustment the polychronic Brazilians have to make when they come to the United States is to the pace of life. People in the United States want to "save time," and they do not want to "waste time." Time is money.

Punctuality and waiting are important elements of informal time, but what constitutes acceptable punctuality or waiting can vary by culture and by situation. Arriving five minutes late for a business appointment in the United States usually elicits a brief apology, and for an employment interview, a first-time meeting, or an appointment where one wants to make a good impression, no degree of tardiness, not even a minute, is acceptable. Typically, the North American will arrive a few minutes early for an important appointment, in order to be cool, collected, and prepared to walk in.

Different perceptions of acceptable punctuality and waiting time can cause people to take offense when none is intended. A punctual North American reacts negatively to being kept waiting when he calls on a Brazilian for a scheduled appointment, unless he has been culturally sensitized. An easy way to transmit a negative message in the United States is to intentionally keep someone who has come for a business appointment waiting.

Punctuality—and the lack thereof—is a source of misunderstanding and frustration between Brazilians and North Americans. The problem, however, is primarily one-way. Punctuality is an "issue" for North Americans but less significant to Brazilians, for whom perceptions of time and the concept of punctuality are very different.

Arriving thirty minutes late in Brazil for an appointment is not unusual (although employees are expected to arrive on time for work). And in Rio de Janeiro or São Paulo, for example, anyone so gauche as to arrive on time for a cocktail party or dinner will be the only guest present and greeted by hosts who are visibly embarrassed—if the hosts are even out of the shower and in a state of dress fit to greet anyone. Horace Sanborn worked as an engineer for Petrobrás in Santos for many years. He was steeped in English and North American punctuality. When he first arrived in Brazil, he and his wife, Felicity, were invited to a dinner party at the home of a Brazilian engineer. The invitation was for 8:00 P.M., which seemed late by Horace and Felicity's standards. He and his wife appreciated this personal invitation and arrived at exactly 8:00 P.M. The hosts' maid answered the door and ushered Horace and Felicity into the living room. To their consternation, they found that no other guests had arrived and the hosts were nowhere to be seen. With Felicity's rudimentary Portuguese it was determined that their hosts were, in fact, still in the shower. The next couple (a Brazilian couple noted for their punctuality) did not arrive until 8:40 P.M. For the rare occasion in Brazil when guests are expected to arrive on time, an invitation will specify Swiss Time, British Time, or American Time[16]—which appear to be in descending order of rigorous observance. And, as discussed above, North Americans frequently specify a beginning and an ending time for an event, whereas it would never occur to a Brazilian to specify a time that a party should end.

When North Americans schedule meetings in Brazil, they should allow for some degree of tardiness. In the United States people are accustomed to strictly adhering to schedules. Maria Brasil comments that in the United States "usually things work better and faster." Brazilians deal routinely with several people and different problems concomitantly, they contend with a cumbersome government bureaucracy, and they wait in interminable lines at banks and in government offices. Maria observes that when you add to this the fact that Brazilians usually spend time—or waste time, depending on your perspective—socializing wherever and whenever they meet, you will have a scenario guaranteed to discomfit North American businesspeople. The best way to deal with this cultural difference is not to become irritated by what appears to be inefficient and a waste of precious time. It is necessary to slow down and adapt to Brazil's pace, even though this may not be an easy attitude to adopt on a business trip with a pressing schedule.[17] A North American would be well advised to allocate more time to accomplish things in Brazil and not plan as tight a schedule as in the United States.

In polychronic Brazil, both business and social calls take time. In Brazil, multiple visits are often required to open the door to do business, whereas one visit would suffice to accomplish the same purpose in the monochronic culture of the United States.

Polychronic cultures have different patterns of turn-taking when speaking than do monochronic cultures. Interrupting another speaker is not uncommon in Brazilian culture and in fact may be taken as an indication of interest and enthusiasm. While some interruption is acceptable in southern Europe and Latin America, conversational overlap is considered ill mannered in northern Europe and in the United States. A Swedish study shows that interruptions frequently frustrated Scandinavian and German negotiators conducting meetings in Italy, Spain, and Greece. The researchers, in recording Spanish-Swedish negotiations, found that the Spaniards interrupted the Swedes five times more often than the reverse.[18] Brazilian–North American interruption patterns parallel the Spanish-Swedish patterns. Trying to carry on a conversation with someone from a culture with a turn-taking rhythm that you have not learned is as awkward as trying to dance with someone when you just cannot get in step.

Ana Carolina Ecósteguy, a communications professor in Porto Alegre, was constantly aware of cultural differences during her six months of study in London. Even the organization of the kindergarten that her daughter attended caused her culture shock. The activities of her three-year-old daughter, Carolina, were linearly and sequentially organized, as were the activities of all the children. First Carolina could play with one toy. Then she was required to finish that activity and put the toy away before she was permitted to select and play with another. "It was so organized!" exclaimed Ana Carolina. She explained that this was so unlike Brazil, where all of the children would typically haul out all of the toys and play with them in any combination of toys and children.

Local time in Brazil is two hours ahead of Eastern Standard Time in the United States. Brazil observes daylight savings during months that include Brazil's summer (winter in the United States). During the summer months, when the United States observes daylight savings time, it is winter in Brazil. When daylight savings time is in effect in the United States, Brazilian time is one hour ahead. When daylight savings time is in effect in Brazil, Brazilian time is three hours ahead. In the United States, daylight savings time begins at 2:00 A.M. on the first Sunday in April; it ends at 2:00 A.M. on the last Sunday in October. In Brazil, daylight savings time usually begins in November or December and ends in February or March. The dates for beginning and ending are not fixed but are set each year. As in the United States, not all states go on daylight savings time. Much of Brazil is in one time zone (out of four), with the Amazon being the sizable exception.

Wilson de Sá commented that he frequently gets in trouble in Brazil because he says good-bye and then actually leaves within the next fifteen minutes. Perhaps, he mused, he has spent too much time in monochronic countries. In Brazil, he explained, you should not rush your departure and you should spend at least forty-five minutes to say good-bye. He joked that in a certain tribe in Africa, the leave-taking ritual is expected to take three days and that when one man left in just two and a half days, he was killed for his breach of social protocol.

If persons are engaged in an activity such as picking others up and organizing to go to a party, then the time to arrive at the party is when they get there, that is, when the activity of getting together and physically arriving is completed. The activity of gathering and going to the party is in and of itself valued.

Annie Nimos was invited to a weeknight dinner for the members of a chapter of the Friendship Force in Brazil. Iracy Saldanha told Annie that she would pick her up on Wednesday evening between 7:00 and 7:30 P.M. At 7:40 Iracy called on her cell phone to tell Annie that she would arrive in approximately twenty minutes. Finally, Iracy and a friend arrived at 8:45. Then Iracy went to pick up another couple at a church where they had gone to a meeting; they needed a ride because their car was being repaired. However, the couple needed to stop at their house to take some cash to their daughters before the group went to the dinner. The group finally arrived at the gathering around 9:45. After eating dinner and talking, people began leaving a little after midnight.

On one of Lourenço Juvenal's first business trips to the United States, he walked into an office supply store and was amazed to see a whole rack of daytimers, agendas, and calendars. "There was every shape, size, and format conceivable. North Americans are paranoid about time," he said. He thinks the difference between the United States and Brazil is one of focus rather than of material wealth. Daytimers and calendars are not marketed so prominently in Brazil. They are simply items in a store, with two or three choices displayed.

Edward A. Riedinger reflects that it is the Brazilian rhythm of life that so differentiates it from other countries and that it seems that in Brazil people live life the way they truly want to, instead of as they have to. The leisure and indulgence that Brazilians enjoy enrich time. He describes Brazil as a third world country with a more aristocratic sense of living than any he has ever seen, which Brazilians welcome others to share.[19]

ALTHOUGH SOME CULTURES attach relatively more importance to words, in *every* culture most communication takes place through nonverbal behavior. When we communicate across cultures, we need to keep in mind that the other person is behaving in accordance with a different set of learned rules.

CHAPTER SIXTEEN

Everyday Communication

"[S]pace is one of the *basic, underlying organizational systems for all living things.*"[1]

Communicating with Space and Body Motion

Space can be formal and fixed, such as in a church, where certain behavior is mandated, or on a basketball court, which invites different behavior. Space can be formal and semifixed, as in the arrangement of furniture in a living room. And space can be informally allocated, such as the way people position themselves in relation to each other so as to interact. In addition to positioning the body at a certain distance from another person, one also uses his or her body to communicate through gestures, posture, eye contact, facial expressions, touch, and smell.

Brazilians and North Americans use some formal spaces differently. As discussed in Chapter 13, Brazilians usually eat only in formally designated spaces, such as dining rooms, breakfast rooms, snack counters, and restaurant tables, whereas North Americans are likely to eat in places not specifically designated for this purpose. North American libraries are quiet spaces where people are expected to speak in hushed tones; utterances at normal volume meet with disapproving glances. Study groups meet behind closed doors, in rooms available for that purpose, to protect library patrons from the sound of conversation. Conversely, in Brazil personal interaction in libraries is noisy and gregarious. Those seeking quiet can use small rooms closed off from the prevailing hubbub.

When discussing Brazilian–North American interaction, Brazilians from many regions volunteer that they think North Americans are more polite than Brazilians. I have heard comments such as, "They are always saying 'excuse me' and 'sorry' when it seems they haven't done anything. We have to learn to say this a lot when we go to the United States."

Brazilians' perception that North Americans constantly use verbal politeness rituals stems in part from the different use of personal space and physical contact in the two cultures. North Americans require more personal space, that is, physical distance from others, just as they both require and tolerate less physical contact than do Brazilians. When North Americans perceive that they have invaded another's personal space or when they inadvertently make physical contact with another person, they excuse themselves, as is expected by their culture. Brazilians do not see the need for these apologies because such physical contact does not offend them and such proximity does not invade their personal space.

Walking along pedestrian streets in downtown Porto Alegre or São Paulo, people brush against and bump into each other and squeeze through narrow spaces between other pedestrians. No one requests permission or excuses himself or herself. When Annie Nimos was waiting in a crowd gathered to gain entrance to the legislative assembly in Porto Alegre to witness an important vote, people stood so close together, body to body, that she felt she could have lifted her feet off the ground and remained supported in her same upright position.

Claudina Junker commented that North Americans walk around inside an invisible bubble that extends two feet out from their bodies. Inside that bubble is their personal territory. Others are not allowed inside unless invited or on intimate terms. She has observed that North Americans react visibly if anyone invades their space. They stiffen and back away.

Robson Rego said that it is easy to measure how close to a Brazilian or a North American you should position yourself. The personal space for North Americans extends about the length of an arm, because one cannot comfortably touch another person at that distance. Brazilian personal space is half that distance or less. Brazilians position themselves when sitting, walking, and standing so that they are close enough to comfortably touch the other person with a relaxed arm, elbow bent.

Robson stood with a Brazilian friend, Armando, at a store counter in the United States. Armando reached across in front of a North American woman to pick something up from the counter. The woman, clearly offended, stiffened and glared at him. Armando had invaded the woman's space unwittingly, because Brazilians would not perceive his action as a transgression.

In the United States the expression "Excuse me" has come to be used as both a request for pardon for an offense and a request for permission for an action. In Brazil, dá licença *is used to request permission and* desculpa *is used to request forgiveness. Felicity Sanborn moved to Santos to live and when she first arrived had learned only some basic Portuguese. She took a bus from the Gonzaga to the downtown Praça Mauá. The bus was crowded and many people were standing, including Felicity. As the bus moved along Avenida Ana Costa, it jolted to a stop. Felicity lost her footing and fell sitting into someone's lap. She said "Dá licença," which provoked smiles. Felicity had mistakenly requested permission to sit on the person's lap, instead of asking for "forgiveness" for her precipitous landing.*

Tânia, a young Brazilian woman whom Annie Nimos had just met, put her hand on Annie's forearm to converse. They were seated side by side at a conference table. Tânia then turned and leaned toward Annie, gripping Annie's thigh with both hands as she spoke with animation. A North American woman who was present later commented to Annie that she would have found a pretext to stand up or to move to a different seat because such close physical contact would have made her uncomfortable. Just watching Tânia's physical interaction with Annie upset the woman.

A Rio resident explained that for the *carioca*, bodily contact is essential for conversing. With only some exaggeration, she counseled that you must position yourself as close as you can to the person with whom you are speaking and lock your eyes on theirs. Touch the other person at least once per phrase, she recommended, by touching on the arm, stroking the forearm, squeezing the person's hands, patting the back or shoulder, touching the chin or face, or patting the chest (she cautions, however, that one should only pat men's chests). For the *carioca* ritual of greeting, she advised, bodily contact is especially important, whether you meet on the street or whether the friend is lunching at a table of six or standing with a group of twenty persons. It is imperative that you make bodily contact with all present, through a handshake, *abraço* (embrace), or kiss on both cheeks, whether you know them or not.[2]

The Brazilian *abraço* between men consists of a handshake with the right hand, while with the left arm each man reaches around and pats the other on the back simultaneously. It is used to greet male family members, friends, and peers. Women greet both male and female family members and friends with cheek kisses. The kiss on the cheek is not actually a kiss but a brushing of cheeks first on the right side and then on the left.

North Americans may greet friends, acquaintances, and colleagues — even family — with just a nod to accompany their verbal salutation. It is common for a son and father who live in different cities to greet each other when visiting with only a brief handshake. Observe two North

American friends on the occasions they try to hug each other. They usually stand so far apart that the only way they can exchange a brief hug is by leaning forward from the waist up. To interact without offending, Maria Brasil advises that Brazilians living in the United States get used to maintaining physical distance from North Americans. If Brazilians occasionally wish to fulfill their need for bodily contact when socializing, she suggests they seek out other Brazilians.[3]

During Annie Nimos's visit to the legislative assembly in Porto Alegre, she watched two of the *deputados* (deputies) greet each other. They shook hands and exchanged hearty *abraços.* They then stood face to face, only some twelve inches apart, and began a discussion. As he spoke, one man placed his hand flat on the other's chest for a few moments and removed it. He shifted feet and then placed his other hand on the man's upper arm for a while as he talked. The two men appeared intensely involved in their discussion. The second deputy then took the lapels of the first man's suitcoat in his hands. After a few moments, he stroked the length of the lapels several times before removing his hands. Both men shifted their weight on their feet and continued speaking. The second deputy then smoothed the front of the first's tie with one hand, before running the length of the tie through his hands two or three times. After several minutes the *deputados* appeared to have concluded their conversation, and each patted the other's left upper arm with his right hand as they broke away to go to their respective seats.

Annie subsequently recounted this use of space and touch to Hal Brandon, her North American friend. She stepped in close to demonstrate the distance at which the two *deputados* stood and touched Hal's chest and arm. She mimed stroking suit lapels and tie. Even though the two were dicussing communication and cultural differences and she had lexically requested permission with the phrase, "Let me show you . . . ," Hal reflexively stiffened and then backed up. Annie was surprised and laughed. She said, "You see how uncomfortable this makes you?" "I couldn't handle it," Hal responded.

In North American use of conversational space, men will frequently allow a female acquaintance to stand somewhat closer than a male, because females can be less "threatening" and because there are no homosexual overtones. Occasionally some touch is allowed at a distance, but it is usually only momentary and on a neutral zone of the body such as the forearm. A North American man would be very uncomfortable in a conversation with a Brazilian man if the Brazilian employed the same use of space and touch as the *deputados.*

Wendy Huggins entered a spacious Saraiva bookstore in Brazil. It immediately struck her that there were several groups of four or five men and women dressed in business attire standing tightly clustered around

Friends cluster close enough to touch while talking in Parque Moinhos de Vento, Porto Alegre, Brazil.

each other here and there. The individuals in each group were standing so close to each other that they appeared to be conspiring. They could have heard each other even if they had been whispering. Wendy wondered what was going on and looked around. As she walked farther into the store, she saw signs announcing a presentation and book signing. She then realized that the tight little clusters were composed of people who had been invited for the event. Many of them knew each other and were just conversing in normal voices, standing at the distance with which Brazilians are comfortable. The physical proximity at which the people in each tight cluster stood, surrounded by plenty of space, was strikingly different from how people in similar small conversation groups would position themselves in the United States—at least at arm's length.

Annie sat on a bench and observed people exercising and enjoying a cool, sunny morning in Parque Moinhos de Vento in Porto Alegre. In the center of an open area, a small group of middle-aged men and women gathered. On arriving, each person shook hands with the other, combined with variations of *abraços* between men and kisses on both cheeks for women. The friends clustered closely together to talk, each positioned some twelve inches from the other. One man stood with his

At Town Lake in Austin, Texas, friends maintain a distance of an arm's length while conversing.

hand on the shoulder of the man next to him. The friends patted and touched each other as they spoke.

A group of men and women who walk together on Town Lake in Austin, Texas, stand and converse before they set out every Sunday morning, promptly at 8:00 A.M. They usually arrive, nod at the others in the group, and say good morning. Each person stands at a distance of two or more feet from the other, and they talk to each other without making physical contact. In fact, one couple who have spent much of their lives overseas, by habit often greet each member of the group with a handshake on arrival. This is so noticeably different from the group's greeting style in this informal setting that one member always reacts with a laugh and jokes that the couple must be campaigning for political office. From the couple's long experience in other cultures, not to individually greet each person present seems rude.

Ana Carolina Ecósteguy commented that language was not a form of communication available to her three-year-old when they first moved to England, because the child did not speak English. And since in England preschoolers do not engage in the same bodily contact among themselves or with their teachers that children in Brazil are accustomed to, her daughter was very limited in how she could communicate with oth-

Men pass *mate* tea back and forth and drink from the same *chimarrão* straw.

ers. Ana Carolina found English children to be less involved with each other than Brazilian children; they often played by themselves, without much physical contact. Ana Carolina's daughter was used to being hugged and kissed by the teacher at school and being touched by the other children. Ana Carolina said that she had the same physical contact at school when she was her daughter's age and that she suffered for her child who seemed so isolated in England.

Brazilians seem comfortable sharing beverages in a way that makes most North Americans uncomfortable—a sort of indirect physical contact. Annie Nimos visited the Galpão Crioulo Restaurant in Porto Alegre with friends. At the entrance, a counter displayed *cuias* (gourds) packed with green *mate* tea pressed into neat geometric designs, each oblong gourd sitting in a stand to hold it upright. Each gourd held a silver "straw" with a spoon-shaped strainer at the end (*bomba*) through which to drink the liquid at the bottom of the gourd when a small amount of hot water was added. The attendant at the counter asked Gisela and Lúcio if they would accept one. They did, so Annie did also. The attendant did not hand Annie the stand with the round-bottomed gourd, so she wondered how she would set the gourd down at the table when she ate. But she soon found out that after you sip on the tea for a while, you return the ensemble to the counter. The attendant then wipes off the end of the silver straw and sets the gourd and straw back in its stand. It is now ready for the restaurant's next customer. The eight to ten gourds set up on the counter are communal and serve all the customers who come into the restaurant. These *chimarrão* setups are offered to the public in other places as well. One gourd and straw may serve all the guests who come to a hotel reception desk. The restaurant attendant said that the worst breach of *chimarrão* etiquette is to touch or wipe the tip of the straw with fingers, which he proclaimed much dirtier than the mouth. His perfunctory wipe of the tip, however, clearly did not sanitize the straw used by the public to savor the beverage.

Friends share a *chimarrão* and drink through the same straw; neighbors of friends offered a *chimarrão* to Annie when she was introduced to them in their front yards; a stranger in the town of Estrela also invited Annie to drink from her *chimarrão* when she stopped to admire the stranger's front yard. Friends in Brazil also share sips of a *caipirinha* cocktail from the same glass.

Sense of Smell

Brazilians are both comfortable with and very aware of their bodies. They pay attention to personal cleanliness and to smell, and they shower one or more times a day. Brazilian hosts receiving international guests from the Servas organization for the requisite two-night stay had complained that they found the odor of some of their guests offensive. They also noticed that their visitors did not always shower daily while staying with them. As a result of host complaints, Servas of Brazil has instituted a written policy requesting that all visitors shower before they arrive at a host's home and again on arrival. In good Brazilian fashion, Servas softens the request with a preface about most of Brazil being hot and tropical, which necessitates frequent bathing, and so on.

Gestures and Customs

Brazilians say that if you tie their hands, they cannot speak. They use hand gestures and broad arm gestures as they talk. North Americans use far fewer gestures, and when they do, the gestures tend to be contained, short, and choppy. Sometimes North Americans will hold up and punctuate a point with the extended index finger for emphasis (*o dedo en riste*) or execute a few short chops with a flat hand like a cleaver. Annie Nimos watched Brazilians' eyes lock onto these gestures when in discussion with North Americans. Claudina Junker observed that Brazilians react to index finger punctuation as somewhat menacing.

A culture assigns specific meaning to some gestures. We often realize that we do not understand the meaning of gestures in a foreign culture. When a foreigner first sees a Brazilian tug at an earlobe with thumb and forefinger, it is clear to the person that he or she does not understand the meaning. This gesture indicates that the communicator thinks that something—usually food—is wonderful. North Americans often form an "O" with thumb and forefinger to indicate "OK" or approval. However, in Brazil this gesture is employed as an obscenity. Some Brazilians now understand this North American gesture because it was widely televised on a dubbed version of *Charlie's Angels.* Similarly, North Americans will sometimes sit and talk, place their elbows on a desk or table, and form a diamond shape by joining their two index fingers up and two thumbs down as they pensively discuss something. This gesture is obscene in Brazil. Not understanding another person may be frustrating, but it usually does not cause ill will. On the other hand, misunderstanding—ascribing meaning that is not there—often provokes hard feelings toward the communicator. Below is a brief guide to Brazilian gestures.[4]

- "Come here"—Brazilians commonly beckon someone with the forearm extended at elbow height and the palm of the hand turned down (North Americans usually do so with the palm turned up).
- "Call me," "You have a telephone call"—Put your thumb to your ear and your little finger to your mouth, with the three middle fingers folded against your palm.
- Two people have a close relationship—With hands at elbow height and palms down, rub the sides of the two index fingers lengthwise, with all the other fingers folded in.
- "I'm on to you," "Keep your eyes open"—Put your index finger to your lower eyelid and pull it down slightly.
- "He [she] doesn't know what he [she] is talking about"—Tap twice under your chin with the back of your fingers.
- "Time to eat"—Point the tips of all five fingers at your mouth, with the hand in an "L" close to your lips and move your fingers up and down a few times.
- "Let's have a *cafezinho*"—Hold your index finger and thumb up near your mouth and indicate a vertical inch of space.
- "Let's have a drink"—Put your thumb near your mouth (just like a child who is going to suck its thumb).
- "This is delicious"—Tug at your earlobe with index finger and thumb.
- "OK," "Great," "I approve"—Give a thumbs up sign.
- To give someone an obscene "finger" gesture—Make the North American OK sign, forming a circle with thumb and index finger. It's close

enough. In fact, Brazilians sometimes laugh when they see a North American politician making this gesture on television and say that that is what the politician is doing to the people.

• To give someone a "banana" is the equivalent of making the obscene "finger" gesture in the United States. Place one hand in the crook of the elbow of the other arm and snap a fist up near the cheek. Not recommended.

• An obscene middle "finger"—Same as in the United States.

• "Screw you," "I got screwed," "I screwed up"—Make a fist and slap the top (index and thumb side) with the palm of your other hand. This is a common benign informal gesture or a gesture used for emphasis in the United States. It should not be used when interacting with Brazilians.

• To wish good luck or protect from bad luck—Put up a fist with the thumb sticking up between the index and middle finger. Despite appearances, this is not obscene but like crossing your fingers.

• "He [or she] is jealous"—Put a fist up near your cheek and rub the elbow with the free hand.

• I am or you are "living well"—Put your thumbs in your armpits and waggle your fingers.

• Someone is a bad driver—Rub the back of your hand against (real or imaginary) whiskers on your cheek. Not recommended in traffic.

• "Expensive"—Hold your hand up approximately chin height and rub your thumb and index finger together.

• "I don't know," "I don't care"—With hands waist high and palms up, drag the backs of your fingers the length of the fingers of the other hand and vice versa.

• Packed full of people—Put the tips of all five fingers together near your chin and open and close them a couple of times. Taxi drivers make this gesture to indicate they have passengers.

• "Quick," "Fast"—Hold your thumb and third finger together and shake your hand to snap the index finger against the third finger.

Toothpicks are not used in fine restaurants, at formal dinners in homes, or anywhere in "polite" society in either the United States or Brazil. Use in both countries tends to be restricted to popular restaurants and informal settings and occasions. Even in Brazil, where the use of toothpicks is more widespread and public than in the United States, Brazilians joke that their etiquette guru, Danuza Leão, mandates, "*Never* use a toothpick, not even alone, in the bathroom, in the dark, with your back to the closed door." Nonetheless, toothpicks seem ubiquitous in Brazilian restaurants. Protocol dictates, though, that one use one hand to mask the mouth while using the toothpick. North Americans con-

"Come here."

"You have a telephone call."

"They have a close relationship."

"You don't fool me."

"He doesn't know what he's talking about."

"It's time to eat."

"Want to go for a *cafezinho*?"

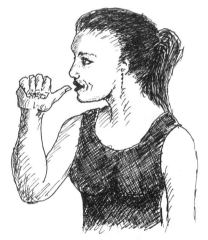

"Let's get something to drink."

"This is delicious."

"Uma banana." (Same as "middle finger" in the United States.)

"I hope so!"

"He's jealous."

"She's living the good life."

"It doesn't matter one way or the other."

"The room was packed full of people!"

sciously notice people sitting in restaurants after a meal with one hand covering their mouth and the other hand using a toothpick, in a manner that seems secretive and odd. Brazilians notice North Americans openly using toothpicks without discreetly screening their mouths and teeth from view. In Brazil, to remove something from the mouth, such as an olive pit or a pebble that was in the beans, one also masks the mouth with one hand. It is not considered polite for either the activity or the inside of the mouth to be visible.

In Brazil homes do not always have doorbells or buzzers, and walls and fences enclose the front yards and even the front doors. To summon the occupants, one stands at the gate and claps loudly to get attention. One should not try to enter the front yard.

Marcelino de Carvalho, a Brazilian writer on etiquette, comments that Anglo-Saxons do not proffer their hands as generously as do Brazilians. In fact, in his opinion, they avoid shaking hands if at all possible. He also writes that Brazilian men frequently kiss a woman's hand in a salon or on other formal occasions. It would be ridiculous, however, to kiss a woman's hand on the beach. For one thing, the parties are in bathing suits, which lends an air of informality to the meeting, and for another, he points out, the woman would probably have oil and sand on her hand. For house guests, he counsels that a man should not kiss the woman's hand if either party is dressed informally, such as in a robe.[5]

Different Strokes

Teresa, who grew up in Brazil, attended a U.S. university and married in the United States. While waiting for the house they planned to move into to become available, she and her husband lived with her husband's parents for a few months. Every morning the young woman would greet her father- and mother-in-law with a kiss on both cheeks, as she was accustomed to doing at home. Her mother-in-law, Antonina, would complain from time to time that Teresa clearly showed she did not like her by the way Teresa treated her. Teresa did not understand what behavior Antonina was criticizing.[6]

Antonina greeted close family, both men and women, with a kiss on the mouth, a custom that came from her Russian heritage and is also common in northern Europe. Antonina construed Teresa's turn of her head and her brush of cheeks as a rebuff that evidenced dislike. For Teresa, a kiss on the mouth was part of an intimate male-female relationship; this was how she kissed her husband. It would not occur to her to kiss family members in that manner. It was a number of years before Teresa realized that her Brazilian morning greeting, a kiss on both cheeks—or more accurately, a brushing of cheeks—was the source of Antonina's complaints about her behavior.[7]

Antonina's and Teresa's greetings were culturally learned and governed by subconscious rules. Antonina's reaction to Teresa's avoidance of contact on the mouth was strong because she interpreted it negatively. Because of her negative perception, routine behavior was raised to a conscious level, although Antonina seemed able to verbalize only her reaction and not the cause. Since the morning greeting was not a negative event for Teresa, for her the ritual passed unnoticed. If Teresa had become consciously aware of the difference between her own and Antonina's cultural conditioning in this regard earlier in the relationship, it would have been helpful. The offense perceived—that is, "taken"—by Antonina added fuel to a fire of long-lasting misunderstandings. Such misunderstanding is typical of how cultural differences impede intercultural communication and also demonstrates that a misunderstanding can clearly be one-way.[8]

Marla, a North American of Scandinavian descent living in the United States, had a group of good friends with whom she and her husband gathered frequently. The small group went to the movies, had dinners in each other's homes, and occasionally took trips together. Whoever from the group was available for such occasions would participate. All were married and knew each other well. One man, Antônio, was a Brazilian married to a North American. When greeting her friends at a birthday party one evening, without thinking Marla pecked a kiss on Antônio's lips, along with the usual hug the persons in the group gave each other. Antônio instantly stiffened and rebuked Marla, "You should not do that."

Antônio's rebuff of her spontaneous kiss stung Marla. Some time later, in recounting the incident in a conversation with Annie Nimos, she said that she realized she had quite unconsciously greeted Antônio as she would greet a close relative—she would not have done so had she thought about it—probably because of the feelings of closeness that the group members had for each other. There was affection but certainly no sexual undercurrents in the way the men and women in the group related to each other. Antônio's reflexive reproof of Marla's brief kiss on the lips as inappropriate stemmed from deep cultural conditioning that such contact is normally confined to intimate and sexual contact in Brazil. Conscious thought did not govern the behavior of either person.

Eye Contact

A *paulistano* writer-in-residence at the University of Texas in Austin told Annie Nimos that for him, the biggest difference between Brazilians and North Americans is how they look at people. Brazilians look people up and down and up again. They openly turn to look at and watch people; they follow them with their eyes. And when Brazilians converse with peers they have intense eye contact. The writer felt that for a Brazilian to look at a North American as he or she would look at a Brazilian invades the sense of privacy that North Americans carry with them even in public places.

Some days, Verlyn Klinkenborg writes, when he walks in Manhattan streets, not an eye meets his. Eyes slip past, he says, frictionless. People wear sunglasses in the rain. "They carry their eyes fixed in their skulls, immobile, unreflective. They let you see that they are purposely not looking. On the subways they bury their heads in books . . . or they read the rum ads over and over again."[9]

When Annie Nimos moved from Brazil to the United States, she felt that something was not quite right when she walked in public places. After a month or two, she realized she felt invisible. No one looked at her. Then she realized that she felt, in particular, that men did not look at her overtly. In Brazil a man would stop on the street and watch a woman walk by, following her with his eyes for a full 180 degrees. His eyes would take her in from head to toe. The woman would not acknowledge the presence of the man, although she was quite aware of it. In the United States, in many circumstances, such an overt demonstration of interest would be considered threatening or inappropriate. The rules of gaze are different in the two countries, and after Annie became accustomed to the difference she no longer felt as if she were invisible.[10]

Even so, Brazilians will lower their eyes as a sign of respect when communicating with an individual in certain situations. One does not challenge authority by looking it directly in the eye. This lowering of the eyes is often misinterpreted by North American employers, teachers, and so on, who tend to interpret avoidance of eye contact as a sign of disrespect, deviousness, or dishonesty.[11] North Americans can recall comments such as, "He's shifty-eyed. I don't trust him." They can also picture a North American adult scolding a child who looks down: "You *look* at me when I speak to you!"[12]

Use of the Voice

Although the vocalics of a language have to do with sounds produced by the human voice, they are nonverbal language in the sense that they convey meaning by actions and interactions other than words. The term "vocalics" encompasses any vocal-auditory behavior except the spoken word. The voice is a rich channel in the system of nonverbal communication, and vocalic cues are among the most powerful in the nonverbal repertoire. Next to body motion language, vocalic cues are the larg-est in number.[13] Vocalics are how something is said rather than what is said. One can articulate the simple phrase "What do you want?" in a va-riety of ways, and each will convey different meaning. These four simple words can express meaning as different as solicitude or impatience or in-sult, and the difference is produced solely through vocalics.

In general, Brazilians employ more vocalizations than do North Americans. Laughing, crying, yelling, moaning, whining, and yawning are all examples of vocalizations.[14] Brazilians also use more vocal sounds such as "un-huh," "shhh," "ooh," "uh," and "mmmm."[15] When con-versing on the telephone in Brazil, the party who is speaking requires that the party who is listening signal their attention and involvement by providing constant feedback through vocalizations and an occa-sional word, such as "Aaaa . . . ," "É . . . ," "Mmmm . . . ," "Isso . . ." If there is no feedback, the other party will stop and ask, "Are you there?" thinking perhaps that they have been disconnected. In Brazil a sibilant "Sssssss . . ." can voice male appreciation of a passing female, although to the North American it may sound like a disapproving hiss.

Vocalics include volume, pitch, rhythm, tempo, resonance, and tone. Loudness of voice is customary in much of Brazil but seems aggressive to North Americans. Vocal rate is the speed at which people speak. A fast talker may be viewed as glib and untrustworthy in one culture but as intelligent and involved in another.[16] Brazilians usually speak at a fast rate, whereas North Americans usually speak in a slower, more deliber-ate manner.

Brazilians generally speak more loudly than North Americans, ac-companied by expansive and vigorous arm and hand movements, and more than one person talks at a time. North Americans often think Bra-zilians are arguing when they are simply having a conversation. Voice volume, pitch, tone, and rate give this false impression. Most North Americans interpret many nonverbal forms of Brazilian communication as signals that a physical or verbal fight may develop. North Americans believe people should "stay cool" when discussing their viewpoints.[17] Ana Carolina Escósteguy commented that when she was living in En-gland, she noticed that the English followed her hand and arm gestures with their eyes. This was so noticeable to her, even though no verbal comment was made, that she became self-conscious of how she gestured when she spoke. But for a Brazilian, the louder voice, visible signs of an-imation and emotion, and expansive arm and hand gestures all signify interest and involvement. Brazilians become uncomfortable when they do not see this nonverbal behavior and find the other person cold and aloof. In contrast, some North Americans may think Brazilians are loud and pushy.

Juliana and Lília were attending a linguistics conference together in Mexico. Juliana is Brazilian and Lília is Mexican. Juliana came down to meet Lília for breakfast in the restaurant of the hotel where they were staying. She walked into the restaurant and saw Lília. Across the room, she announced to Lília, "I'm so cold. I'm just freezing. Why is it so cold in here?" Everyone in the restaurant paused and looked at her.

She joined Lília and sat down at the table. "I can't understand why it's so cold. I need a jacket."

Lília commented softly to Juliana, "In Mexico, you know, people speak more softly, not across a room."

Juliana shrugged. "But this is *my* culture. I'm Brazilian and I communicate like a Brazilian. You can't change my culture."

WE ARE UNCONSCIOUS of most of our culturally programmed behavior in our everyday interactions with people. In transnational communication, small differences are frequently misunderstood and may provoke large, needless rifts. Being aware that such differences exist will forestall much miscommunication.

CHAPTER SEVENTEEN

More Daily Interaction

Brazilians react negatively to what they perceive as North American coldness.

Immediacy

Much of nonverbal communication contributes to a person's immediacy, that is, his or her apparent availability and positive disposition toward communicating. The most significant clash of cultures in Brazilian–North American communication is immediacy. Brazilians find North Americans distant, both literally and figuratively. In general, North Americans do not display as much emotion as do Brazilians. They are more reserved and contained. Their body posture is stiffer and straighter. They do not touch as much. They do not use as much volume and variation in voice, tone, and pitch. They do not gesture as expansively or display as much facial expression. Brazilians react to containment, reserve, and distance in interpersonal communication as though they have been doused with cold water. They frequently interpret this "distance" as criticism.

Relationships between cultures are relative. While the French complain of the superficiality of North Americans' "instant friendliness,"[1] Brazilians complain that North Americans are not friendly enough. Despite these opposite perceptions of North Americans, Brazilians and the French have a great affinity for each other, due in part to both cultures' strict observance of the steep hierarchies of their societies, their collective organization, and Brazil's history of francophilia among the educated.

Ana Carolina Escósteguy recounted that during her six-month sojourn in England, she always had a feeling of unease. Brazilians, she explained, are expansive, outward looking, spontaneous, open, and effusive. In contrast, the English are contained, inward looking, deliberate, and reserved. Although they are courteous and attentive, they maintain distance. Their style of communication is ironic and so forthright (*con-tundente*) that Brazilians are taken aback. In contrast, even casual socializing in Brazil is "warm" and "close."

Annie Nimos was in contact with Joaquim Santos, a professsor at a Catholic university. They first corresponded through e-mail and then spoke by telephone to coordinate a visit to discuss communication. Santos addressed Annie formally as "a Senhora," and she addressed him as "o Senhor." Nonetheless, the professor ended their telephone conversation with the expression "um abraço" (an embrace), in warm Brazilian fashion.

In talking with some Brazilian students of English at ICBNA, Antônio told Annie Nimos that his sister, Gabriela, had a North American admirer, Stuart, who had lived with his family as an exchange student in Brazil for months. Antônio and Stuart had been friends in Brazil and knew each other well. After Stuart returned to the United States, he would call Gabriela, and Antônio would sometimes answer the telephone. Antônio said that Stuart would say "Hi" and ask for Gabriela without conversing with him, no "How are you?" or "What have you been doing?" Antônio was hurt that Stuart did not express warmth and interest by engaging in personal conversation before asking for Gabriela. A Brazilian would never do this, Antônio said. There was general agreement in the classroom that this behavior is typical of North American coldness.

But to again illustrate relativity, the British-born journalist Henry Fairlie finds North Americans warm in manner. He writes that in the United States, the friendly word "Hi!" represents democracy.

> I come from a country where one can tell someone's class by how they say "Hallo!" or "Hello!" or "Hullo," or whether they say it at all. But [in the United States] anyone can say "Hi!" Anyone does.[2]

Like many foreigners, Fairlie was struck by the egalitarianism that prevails among most North Americans. He recounted his first meetings with the Suffragan bishop of Washington and with President Lyndon B. Johnson. Both men greeted him, "Hi, Henry!" Fairlie remarked that such a thing simply would not happen in most countries.[3]

Gisela Hauptman commented that North Americans often say "Hi" to people they do not know in various public circumstances. Paradoxically, gregarious Brazilians do not greet or verbally acknowledge the presence of strangers in the street or in public places. Gisela explained, "If you say 'Hi' to a person you do not know, then they will have to tell you the story of their whole life, and become intimate right away. You will never finish." Annie Nimos confirmed Gisela's statement. When she stayed in an executive apartment in Porto Alegre for two months while doing research, she noted that people who saw each other every day for weeks or months in the small room where breakfast was served did not greet or acknowledge each other. Because Brazilians conceive of friendship as an intimate relationship, they may interpret friendly gestures made by strangers as signaling an attempt to become more intimate, whereas North Americans do not make the same assumption about casually friendly behavior.

While Brazilians find North Americans distant and reserved, North Americans find the British, the French, and the Germans distant and reserved, primarily because of the steeper hierarchy of those cultures. North Americans are much more comfortable with the immediacy of their compatriots. Brazilians also find the Portuguese more reserved than themselves. A Brazilian engineer joked that if you ask a Portuguese if he has the time, the person will answer, "Yes." If you want a Portuguese to tell you the time, you must expressly ask, "Please tell me what time it is." But, they say, if you ask a Brazilian for the time, he or she will not only tell you the time, but proceed to inquire if you need any other information or assistance.

But surface characteristics of a culture can be deceptive. The North American may be disappointed if he or she does not learn to distinguish between Brazilians' warm and engaging manner and genuine interest or a friendship that takes time to build.

Appearance and Extensions of the Physical Self

In addition to communicating with words, through how we use time and space, and through body behavior, we also communicate through appearance. Since communication studies demonstrate that our perception of similarity correlates to how much we desire (or not) to communicate with another person, appearance can make a person seem more or less similar and therefore more or less "approachable" for communication.

We are born with some aspects of our physical appearance, such as eye and skin color, hair texture, and stature, that we do not control. A woman with blond hair and blue eyes visited a district of Raiatea in French Polynesia that was accessible only by boat. It had been many years since a Westerner had been there. The small children of the village stared at her fearfully and ran into their huts crying out "Tupapao, tupapao" (Ghost, ghost). A Guatemalan woman who went to Leningrad to study recounted that people would walk up to her, gaze at length at her brown eyes, and even make comments, because brown eyes were so unusual in that city. Similarly, an Asian's physical appearance may be remarkable in many small towns in the United States. People everywhere need to overcome their provincialism in order not to be intimidated or repelled by significant differences in physical characteristics.

We also communicate through extensions of our physical selves, or artifacts. Artifacts can include clothes, jewelry, perfume, makeup or lack thereof, briefcases, and even the car we choose to drive. Of great importance are the aspects of our physical selves that we control daily: grooming, haircut and style, smell, and clothing. These factors contribute positively or negatively to the communication between foreigners and Brazilians, as they do with people of all cultures.

Wedding rings are artifacts that signal marital status. Brazilian men and women wear their wedding rings on the ring (third) finger of the left hand, as do North Americans. The ring is usually a simple band. The ornate wedding rings commonly worn by many North American women are not always recognized as such. In Brazil the wedding band is presented to the woman at the time of the couple's engagement. It is worn on the ring finger of the right hand until the wedding, at which time the ring is placed on the left hand.

Maria Brasil writes that Brazilians follow European styles and dress in the latest fashions (of course, this does not apply to the marginalized poor). They select clothing of quality fabric and impeccable cut. They often wonder aloud why North Americans, who are citizens of a wealthy nation, dress poorly. When traveling to Brazil, depending on the time of year and region, women should wear a good-quality suit or dress with a jacket. For blouses and dresses, elegant, simple lines are appropriate. São Paulo and regions farther south can get chilly in the winter, so lightweight wool is a good choice. Lightweight linen and cotton are comfortable for hot weather; these garments should be crisply ironed. Men should wear a good suit of European cut with a quality silk tie.[4] However, this appreciation of quality in clothing presents a dilemma. Despite the Brazilian predilection for dressing well, Brazilians and visitors alike often dress down to go out into the street, because they are then less likely to be mugged.

In Rio and the North, where it gets very humid and hot, women wear dresses or short skirts with sandals to work. A foreign woman should wear hose and pumps the first day and then take her cue from the Brazilian women in the social and business environments she is visiting. A good pair of sandals with a medium heel can serve for both day and evening use.[5]

For casual wear, jeans are very popular with Brazilians of all ages, but the jeans are ironed and worn with belts and do not have patches or holes.[6] In general, Brazilians wear their clothes fitted more tightly than do North Americans, and they wear clothing that is more revealing.

When Vicente and Lúcia Almeida moved to Wichita, Kansas, to join their two sons who were going to school, the sons told their mother she could not wear the clothes she was accustomed to wearing in steamy (literally and figuratively) Rio de Janeiro. When Lúcia dressed to go out on a hot day, her sons would stand in the living room and veto tube tops, halter tops, short shorts, and some dresses and sundresses. Nor was it even a remote consideration that she wear a Brazilian bikini to the swimming pool in this heartland of the United States.

For women traveling in Brazil, Maria Brasil recommends a good-quality tote bag that zips closed. A bag that will carry a laptop computer but that can also be used to go out is a good choice. Maria considers attaché cases too masculine and says they have "foreign businesswoman" written all over them. She also instructs, "Don't carry a backpack, unless it sports a famous European label." Wearing good-quality costume jewelry is preferable to the risk of expensive jewelry. Women often wear bright prints and colors in Brazil, but the colors of the Brazilian flag, green and yellow together, are inappropriate for clothing. Maria also reminds visitors that not all of Brazil is the Amazon jungle. They can purchase an item of clothing if they need it.[7]

A man should never wear a tie with a short-sleeved shirt or he will be taken for a missionary, and he should leave undershirts and white socks at home. Wearing socks with sandals is like wearing a sign that says "Tourist." A man should wear no more than an inexpensive watch for jewelry. Good shoes and a good leather belt are imperatives, as are a good haircut, impeccable personal grooming, and immaculate fingernails at all times.[8]

Looking young in Brazil is an obsession. In Rio de Janeiro especially, life is a continuous beauty pageant along the city's beaches. Much of the population eats sparingly to stay slim and works out vigorously in gyms to sculpt their bodies. Most women who are over forty years of age and of privileged economic means seek the scalpel of the plastic surgeon at least once to prolong their youthful appearance.[9]

Rituals

In every culture, communication takes place through its rituals and its rules of behavior. How and if they are carried out communicates volumes to those who understand them. Those who do not may not understand or misunderstand what is being communicated. Hall admonishes that there is not much flexibility in cultural rules.[10] One must learn the rules of a target culture in order to communicate effectively with a person from that culture.

A film produced in Brazil depicts a Brazilian cultural attaché telling the U.S. ambassador that he cannot give a truly elegant party for the Rio elite if he invites too many North Americans. The attaché is referring here to the difference in the rules of courtesy and custom that Brazilian and North American culture dictate. North Americans customarily do not observe the same protocols that are used in Brazil, such as greeting rituals, forms of address, respect for hierarchy, conversational styles, attire, table manners, and leave-taking, and Brazilians often note these differences.

Ignorance of a culture's rituals of courtesy can directly affect the participants. Manoel Freitas of the Friendship Force remarked to Annie Nimos that Brazilians frequently go hungry when visiting the United States: "In a North American home, the hosts might ask if you would like something to drink or eat. In good Brazilian fashion we respond, 'Thank you. It is not necessary' [Obrigado. Não precisa]. We are thirsty and hungry, but North Americans accept our answer and move on to the next person or other things."

Manoel laughed and continued, "They don't ask again. Too late. Finally, we learn that you only get one chance to eat or drink, and you had better take it. This is strange for us."

In Brazil the ritual is to ask people if they want something to eat or drink. Often the first response of convention is to decline or say that it is not necessary (meaning, I don't want you to go to any trouble on my behalf). The host will then insist, and eventually the guest will accept. Or, hearing a negative answer, hosts frequently respond that their guests must want or need something and serve them anyway.

There are a multitude of courtesies and customs to learn in another culture. In Brazil when a guest departs from the home, the host must go to the door with the guest and the host must open the door. This custom is based on the superstition that if the host wants someone to return, the host must physically open the door for the person. When going to a party, Brazilians think nothing of bringing an unannounced friend or visiting relative with them. The more the merrier. Also, Brazilians consider good table manners, like good grammar, a sign of a good education and upbringing and therefore as a sign of good social standing.

Through Brazilian Eyes

On May 19, 2000, before a presentation I was giving on intercultural communication, fifty-nine teachers and directors of the Instituto Cultural Brasil–Norte América responded in writing to three open-ended questions. The respondents had not been notified that they would be asked to fill out a questionnaire, and they gave quick, spontaneous answers. The concepts contained in the group's answers were sorted into

TABLE 17.1 May 19, 2000, Questionnaire, Instituto Cultural Brasil–Norte America

Cultural Category	Number of Mentions	Explanation and Comments
Immediacy	52	Brazilians nonverbally display great availability/desire for communication. Americans seem cold and distant to them.
Touch	40	Brazilians touch others when interacting and need physical touch, such as hugs and kisses. "All Brazilians need body contact to communicate."
Vocalics	28	Brazilians speak loudly. They are very talkative.
Emotional directness	27	Brazilians express their emotions—what they really think and feel. Americans do not communicate their emotions. "Brazilians are more heart and Americans are more reason."
Space	24	Brazilians need to get close to each other physically to talk and interact. Americans stand farther away; they are more reserved.
Adaptability	19	Brazilians are spontaneous and flexible.
Attitude	19	Brazilians are a happy, optimistic, enthusiastic people. They "enjoy life no matter how hard it is."
Directness/indirectness	16	Brazilians rarely go straight to the point in conversation or negotiation. Americans are very objective.
Rules	15	Brazilians perceive themselves as less formal in their behavior than do North Americans, and say that North Americans are more polite. Brazilians comment that North Americans use more expressions of (verbal) politeness, such as "please," "thank you," "you're welcome," "sorry," "excuse me."
Collectivism/individualism	14	Brazilians maintain strong family ties and have more obligations than do Americans. Friends are more important to Brazilians. Brazilians want to know people to do business.
Time	14	Brazilians are flexible about time. They are polychronic. North Americans tend to be monochronic; they observe time more strictly and act in an organized and sequential manner.
Ethnocentrism	10	Brazilians are open to and curious about other cultures. North Americans are self-centered and do not know much about Brazil.
Worldview	8	Brazilians use jeito to solve problems or to take advantage of situations. They break rules and laws.
Body motion communication	7	Brazilians use more body motion than do North Americans to communicate.
Context	6	Brazilians use words for effect that are not intended to be information-specific.

the cultural categories listed in Table 17.1 and then tallied as to how frequently the category was cited. If one respondent volunteered the same category as a response to two different questions, two responses were counted for that category. The categories that were volunteered most frequently were then ranked by their score.

The questions asked were as follows:

• What do you think are the two greatest problems in communication between Brazilians and North Americans, caused by cultural differences?
• What do you think are the two cultural characteristics that are most characteristic of Brazilians?
• What do you think is the one greatest difference in Brazilian communication/cultural style and the communication/cultural style of other nationalities in general?

By virtue of their association as teachers or directors of an organization that teaches language and cultural concepts, this group had had exposure to North American and other cultures, was conscious that cultural differences exist, and had ostensibly given some thought to such differences at some time. Table 17.1 represents their one-way, spontaneous perception of Brazilians' most characteristic cultural traits and what they perceive as common areas of difficulty in cross-cultural communication with North Americans.

Clearly, Brazilians exhibit and seek extensive nonverbal displays in their communication, as evidenced by the cultural categories that rank as the first five in Table 17.1. Immediacy is extremely important: Brazilians require multiple signals of availability for communication, such as voice intonation, facial expression, eye contact, proximity, body posture, and gestures in order to feel comfortable communicating with someone. It is also extremely important for them to touch and be touched and to display and perceive emotion when interacting.

IT IS IMPORTANT to pay attention to the function and importance of immediacy displays in Brazilian culture and to consciously observe and adapt to Brazil's cultural rituals. To do so will both improve one's communication skills and increase the enjoyment of cross-national interaction.

PART IV.

Conclusion

CHAPTER EIGHTEEN

In a Nutshell

The fundamental and dominant character of the Brazilian is an enormous zest for life.[1]

The Brazilian Experience

Having considered from many angles the factors that affect communication with Brazilians, I now propose to distill the cultural characteristics of this country of continental proportions and diverse people.

Although Brazil may have Latin America's largest economy, it is a country full of poor people. Brazilians have had to cope with many chronic and acute political and economic problems. They survived a repressive military dictatorship from 1964 to 1985 and rampant inflation that peaked at 2500 percent per annum in 1993. They developed *jeito* to find a way around laws, to bend rules, to deal with a bureaucracy that is often absurd, and to extricate themselves from the unwelcome vagaries of their lives.

Brazil has developed industry and many conveniences in its large and affluent cities. But urban convenience also brings the great concern for personal safety that permeates current daily life. This is a consequence of the juxtaposition of the privileged and the deprived in densely populated urban areas.

Handling the Hierarchy

Brazilians are very gracious. The fundamental rule for interpersonal communication in Brazil is to maintain cordiality and to avoid friction. Brazil charms with its pleasant surface culture, but society undergirds this smooth daily interaction with a strict, steep hierarchy—in which everyone knows and stays in his or her place. Hidden beneath Brazilian cultural uniformity are profound social distances that are more unbridgeable than racial differences.[2] In the United States the belief prevails that anyone who is willing to work can better her or his economic and social situation, but in Brazil it is extremely difficult, if not impossible, to escape from the traps of poverty and social circumstance.

Brazil's upper classes demand deference from the lower classes, which is manifested in verbal and nonverbal communication styles between the social strata. Because in the United States the hierarchy is flatter and a more egalitarian attitude prevails, North Americans appear less respectful of persons and authority than do Brazilians. Brazilians ubiquitously employ such forms of courteous address as "Dona Teresa" and "Seu Armando." A foreigner should always err toward the more formal when addressing Brazilians, using titles and honorifics until invited to do otherwise, which will usually be the case when communicating with social peers. And because of the greater power inherent in the upper levels of Brazil's steep hierarchy, Brazilians interpret and place more importance on the statements and moods of those in authority than do North Americans.

Pleasant daily communication between people in Brazil can mask racial discrimination. Even so, Brazilians do not draw color lines; they do not categorize as black anyone with an African ancestor. They do not discuss multiculturalism and diversity, because these are part of daily life. Nor do they use affirmative action, because it would be impossible to categorize the general population as to race.

Personal Relationships

Family and friends are of paramount importance in Brazil, and both kinship and friendship carry mutual rights and obligations. This commitment affects Brazilians in the workplace, because culture obligates them to take more time away from work to assist extended family and friends than is usual in the United States.

Brazilians do not want or need the same emotional and physical privacy that North Americans cherish. They seem to regenerate through interpersonal contact; they require emotionally close friendships and family relationships for a sense of well-being. So much closeness can overwhelm North Americans.

In the United States the perception of who a person is, is frequently based on what the person does. In Brazil identity is derived from the person's network of family, relatives, friends, and colleagues. And as a society of collective in-groups, Brazilians are motivated more by appealing to their spirit of cooperation than by individual competition.

Emotion—liking and disliking—dictates all forms of personal association in Brazil. A purely business relationship has to be mixed with a personal relationship to succeed.[3]

Because Brazilians personalize interaction, they prefer to communicate first by speaking in person, second by telephone, and last by letter or e-mail. Personal contact provides the channel richest in the nonverbal cues that are so important to Brazilian communication.

Perception of Time

Brazilian culture falls on the polychronic side and North American culture on the monochronic side of the time-perception spectrum. Symbolic time as measured precisely by a clock is of paramount importance to North Americans but of less importance to Brazilians, with *paulistas* being a possible exception. North Americans generally prefer linear, sequential activities, carried out one at a time. Brazilians typically multitask with ease and by preference, adeptly juggling a number of activities at once in what appears to North Americans to be chaos. Monochronic and polychronic treatments of time, however, are not mutually exclusive. North Americans live on time; Brazilians live in time.

Time cues frequently provoke strong emotional reactions in persons from predominantly monochronic cultures. The difference in time perception in Brazil and the United States is significant. North Americans commonly deplore Brazilians' allocation of time, but Brazilians view North Americans' precise treatment of time as more of a curiosity than a problem.

The Brazilian lives in the present and does not dwell much on the past or project much into the future.[4] North Americans do not dwell on the past either, but they plan extensively for the future.

In Brazil calling on a person to initiate or conduct business will both take more time per visit and require more visits than in the United States. North Americans should consider this cultural factor when setting their schedules in Brazil.

Directness versus Indirectness

In Brazil, one has to learn when "yes" means "no."

North American communication, especially in business, is direct and information-specific; Brazilians tend to be indirect and less specific, and they can be overly optimistic in their assessments. North Americans like "yes" and "no" answers, and their thinking patterns tend to categorize concepts and events as either black or white. Brazilians tend to perceive matters along a spectrum of grays.

When communicating with Brazilians, one must consider the entire context of what is being said rather than focus on specific word content alone. North Americans should be aware that "no" is usually communicated indirectly. To communicate effectively, they need to learn to distinguish language that Brazilians intend to be information-specific from words that Brazilians use as nonspecific and intend primarily for pleasantness of interaction. Since a Brazilian will rarely say "no," North Americans should be alert for rituals such as postponing an answer, saying that something might be difficult, or alluding to an imprecise future commitment, which by convention are used to indirectly communicate a "no" answer. Brazilians spontaneously make promises they may not keep to contribute to the enjoyment of the present, or because they are unable or unwilling to help.[5] In turn, Brazilians should bear in mind that North Americans tend to take words specifically and literally and that they place great importance on verbal commitments.

Brazilians engage in more preliminary social interaction than is necessary in the United States both for business and for personal contact. On meeting, they find going straight to the point too direct and brusque. In placing a telephone call, etiquette requires that one make preliminary personal conversation and inquire about the other person before bringing up the subject of the call. North Americans are often reluctant to "waste" someone's time in this manner, but it is essential to personalize interaction and take the time to earn a place even at the fringes of a Brazilian's in-group to interact and communicate effectively.

Brazilians and North Americans commonly use different presentation styles to make a point. Brazilians tend to present supporting information first and subsequently come to the point (information > point). North Americans usually present the point first and support it with only as much information as seems necessary (point > information). Since we listen and make sense of what we hear in the same format that we present it, the difference in style causes confusion on both sides, but it causes more difficulty for North Americans than for Brazilians in communicating with each other. The familiar North American interjection "Get to the point!" well represents their point-making style, their directness, and their treatment of time.[6]

While North Americans may be direct and specific in communicating information, Brazilians find them indirect when it comes to communicating emotions. Brazilians are more emotionally open and direct with their peers than are North Americans, and they do not feel they have really communicated with someone if they do not know what that person's feelings and personal opinions are. North American lack of self-disclosure discomfits Brazilians. Since North Americans lament that Brazilians are indirect in communicating information and Brazilians complain that North Americans are not direct in revealing what they "really think," that is, their emotions, the mutual perception of indirectness is a two-way communication problem between Brazilians and North Americans.

Another difference in general thought patterns is that North Americans like to analyze and plan methodically, whereas Brazilians adeptly deal with problems that require quick innovation, although such focus and abilities can overlap.[7]

Physicality

To feel comfortable communicating, Brazilians require more immediacy displays than most North Americans employ. Brazilians are accustomed to more variation in voice intonation, volume, and pitch and more animated facial expressions, gestures, and body movement, and they stand closer and touch more. Their body posture is more forward leaning as opposed to straight-backed and reserved in physical attitude. Visible displays of animation, enthusiasm, and indications of interest in the person with whom one is communicating will go a long way for foreigners in Brazil.

Satisfactory Brazilian communication generally requires the use of touch, which Brazilians give and receive from each other. They also position themselves closer to the person with whom they are communicating than do North Americans. North Americans require more distance from others, and they are usually uncomfortable with touch, except with immediate family members and some close friends. As a result, they often retreat from interaction with Brazilians, which Brazilians may interpret as criticism or which may lead them to feel they have not communicated successfully.

Experiencing and displaying emotion is important in the lives of Brazilians. While the Brazilian rebels against arbitrary order, systems, and discipline, he or she responds especially well to emotional appeals. The Brazilian also alternates easily between euphoria and depression. Outbursts of anger quickly fade, and Brazilians rarely hold a grudge.[8]

Eye contact is used differently in Brazil and in the United States. When communicating with anyone in authority, a Brazilian will usually lower his or her eyes to indicate respect and to avoid challenging the person. However, in social settings and in public, Brazilians watch each other more than do North Americans. Brazilian men overtly look at and follow women with their eyes in a way that would seem invasive in the United States. Brazilian women, however, usually avoid eye contact with men they do not know, such as men encountered on the street.

Rituals

In Brazil the rituals of greeting and leave-taking are more demanding than in the United States. One should greet and make physical contact with every person present in a social gathering by shaking hands, using an *abraço* or cheek kiss as appropriate, and one should say good-bye in the same manner. Obviously, common sense should prevail. It would be ridiculous to attempt to greet and say good-bye to one hundred people, but to comply with Brazilian courtesy rules, one should still take the time to say good-bye personally to all of the people whom one knows and those accompanying them. This practice often makes North Americans feel awkward, as if they are importunate. They may try to depart in a discreet manner so as not to "bother" people or "break up the party," but "discreet" leave-taking can be interpreted by Brazilians as disinterest or bad manners.

When offering food or drink to a Brazilian, North Americans should not take a ritual refusal literally. They should repeat their offer several times, which may seem too insistent by North American standards, and it may be advisable to serve a Brazilian guest who declines in spite of the guest's protests.

The ritual of eating in Brazil is affected both by society's organization in collective groups and the perception of the appropriate use of formal space. Brazilians rarely eat alone. They eat primarily in designated eating spaces rather than in cars or walking in the street. At a meal, North Americans are advised to eat everything with a fork and knife; Brazilians do not often eat foods with their fingers. And one should not eat in front of others without offering to share.

Brazil is a land of paradox, where reality often is not what it appears to be:

• Brazil is a rich country full of poor people.
• Although democracy successfully deals with some of the country's needs and problems, people constantly seek a way (*um jeito*) around regulations and laws.
• Brazilians are known for their gentleness, but Brazil's history demonstrates a capacity for violence.[9]
• Smooth personal interaction and the seeming informality that predominates among peers mask a steep and intransigent hierarchy.
• Most interracial encounters are relaxed and pleasant, but this comfortable interaction may dress underlying discrimination.
• Although Brazilians observe that they are an individualistic and self-centered people, Brazil's social structure is collectively organized into

in-groups of family, kin, and friends. Each in-group focuses primarily on its own well-being. Brazilians may act as individualists outside of their in-groups, but they function as collectivists within them.

• Brazilians rarely identify constructively with the suffering of others, but they treat family and friends with profound sentiment and generosity.[10]

• The Brazilian operates as the quintessential cordial person in the world of personal relationships that exists in *a casa* but may callously and abrasively function in the impersonal world of *a rua*.[11]

• Although Brazilians seem immediately warm and friendly, real friendship accords rights and imposes obligations.

• Brazilians behave as extroverts, but they are self-critical and often lack confidence.[12]

• "Yes" may mean "no," depending on the context.

• Brazilians find North Americans more polite in the use of words such as "please," "thank you," and "excuse me," but Brazilian culture is more exigent in the use of courtesy rituals of nonverbal behavior.

• Brazilians are optimistic and happy, even when social and economic circumstances do not warrant it.

Bridging the Culture Gap

Exposure to another culture does not guarantee better communication and may result in friction without adequate preparation. Since anything that can properly be called cultural is learned,[13] it is necessary to learn Brazil's nonverbal language of behavior. We do not take most of our actions based on free choice. Culture governs our perceptions and our thinking and mandates the preponderance of our behavior at a subconscious level. Furthermore, we tend to react negatively to any behavior that differs from our own, because our culture trained us in great part through negative feedback.

Since culture can be broken down into categories of perception and behavior, it is useful to examine Brazilian culture in categories. It is easy to identify cultural differences, but to use any such list to improve communication, we must understand how such categories function in the whole of Brazilian society. And to communicate effectively across cultures, we need to increase our understanding of our own unconscious cultural patterns.[14]

Some familiarity with Brazilian culture will reduce the uncertainty that most people try to avoid in personal interaction. Attitude is also important; we should seek to understand differences rather than to judge them. For the most part, we can choose a positive attitude just as we can choose to be flexible, attributes that greatly help cross-cultural communication.

When we get to know someone personally, we no longer stereotype him or her. We see the person as an individual and begin to empathize. Brazilians comment that when you get to know North Americans, they are very nice.

We should bear in mind that communication style is culturally shared and personally differentiated.[15] Therefore, some characteristics of an individual's communication style may be correctly attributed to the individual rather than to the culture. Ideally, we will learn to suspend judgment about unfamiliar behavior and an individual and ask ourselves what function the behavior in question serves in Brazilian culture. We must, above all, remember that another culture can be different without being defective.[16]

Checklist of Brazilian Cultural Characteristics

Cordiality is maintained and friction avoided in personal interaction.

The hierarchy of Brazilian culture requires formality of address. Use titles and honorifics unless invited to do otherwise.

There is more social distance between class than race.

Culture imposes more obligations to extended family and close friends in Brazil than in the United States.

Seeking cooperation as a team can motivate Brazilians.

Brazilians seek more emotional connection than do North Americans.

Emotion dictates all forms of personal association.

Brazilians measure time more by activity than the clock.

Brazilians live in the present.

Brazilians are very adaptable.

There is always *um jeito.*

Brazilians rarely say "no" directly.

Language is often used for pleasantness rather than to convey specific information. Projections and forecasts can be overly optimistic.

Personal interaction is required before "getting to the point."

Point making commonly presents supporting information first and concludes with the point.

Brazilians prefer personal over written communication.

Visible and abundant displays of animation, enthusiasm, and interest are necessary for satisfactory communication.

Brazilians position themselves at a close physical distance to communicate in person.

For most communication, Brazilians touch and expect touch.

The eyes may be lowered to respect and to recognize authority, but Brazilians watch people more than do North Americans.

One must greet and take leave of every person in a small group or gathering.

It is customary to offer food and drink several times if it is initially refused.

Brazilians eat primarily in designated areas and use a fork and knife.

Brazilians do not eat in front of others without offering to share.

A Prescription for Intercultural Communication

We can summarize the prescripts for more successful and enjoyable transnational communication as follows:[17]

Be conscious of your own peculiar cultural conditioning.

Have a positive and respectful attitude toward Brazilian culture.

Make an effort.

Overcome ethnocentrism through education and knowledge.

Learn the rules of Brazilian interaction. Try to describe Brazilian culture in all of the categories shown in Table 2.1.

Look for meaning in the verbal and nonverbal context of what is said.

Be flexible: Adaptability is the metacompetence for intercultural communication.

Take responsibility for communicating successfully.

THE MIND-SETS that are the most universal for achieving successful intercultural communication are a positive attitude, adaptability, effort, and assuming responsibility.

Delightfully Different

Judging Brazil by quantitative data focuses on a wasteful government, a history of uncontrolled inflation, and extensive poverty. Alternatively, one can construct Brazil's identity with qualitative factors such as the country's good food, its engaging music, the physical beauty of the land and its abundance, the *saudade* (yearning) of the people that humanizes time and death, and the importance of family and friends with whom one can face all the rigors of life.[18] All of these qualities comprise the seductive charm of Brazil.

Summarizing from Roberto DaMatta,

[I know] that I am Brazilian and not North American because I like to eat *feijoada* and not hamburgers; because I speak Portuguese and not English; because football is a game played with the feet and not the hands; because at Carnival I bring into the light my social and sexual fantasies; because I believe that "no" never exists in the face of formal barriers, and that there is no such barrier that cannot be overcome with *jeitinho* through the use of personal relationships or friendships; because I believe both in Catholic saints and in African *orixás*; because I know that destiny exists and yet I still have faith in study, education, and the future of Brazil; because I am loyal to my friends and cannot deny anything to my family; because, finally, I know that I have personal relationships that will not let me walk alone in this world, as do my North American friends, who perceive themselves and live their lives as individuals.[19]

Glossary

Adaptability: Adaptability is the capability to alter the psyche to meet the demands of the environment and to suspend or modify cultural ways to creatively manage the dynamics of cultural difference. Self-altering, creative adaptation capacity is the metacompetence for intercultural communication.[1]

Anxiety: Unfamiliarity and uncertainty produce anxiety and stress in communicators, which compounds the problems presented by other intercultural communication obstacles.[2]

Artifacts: *See* Extensions of physical self.

Attitude: Attitudes are psychological states that influence overt behavior and distort perception. They cause interpretation of events in predisposed ways. *See* Preconceptions.[3]

Body motion language (Kinesics): Body motion language, like vocalic language, in every culture is composed of distinctive elements that can be combined in a virtually infinite number of ordered combinations that rule the communicative aspects of human behavior. We can term verbal language digital and body motion language analogic.[4]

Collectivism: One of the most fundamental ways in which cultures differ is in collectivism versus individualism. Collectivists interact closely and are interdependent.[5] They are best encouraged by requesting cooperation and appealing to their group spirit.[6]

Communication: Communication takes place when communicators arrive at acceptable shared meaning of an intended message, or when an unintended message has been correctly interpreted.

Context: Nonverbal behavioral context communicates on its own, affects, amplifies, explains, and supplements verbal language. It is estimated that some three-fourths of communication is through context. Different cultures use proportionally more or less context to communicate, and this difference can hinder intercultural communication.

Cross-cultural: This term is used synonymously with *intercultural.*

Culture: Culture is the logic by which we give order to the world.[7] "Culture is the whole view of the universe from which people assess the meaning of life and their appropriate response to it."[8] Put simply, culture is just "the way we do things around here."[9] Culture is communication and communication is culture.[10] Culture governs communication and communication in turn creates, reinforces, and re-creates culture.[11]

Customs: *See* Rules.

Directness: Low-context communicators most often use words literally; the contents of their verbal messages are direct and information-specific. High-context communicators are less direct and frequently communicate their intended message by context; they often use words as a ritual that is information-nonspecific. In some cultures, directness is considered rude.

Ethnocentrism: When perceptions learned through acculturation are narrow and cause rigid behavior they are ethnocentric.[12] Ethnocentrism is the opposite of empathy.

Eye contact: Cultures have explicit rules regarding eye behavior such as staring, frequency of contact, and lowering the eyes. The same behavior can have different meanings in different cultures, giving rise to misinterpretation. Direct eye contact can signify honesty and attentiveness or disrespect and boldness, depending on the culture.

Extensions of physical self: People communicate consciously and unconsciously through physical extensions of themselves,[13] such as dress, gifts, or cars. These extensions are interpreted differently in different cultures.

Face: Face is a person's value, standing, or prestige in the eyes of others. In many cultures maintaining face is of great importance, and one must take great care not to openly disagree, criticize, or compete.[14]

Gender: Cultures regard some behaviors as masculine or feminine and frequently assign roles based on gender. Behavior associated with one sex is usually considered inappropriate for the other.[15]

Gestures (Emblems): A culture can assign specific meaning to a gesture. We know when we do not understand a foreign gesture. Homomorphic gestures are those that are the same or similar in form but carry different meaning. Homomorphic gestures frequently generate misunderstanding.[16]

Hierarchy: All living things have a ranking order,[17] and the use of hierarchy differs from culture to culture. The concept of hierarchical distance affects the degree of formality in communication.[18] Steep hierarchy in a society encourages respect of classification, rank, order, and harmony. A flat hierarchy has a decentralized and democratic perspective that encourages participation based on declassification, equality, exploration, and adventure. There is, of course, some overlap. The use of language and ritual courtesies can change or reinforce the steepness or flatness of hierarchy.

Immediacy: Actions that simultaneously communicate warmth, closeness, and availability for communication are immediacy behaviors that signal approach rather than avoidance. Strong immediacy displays are typical of cultures that have high physical contact.[19] Persons tend to approach things they like and avoid things they dislike, so people interpret immediacy behaviors as communicating positive or negative evaluations of the interaction partner.

Individualism: One of the most fundamental ways in which cultures differ is in the dimension of individualism versus collectivism. Individualists tend to be independent, distant in their personal interactions with others, and self-motivated and can be stimulated to achieve by individual competition.[20]

Information-specific: *See* Directness.

Intercultural: A macro definition of "intercultural" is used. This book addresses the obstacles in communicating across cultures that are *inter-* or *trans*national, rather than targeting diverse, *intra*national subcultures (sometimes called co-cultures) that share the experience of living in the same polity.

Intercultural communication: Intercultural communication is "a transactional, symbolic process involving the attribution of meaning between people from different cultures."[21]

Intracultural communication: Communication between people who share a common culture.

***Jeito* or *jeitinho*:** This is the Brazilian concept that one can always figure out some way to do what one wants to, that there is a quick solution to a problem or a way out of a dilemma. The use of the diminutive *jeitinho* connotes that one does not consider the method chosen a serious transgression, even when bending rules and circumventing laws.

Judgment: *See* Preconceptions.

Language, verbal: Language should be considered a mirror of its culture.[22] Not only is language a product of culture, culture is a product of language.[23] The Sapir-Whorf hypothesis states that language is a guide to social reality and builds up the real world through the language habits of a group. No two languages are sufficiently alike to consider that they represent the same social reality.[24] One must learn to "speak" the culture to learn its verbal language well.[25]

Manners: *See* Rules.

Materialism: *See* Values.

Miscommunication: Miscommunication occurs when a receiver attributes erroneous meaning to a verbal or nonverbal message, whether the message was intended or unintended, and whether or not the message was adequately or properly encoded and transmitted.

Monochronic: This is a linear and sequential approach toward time that is rational, suppresses spontaneity, and tends to focus on one activity at a time. People of monochronic cultures are punctual, value efficiency, and "get to the point" quickly.

Motivation: Willingness or desire to make the effort required to reduce uncertainty in intercultural interaction.

Nonverbal communication: The nonverbal behavior through which a person communicates; this includes such behavior as gestures, facial expressions, tone of voice, dress, body language, and the rituals (such as courtesies) one observes.

North American: This term refers to an English-speaking citizen of the United States (not someone from Canada or Mexico, both of which are in

North America), sometimes called an anglophone. An anglophone can be of any ethnic origin or ancestry; however, in common U.S. usage, the shortened term "anglo" usually refers to a North American of northern European origin and has a different connotative meaning (usually pejorative) than the word "anglophone."[26]

Perception: Perception is the internal process by which we select, evaluate, and organize the stimuli of the outside world. From the time we are born, we learn our perceptions and the resulting behaviors from our cultural experiences.[27]

Phenotype: *See* Physical appearance.

Physical appearance: A person's physical features such as hair or skin color can be "markers" that accentuate perceptions of cultural difference.[28] Markers of difference can discourage interaction, because the higher the perceived similarity between two individuals, the greater their attraction to each other to communicate.[29]

Polychronic: This is a multiple-activity, "matrix" concept of time. Polychronic cultures only loosely measure time with the symbols of a formalized system. Business relationships are personalized, based on trust, and take "time" to establish. It is "time" to move on to the next activity when the current set of activities is over. Activity is more important than the abstract measure of time by a clock. Persons in polychronic cultures frequently carry on many activities at the same time.

Power: A significant discrepancy in power or status between groups causes acute intergroup posturing tendencies, which can create obstacles to intercultural communication.[30]

Preconceptions: People tend to see what they expect to see and, furthermore, to discount that which conflicts with these preconceptions, stereotypes, or prejudices toward persons.[31]

Prejudice: *See* Preconceptions.

Process: Differences in the behavioral units (categories) of cultures create obstacles in the process of verbal and nonverbal communication between persons. A behavioral unit is the smallest viable element of a culture that can be analyzed, taught, and transmitted as a complete entity.[32] Examples of such units are greeting, touch, eye contact, and table manners.

Rituals: *See* Context; Rules.

Role: Prescribed roles for persons can vary culturally, such as by gender, social class, or race.[33]

Rules: Cultural rules are based on ideas.[34] They govern formality and ritual and what types of interaction take place when and where.[35] There is not much flexibility in cultural rules,[36] and one must learn the rules of a target culture in order to communicate effectively.

Saudade: A nostalgic yearning for what was or what might be, characteristic of Portuguese and Brazilian culture.

Similarity assumptions: To assume that surface similarity in communication or behavior means the same thing in different cultures can result in misinterpretation. Likewise, surface differences may represent underlying similarity. Unless assumptions are overtly reported, there is no chance of correcting misinterpretations.[37] It is easy to underestimate the effect of an unfamiliar cultural environment on communication.

Space sense (Proxemics): People of different cultures communicate differently through use of space.[38] Culture dictates what behavior is appropriate in what formally designated space. Culture also governs the use of informal space, such as the distance maintained in interpersonal encounters.[39] In some cultures people stand and sit very close when interacting, and they judge those who interact at a greater distance to be cold, condescending, or disinterested. Other cultures perceive close interaction as pushy, disrespectful, or sexually aggressive.[40] Culture usually determines whether people wait in line or jockey for the best position to be served.[41]

Stereotyping: *See* Preconceptions.

Thought patterns: Different cultures arrive at their concepts of reality in different ways. A culture's perception of reality may come through faith or belief, independent of fact. It may come from fact based on evidence, which is the most predictable concept of reality. Or a culture may perceive reality primarily through feelings or instinct, which is the most common basis for reality perception in the world.[42]

Time sense (Chronemics): Formal time is measured abstractly by units such as hours, days, months, and years and by different calendars. Informal time is measured by systems such as seasons or customs. People easily understand the differences in formal time between cultures but find it more difficult to understand a foreign culture's informal time system. Informal time elements are loosely defined by a culture, not explicitly taught, and typically operate outside consciousness. Time cues can be intentional or unintentional and are often ambiguous. Time cues often evoke strong emotional reactions in people of monochronic cultures.[43]

Touch (Haptics): Although all human beings are born with a need for touch, cultures train humans as to what and how much touch is acceptable as they mature. People in collective cultures touch each other more than those in cultures that stress the individual.[44]

Uncertainty: People have a strong need to understand both the self and the Other in interpersonal interaction. To reduce uncertainty, they strive to increase predictability—which is often difficult with people of other cultures.[45] Culture teaches individuals to behave in prescribed ways that permit the other group members to recognize and anticipate the individual's behavior.[46] Most people prefer to interact in predictable social environments.

Values: Values are the learned (through acculturation) organization of rules for making choices and resolving conflicts,[47] and differences in values can be an obstacle to intercultural communication.[48] Religious values are manifested not only in dogma but also in living patterns and outlook.[49] Materialism places value on money, work, and material success. To respect another culture's values can conflict with one's own values as a basis for judgment. There is much debate over relative and absolute values.[50]

Verbal communication: This is communication by verbal (word) symbols of meaning, both written and oral.

Vocalics: The term "vocalics" encompasses any vocal-auditory behavior except the spoken word.[51] Vocalics also refer to how something is said rather than the actual meaning of the words.[52] The voice is a rich channel in the system of nonverbal communication. Vocalic cues are among the most powerful cues in the nonverbal repertoire and, next to body motion communication cues, are the largest in number. Some vocalic cues are so brief as to be missed in intercultural communication.[53]

Worldview: This is a culture's understanding of the meaning of life and being.[54]

Notes

Preface

1. D. Ribeiro (2000). *The Brazilian People: The Formation and Meaning of Brazil.* (Gregory Rabassa, Trans.) Gainesville: University Press of Florida, p. 322. (Originally published 1995.)

2. J. Amados, cited in G. Wells (1997). Continental drift. In Annette Haddad and Scott Dogett (Ed.), *Travelers' Tales Brazil: True Stories of Life on the Road* (pp. 67–78). Redwood City, CA: Travelers' Tales, Inc., p. 68.

3. C. Storti (1989). *The Art of Crossing Cultures.* Yarmouth, ME: Intercultural Press, Inc.

4. E. T. Hall (1959). *The Silent Language.* 1st ed. Garden City, NY: Doubleday.

Chapter 1

1. U.S. Department of Commerce (1999, July 15). *Brazil: Country Commercial Guide Fiscal Year 2000.* São Paulo, Brazil: U.S. Commercial Service.

2. W. A. Selcher (1995). Brazil in the world. In G. H. Summ (Ed.), *Brazilian Mosaic: Portraits of a Diverse People and Culture* (pp. 166–171). Wilmington, DE: Scholarly Resources, Inc.

3. U.S. Department of Commerce, 1999.

4. Ibid.

5. Ibid.

6. Ribeiro, 2000, p. 186.

7. R. DaMatta (1998). *O que faz o brasil, Brasil?* [What makes brazil Brazil?]. Rio de Janeiro: Editora Rocco Ltda.

8. P. Watzlawick, J. B. Bavelas, and D. D. Jackson (1967). *Pragmatics of Human Communication: A Study of Interactional Patterns, Pathologies, and Paradoxes.* New York: W. W. Norton and Company.

9. T. Novinger (2001). *Intercultural Communication: A Practical Guide.* Austin: University of Texas Press.

10. E. T. Hall (1976). *Beyond Culture.* Garden City, NY: Doubleday.

11. G. Hofsteder, cited in I. Varner and L. Beamer (1995). *Intercultural Communication in the Global Workplace.* Chicago: Irwin.

12. W. B. Gudykunst and Y. Y. Kim (1984). *Communicating with Strangers: An Approach to Intercultural Communication.* Reading, MA: Addison Wesley Publishing.

Chapter 2

1. DaMatta, 1998.
2. Hall, 1959.
3. R. H. Pells (1997). *Not Like Us: How Europeans Have Loved, Hated, and Transformed American Culture since World War II.* New York: Basic-Books.
4. Ibid.
5. J. K. Conway (1994). *True North: A Memoir.* New York: Vintage Books, p. 93.
6. Ibid., p. 166.
7. T. Sowell (1994). *Race and Culture: A World View.* New York: Basic-Books.
8. R. L. Birdwhistell (1970). *Kinesics and Context: Essays on Body Motion Communication.* Philadelphia: University of Pennsylvania Press.
9. K. S. Sitaram (1972). What is intercultural communication? In L. A. Samovar and R. E. Porter (Eds.), *Intercultural Communication: A Reader* (pp. 18–23). Belmont, CA: Wadsworth Publishing.
10. R. Carroll (1987). *Evidences invisibles: Américains et français au quotidien.* Paris: Editions du Seuil. [Available in translation: R. Carroll (1988). *Cultural Misunderstandings: The French-American Experience.* (C. Volk, Trans.) Chicago: University of Chicago Press.]
11. Varner and Beamer, 1995, p. 13.
12. M. Tixier (1993). Obstacles to internal communication among subsidiary and headquarters executives in western Europe. In P. Gaunt (Ed.), *Beyond Agendas: New Directions in Communication Research* (pp. 101–116). Westport, CT: Greenwood Press, p. 101.
13. Hall, 1959.
14. Novinger, 2001.
15. J. Streeck (1994). Culture, meaning, and interpersonal communication. In M. L. Knapp (Ed.), *Handbook of Interpersonal Communication* (pp. 286–319). Thousand Oaks, CA: Sage.
16. Sitaram, 1972.
17. Hall, 1976.
18. Birdwhistell, 1970.
19. Hall, 1976.
20. F. Boas (1940). *Race, Language and Culture.* New York: Free Press.
21. Hall, 1976.
22. Novinger, 2001.
23. Hall, 1976.
24. Ibid.
25. Ibid.
26. Hall, 1959.

27. Sowell, 1994.

28. K. L. Pike (1956). *Language and Life.* Glendale, CA: Summer Institute of Linguistics.

29. Ibid.

30. Y. Y. Kim (1991). Intercultural communication competence: A systems-theoretic view. In S. Ting-Toomey and F. Korzenny (Eds.), *Cross-Cultural Interpersonal Communication* (pp. 259–275). Newbury Park, CA: Sage.

31. Hall, 1976.

32. T. Novinger (1996). Intercultural communication: The cultural factors that create obstacles between Mexico and the United States. Master's thesis, Wichita State University, Wichita, KS; T. Novinger, 2001.

33. T. H. Inman, A. C. Ownby, H. R. Perreault, and J. N. Rhea (1991). Internationalizing the business communication curriculum. *Business Education Forum, 46*(2), 19–22.

34. Novinger, 2001.

35. L. A. Samovar and R. E. Porter (1991). *Communication between Cultures.* Belmont, CA: Wadsworth Publishing.

36. Pells, 1997.

37. Novinger, 2001.

38. Hall, 1959.

39. Ibid.

Chapter 3

1. Pells, 1997.

2. Novinger, 1996.

3. Samovar and Porter, 1991.

4. T. P. R. Caldeira (2000). *City of Walls: Crime, Segregation and Citizenship in São Paulo.* Berkeley: University of California Press.

5. Ibid.

6. Ibid.

7. L. M. Barna (1988). Stumbling blocks in intercultural communication. In L. A. Samovar and R. E. Porter (Eds.), *Intercultural Communication: A Reader* (5th ed.) (pp. 322–329). Belmont, CA: Wadsworth Publishing; Y. Y. Kim, 1991; T. Pettigrew (1986). The intergroup contact hypothesis reconsidered. In Hewstone and R. Brown (Eds.) *Contact and Conflict in Intergroup Encounters* (pp. 169–195). Oxford: Basil Blackwell.

8. C. R. Berger and R. Calabrese (1975). Some explorations in initial interaction and beyond. *Human Communication Research, I,* 99–112; H. O. Lee and F. J. Boster (1991). Social information for uncertainty reduction during initial interactions. In S. Ting-Toomey and F. Korzenny (Eds.), *Cross-Cultural Interpersonal Communication* (pp. 189–212), Newbury Park, CA: Sage.

9. W. Gudykunst and S. Ting-Toomey (1988). *Culture and Interpersonal Communication.* Beverly Hills, CA: Sage.

10. R. E. Porter (1972). An overview of intercultural communication. In L. A. Samovar and R. E. Porter (Eds.), *Intercultural Communication: A Reader* (pp. 3–18). Belmont, CA: Wadsworth Publishing.

11. Porter, 1972.

12. B. Wedge (1972). Barriers to understanding. In L. A. Samovar and R. E. Porter (Ed.), *Intercultural Communication: A Reader* (pp. 3–18). Belmont, CA: Wadsworth Publishing.

13. Y. Y. Kim, 1991; Lee and Boster, 1991.

14. G. Althen (1998). *American Ways.* Yarmouth, ME: Intercultural Press, Inc.

15. Ibid.

16. Ibid.

17. H. J. Kim (1991). Influence of language and similarity on initial intercultural attraction. In S. Ting-Toomey and F. Korzenny (Eds.), *Cross-Cultural Interpersonal Communication* (pp. 213–229). Newbury Park, CA: Sage.

18. Novinger, 2001.

19. Varner and Beamer, 1995, p. 13.

20. Samovar and Porter, 1991.

21. Storti, 1999.

22. Hall, 1959.

23. R. J. Lores (2000, March 29). E eles culpam o Brasil [And they blame Brazil]. *Veja,* Edition 1642, Year 33, No. 13, pp. 186–195. Brazil.

24. G. Franco (2000, March 29). Sobre o nacionalismo [On nationalism]. *Veja,* Edition 1642, Year 33, No. 13, p. 196. Brazil.

25. Pells, 1997.

26. Barna, 1988. R. Schneller (1989). Intercultural and intrapersonal processes and factors of misunderstanding: Implications for multicultural training. *International Journal of Intercultural Relations, 5,* 175–191.

27. R. T. Moran and J. D. Abbott (1994). *NAFTA: Managing the Cultural Differences.* Houston, TX: Gulf Publishing Company.

28. Ibid.

29. Y. Y. Kim, 1991.

30. J. A. Page (1995). *The Brazilians.* Reading, MA: Addison Wesley.

31. L. S. Rega (2000). *Dando um jeito no jeitinho: Como ser ético sem deixar de ser brasileiro* [Finding a way to find a way: How to be ethical without giving up being Brazilian]. São Paulo: Mundo Cristão.

32. E. A. Riedinger (1997). Once upon a time in Ipanema. In A. Haddad and S. Dogett (Eds.), *Travelers' Tales Brazil: True Stories of Life on the Road* (pp. 18–26). Redwood City, CA: Travelers' Tales, Inc.

33. Y. Y. Kim, 1991.

34. P. M. Garcez (1996). Brazilian manufacturers and United States importers doing business: The co-construction of arguing sequences in negotiation. Ph.D. dissertation, University of Pennsylvania. Ann Arbor, MI: UMI Dissertation Services.

35. L. Szalay (1995), cited in Varner and Beamer, 1995, p. 115.

36. Varner and Beamer, 1995.

37. P. Andersen (1988). Explaining intercultural differences in nonverbal communication. In L. A. Samovar and R. E. Porter (Eds.), *Intercultural Communication: A Reader* (5th ed.) (pp. 272–287). Belmont, CA: Wadsworth Publishing.

38. Samovar and Porter, 1991.

39. M. Argyle (1988). Intercultural communication. In L. A. Samovar and R. E. Porter (Eds.), *Intercultural Communication: A Reader* (5th ed.) (pp. 31–44). Belmont, CA: Wadsworth Publishing; J. Johnston (1988). Japanese firms in the U.S.: Adapting the persuasive message. *Bulletin of the Association for Business Communication, 51*(3), 33–34.

40. Hall, 1959.

41. J. P. Bowman and T. Okuda (1985). Japanese-American communication: Mysteries, enigmas, and possibilities. *Bulletin of the Association for Business Communication, 48*(4), 18–21.

42. Varner and Beamer, 1995.

43. Ibid.

44. Y. Y. Kim, 1991.

45. R. A. Pastor and J. G. Castañeda (1988). *Limits to Friendship: The United States and Mexico.* New York: Knopf.

46. Barna, 1988; Wedge, 1972.

47. Varner and Beamer, 1995.

48. Inman et al., 1991; Porter, 1972.

49. Argyle, 1988; Inman et al., 1991.

50. Bowman and Okuda, 1985.

51. Hall, 1959.

52. Ibid.

53. S. I. Hayakawa (1958). Communication and the human community. *Etc., 60,* 5–11.

54. L. Moreira (1995). Living avidly in the present. In G. Harvey Summ (Ed.), *Brazilian Mosaic: Portraits of a Diverse People and Culture* (pp. 185–188). Wilmington, DE: Scholarly Resources, Inc.

55. T. Morrison, W. Conway, and G. A. Borden (1994). *Kiss, Bow, or Shake Hands: How to Do Business in Sixty Countries.* Holbrook, MA: Bob Adams, Inc.

56. Samovar and Porter, 1991.

57. Barna, 1988; E. T. Hall and W. F. Whyte (1960). Intercultural communication: A guide to men of action. *Human Organization, 19,* 5–20.

58. I. Torbiorn (1987). Culture barriers as a social psychological construct. In Y. Y. Kim and W. B. Gudykunst (Eds.), Cross-cultural adaptation: Current approaches. *International and Intercultural Communication Annual, XI,* 168–190.

59. W. Feinberg (1989). A role for philosophy of education in intercultural research: A reexamination of the relativism-absolutism debate. *Teachers College Record, 91,* 161–176.

60. Samovar and Porter, 1991.

Chapter 4

1. T. E. Skidmore (1999). *Brazil: Five Centuries of Change.* New York: Oxford University Press, p. xiii.

2. Page, 1995, p. 14.

3. Pells, 1997.

4. G. Freyre (1956). *The Master and the Slaves: A Study in the Development of Brazilian Civilization.* (Samuel Putnam, Trans.) 2d English-language ed., rev. New York: Knopf.

5. Ibid.

6. Ibid.

7. Ibid.

8. M. Eakin (1998). *Brazil: The Once and Future Country.* New York: St. Martin's Press.

9. Ibid.

10. Ibid.

11. Page, 1995.

12. Eakin, 1998.

13. Page, 1995.

14. Ibid.

15. Eakin, 1998.

16. Ibid.

17. DaMatta, 1998.

18. Eakin, 1998.

19. Ibid.

20. U.S. Department of Commerce, 1999.

21. Skidmore, 1999, p. 160.

22. Skidmore, 1999.

23. Ibid.

24. Caldeira, 2000, p. 3.

25. Caldeira, 2000.

26. Eakin, 1998.

27. Ribeiro, 2000, p. 3.

28. J. Krich (1997). The girl from Ipanema. In A. Haddad and S. Dogett (Eds.), *Travelers' Tales Brazil: True Stories of Life on the Road* (pp. 336–347). Redwood City, CA: Travelers' Tales, Inc.

29. Eakin, 1998.

30. Ribeiro, 2000.

31. Eakin, 1998.

32. Page, 1995.

33. R. Freire (1998). *Viaje na viagem: Auto-ajuda para turistas* [Travel on the trip: Self-help for tourists]. São Paulo: Mandarim.

34. Page, 1995.

35. L. Dias and R. Gambini (1999). *Outros 500: Uma conversa sobre a alma brasileira* [Another 500: A discussion of the Brazilian soul]. São Paulo: Editora SENAC.

36. G. Freyre (1981). *Casa grande e senzala em quadrinhos* [The masters and the slaves in comic strips]. Rio de Janeiro: Editora-América.

Chapter 5

1. Cited in Wells, 1997, p. 69. Original emphasis.
2. Eakin, 1997.
3. Freyre, 1981.
4. H. S. Klein, cited in Satomi Furuichi (1999). On understanding racial inequality in Brazil. Ph.D. dissertation, University of Texas, Austin.
5. F. Gonzalez (2001, April 20). From Brazil, a musician's colorful call. *Washington Post*, p. G01. www.washingtonpost.com, April 20, 2001.
6. M. Mendonça and V. Franco (Directors) (2000). *Nascí mulher negra* [I was born a black woman]. Brazil: Global Exchange Video.
7. Page, 1995.
8. Furuichi, 1999.
9. Eakin, 1997.
10. Ribeiro, 2000, p. 2.
11. T. G. Sanders (1995). The social functions of futebol. In G. H. Summ (Ed.), *Brazilian Mosaic: Portraits of a Diverse People and Culture* (pp. 159–162). Wilmington, DE: Scholarly Resources, Inc.
12. Eakin, 1997, p. 130.
13. Page, 1995.
14. DaMatta, 1998.
15. Ibid.
16. Page, 1995.
17. Ribeiro, 2000.
18. Freyre, 1956.
19. Ibid.
20. Furuichi, 1999.
21. J. Fiola, cited in Furuichi, 1999.
22. DaMatta, 1998.
23. Ibid.
24. Page, 1995.
25. Dias and Gambini, 1999.
26. Furuichi, 1999.
27. G. R. Andrews, cited in Furuichi, 1999.
28. Furuichi, 1999.
29. Page, 1995.
30. Ibid.
31. Dias and Gambini, 1999.
32. Page, 1995, p. 73.
33. Ribeiro, 2000.
34. Skidmore, 1999, p. 207.
35. Page, 1995, p. 57.

Chapter 6

1. Eakin, 1997, p. 105.
2. Flor (2000, June 29). Desigualdade cresce no Brasil [Inequality grows in Brazil]. *Zero Hora.* Porto Alegre, Brazil, pp. 50–51.
3. Flor, 2000.
4. *Zero Hora,* Staff (2000, June 30). Subdesenvolvimento humano [Human underdevelopment]. Porto Alegre, Brazil, p. 24.
5. U.S. Central Intelligence Agency (2000, 9 November). *The World Factbook.* U.S. Government: www.odci.gov/cia/publications/factbook/geos/us.num.
6. *Zero Hora,* Staff (2000, June 30), p. 24.
7. T. Rubin (2001, 24 June). Rio de Janeiro is a town of two worlds. *Austin American-Statesman,* p. A11.
8. Eakin, 1997.
9. J. L. Rich (2001, 16 August). *New York Times.* www.nytimes.com/2001/08/16/business/worldbusiness/16BRAZ.html.
10. L. Alder (2000, Fall). Go south young business people. *Texas: The McCombs School of Business Magazine,* pp. 14–15.
11. Rubin (2001, June 24), p. A11.
12. L. Ertel (2000, June 16). Informe económico [Economic Report]. *Zero Hora.* Porto Alegre, Brazil, p. 24.
13. *Zero Hora,* Staff (2000, June 30), p. 24.
14. Flor (2000, June 29), pp. 50–51.
15. *Zero Hora,* Staff (2000, June 30), p. 24.
16. Eakin, 1997.
17. Dias and Gambini, 1999.
18. M. Margolis (1997). Young, down and out. In A. Haddad and S. Dogett (Eds.), *Travelers' Tales Brazil: True Stories of Life on the Road* (pp. 370–375). Redwood City, CA: Travelers' Tales, Inc., p. 372.
19. Page, 1995.
20. J. F. Santos (1995). Bypassing the system. In G. Harvey Summ (Ed.), *Brazilian Mosaic: Portraits of a Diverse People and Culture* (pp. 142–148). Wilmington, DE: Scholarly Resources, Inc., 1995.
21. Ibid.
22. Ibid.
23. Rega, 2000.
24. U.S. Department of Commerce, 1999.
25. P. A. Goslin (1993). *Rau tchu bi a carioca* (*How to be a Carioca): O guia alternativo para a turista no Rio* [The alternative guide for the tourist in Rio]. Rio de Janeiro: Editora Livros TwoCan Ltda., p. 49.
26. Ronald Harry Coase, cited in Rega, 2000, p. 99.
27. L. Ritzel (2000, July 2). Seis anos do plano real [Six years of the real plan]. *Zero Hora.* Porto Alegre, Brazil, p. 22.
28. U.S. Department of Commerce, 1999, p. I.
29. Ibid.
30. Page, 1995.

31. Rega, 2000, p. 95.

32. Eakin, 1997.

33. *Zero Hora,* Staff (2000, June 11). O modelo francês [The French model]. Porto Alegre, Brazil, p. 18.

34. Riedinger, 1997.

35. *Zero Hora,* Staff (2000, June 18). Atividade não é regulamentada [Activity not regulated]. Porto Alegre, Brazil, p. 49.

36. Ibid.

37. Rega, 2000.

38. Skidmore, 1999.

39. L. Rohter (2000, July 1). Energy crisis is just one more thing for Brazil. *New York Times.* www.nytimes.com/2001/07/01.

40. Ibid.

41. Ibid.

42. Eakin, 1997, p. 210.

Chapter 7

1. Rogério Ekberg, cited in Rega, 2000, p. 63.

2. Rega, 2000, p. 99.

3. *Zero Hora,* Staff (2000, June 20). A epidemia de violência [The epidemic of violence]. Porto Alegre, Brazil, p. 16.

4. *Zero Hora,* Staff (2000, June 26). Onze homicídios marcam o fim de semana no estado [Eleven homicides mark the weekend in the state]. Porto Alegre, Brazil, p. 1.

5. *Zero Hora,* Staff (2000, June 18). Eleições 2000: Segurança é maior preocupação do eleitor [2000 elections: Security is greatest concern of the voter]. Porto Alegre, Brazil, p. 10.

6. H. Trezzi (2000, June 18). A escalada da criminalidade: Violência no Brasil triplicou em duas décadas [The escalation of crime: Violence in Brazil tripled in two decades]. *Zero Hora.* Porto Alegre, Brazil, p. 50.

7. K. Santos (2000, June 18). Entrevista: Renan Calheiros [Interview: Renan Calheiros]. *Zero Hora.* Porto Alegre, Brazil, p. 51.

8. Economist (2001, August 18). Security in Brazil: Bullet-proof in Alphaville, p. 28.

9. CNN.com (2001, August 17). Brazil bandits take crime to new heights on plane. cnn.com/2000/WORLD/Americas/08/17/brazil.hijacking.reut/.

10. Caldeira, 2000, p. 297.

11. J. Mariani (2000, June 9). As feras no portão [The beasts at the gate]. *Zero Hora.* Porto Alegre, Brazil, p. 21.

12. D. Freitas (2000, June 25). Penas de morte [Death penalties]. *Zero Hora.* Porto Alegre, Brazil, p. 23.

13. Althen, 1998.

14. A. C. B. Martes (1999). *Brasileiros nos Estados Unidos: Um estudo sobre imigrantes em Massachusetts* [Brazilians in the United States: A study of immigrants in Massachusetts]. São Paulo: Paz e Terra.

15. Ibid.

16. Ibid.

17. R. DaMatta, cited in Rega, 2000.

18. P. Kellemen, cited in Rega, 2000.

19. Goslin, 1993.

20. T. Vasques, cited in Rega, 2000, p. 57.

21. Rega, 2000.

22. S. Buckley (2000, October 1). In Brazil, a miracle in the war on AIDS. *Austin American-Statesman*, p. J1.

23. *Zero Hora*, Staff (2000, June 27). Unaids destaca sistema brasileiro [Unaids distinguishes Brazilian system]. Porto Alegre, Brazil, p. 40.

24. Buckley, 2000.

25. S. Gobetti (2000, June 16). Cônsul divulga plano de Cuba para ensinos [Consul discloses Cuba's plans for teaching]. *Zero Hora*. Porto Alegre, Brazil, p. 12.

26. R. V. Soldatelli (2000, June 14). Palavra do leitor [Letter to the editor]. *Zero Hora*. Porto Alegre, Brazil, p. 2.

27. M. R. D. Z. Flores (2000, June 8). Palavra do leitor [Letter to the editor]. *Zero Hora*. Porto Alegre, Brazil, p. 2.

28. Page, 1995.

29. J. Carrion (2000, June 16). Palavra do leitor: Orgulho [Letter to the editor: Pride]. *Zero Hora*. Porto Alegre, Brazil, p. 2.

Chapter 8

1. R. DaMatta (1995). Do you know who you're talking to?! In G. H. Summ (Ed.), *Brazilian Mosaic: Portraits of a Diverse People and Culture* (pp. 138–142). Wilmington, DE: Scholarly Resources, p. 139.

2. Andersen, 1988.

3. Samovar and Porter, 1991.

4. J. K. Burgoon, D. B. Butler, and W. G. Woodall (1996). *Nonverbal communication: The Unspoken Dialogue*. New York: McGraw-Hill.

5. Varner and Beamer, 1995.

6. DaMatta, 1998.

7. Carroll, 1987.

8. C. Wagley (1995). A most personal people. In G. H. Summ (Ed.), *Brazilian Mosaic: Portraits of a Diverse People and Culture* (pp. 148–153). Wilmington, DE: Scholarly Resources, Inc.

9. Santos, 1995.

10. Moreira, 1995.

11. DaMatta, 1998.

12. Ibid.

13. Ibid.

14. Burgoon et al., 1996.

15. Althen, 1998, p. 7.

16. Althen, 1998.

17. Ibid.
18. Eakin, 1998.
19. Ibid.
20. Page, 1995.
21. DaMatta, 1998.
22. www.maria-brazil.org/birthday.htm, 2000.
23. Althen, 1998.
24. Ibid.
25. Ibid.
26. Ibid.
27. Ibid.
28. Ibid.
29. www.maria-brazil.org/intercul.htm, 2000.
30. Wagley, 1995.
31. Rega, 2000.
32. Hall, 1976.
33. DaMatta, 1998.

Chapter 9

1. DaMatta, 1998.
2. Hall, 1959.
3. A. R. Brown-Gort (1998). The role of culture in the political and administrative transformation of the Mexican state. Master's thesis, University of Texas, Austin.
4. Hall, 1959.
5. Eakin, 1997.
6. Ribeiro, 2000.
7. Caldeira, 2000, p. 10.
8. Ibid., p. 142.
9. D. Maybury-Lewis (1995). The persistent patronage system. In G. H. Summ (Ed.), *Brazilian Mosaic: Portraits of a Diverse People and Culture* (pp. 153–159). Wilmington, DE: Scholarly Resources, Inc.
10. DaMatta, 1998.
11. Ibid.
12. Tixier, 1993.
13. Burgoon et al., 1996.
14. Ribeiro, 2000, p. 120.
15. Novinger, 2001.
16. Burgoon et al., 1996.
17. C. Richard (1991). *Cultures of the World: Brazil.* New York: Marshall Cavendish Corporation.
18. Pells, 1997.
19. J. W. Fesler and D. F. Kent, cited in Brown-Gort, 1998.
20. H. Wilensky, cited in Brown-Gort, 1998.
21. Burgoon et al., 1996.

22. L. F. Veríssimo (2000, June 23). A boca do Bush [The mouth of Bush]. *Zero Hora*. Porto Alegre, Brazil, p. 3.

23. Eakin, 1997.

24. Tixier, 1993.

25. R. DaMatta, cited in Eakin, 1997.

26. DaMatta, 1998.

27. P. M. Garcez (1991). Conflicting conversational styles in a cross-cultural negotiation. Master's thesis, Universidade Federal de Santa Catarina, Florianópolis, Santa Catarina, Brazil, p. 139.

28. Ibid.

29. Pells, 1997.

30. Martes, 1999.

31. Althen, 1998.

32. Dias and Gambini, 1999, p. 175.

33. Skidmore, 1999.

34. L. Rohter (2000, November 26). Mayor most rare: Sexologist and monied Marxist. *New York Times*. www.nytimes.com, November 26, 2000.

35. www.maria-brazil.org/intercul.htm, 2000.

36. Ibid.

37. Dias and Gambini, 1999.

Chapter 10

1. Novinger, 2001.

2. Torbiorn, 1987.

3. Novinger, 2001.

4. Carroll, 1987.

5. Barna, 1988; Wedge, 1972.

6. Y. Y. Kim, 1991.

7. Samovar and Porter, 1991.

8. Althen, 1998.

9. Novinger, 2001.

10. A. Kardiner and R. Linton, cited in Moran and Abbott, 1994.

11. Moran and Abbott, 1994.

12. Page, 1995.

13. Althen, 1998.

14. Hall, 1959.

15. Althen, 1998; Pells, 1997.

16. www.maria-brazil.org/intercul.htm, 2000.

17. Class studying Brazil–United States cultural differences at Instituto Cultural Brasileiro Norte-Americano, Petropolis, Porto Alegre, Brazil, June 8, 2000.

Chapter 11

1. Samovar and Porter, 1991.

2. Novinger, 2001.

3. Hayakawa, 1958.
4. DaMatta, 1998.
5. Ibid.
6. Ibid.
7. Ibid.
8. Page, 1995.
9. DaMatta, 1998; Page, 1995.
10. Eakin, 1997.
11. Ibid.
12. Page, 1995.
13. Eakin, 1997.
14. Page, 1995.
15. G. Freyre, cited in Eakin, 1997.
16. Ribeiro, 2000, p. 18.
17. Page, 1995.
18. DaMatta, 1998.
19. N. Scheper-Hughes (1995). The everyday violence of life. In G. H. Summ (Ed.), *Brazilian Mosaic: Portraits of a Diverse People and Culture* (pp. 194–202). Wilmington, DE: Scholarly Resources, Inc., p. 201.
20. Rega, 2000.
21. Ibid.
22. Scheper-Hughes, 1995.
23. Ibid.
24. Ibid., p. 200.
25. L. Barbosa (1992). *O jeitinho brasileiro—A arte de ser mais igual que os outros* [Brazilian *jeitinho:* The art of being more equal than others]. Rio de Janeiro: Campus.
26. Page, 1995, p. 10.
27. Rega, 2000, p. 57.
28. J. C. O. Tôrres, cited in Rega, 2000, p. 52.
29. Rega, 2000.
30. Caldeira, 2000, p. 317.
31. DaMatta, 1998.
32. Ibid.
33. Rega, 2000.
34. Page, 1995.
35. Rega, 2000.
36. Ibid.
37. B. H. Burns, cited in Rega, 2000.
38. Rega, 2000.
39. Ibid.
40. Ibid.
41. Ibid.
42. Ibid.
43. Ibid.

Chapter 12

1. Samovar and Porter, 1991.
2. Torbiorn, 1987.
3. Althen, 1998.
4. Pells, 1997.
5. Page, 1995.
6. Ibid.
7. Ibid.
8. J. Harding, cited in Page, 1995, p. 9.
9. DaMatta, 1995.
10. Rega, 2000.
11. Martes, 1999.
12. Page, 1995.
13. Santos, 1995.
14. Page, 1995.
15. Ibid.
16. Caldeira, 2000.
17. Santos, 1995.
18. Page, 1995.
19. Argyle, 1988; Inman et al., 1991.
20. Bowman and Okuda, 1985.
21. Hall, 1959.
22. Hall, 1954.
23. Goslin, 1998.
24. Ibid.
25. Ibid.
26. Caldeira, 2000.
27. Ibid.
28. Rega, 2000.
29. Page, 1995.
30. Moreira, 1995.
31. Ibid, p. 186.
32. Moreira, 1995.
33. *Washington Post* (2001, April 1). Brazil rediscovers its culture. www.washingtonpost.com.
34. Page, 1995.
35. L. Valenzuela, cited in Page, 1995.
36. Page, 1995.
37. Dias and Gambini, 1999.
38. M. C. Proença (1969). *Roteiro de Macunaíma* [Guide to Macunaíma]. Rio de Janeiro: Editora Civilisação Brasileira.
39. Dias and Gambini, 1999.
40. Freire, 1998.
41. DaMatta, 1998.
42. Ibid.

Chapter 13

1. DaMatta, 1998.
2. Page, 1995.
3. Freyre, 1981.
4. Dias and Gambini, 1999.
5. Page, 1995.
6. Dias and Gambini, 1999.
7. Goslin, 1993.
8. Page, 1995.
9. Ibid.
10. www.maria-brazil.org/bikini.htm, 2000.
11. *Mãe* (2000). Ano VII, Número 74, front cover. Brazil.
12. S. Buckley (2001, April 16). Flirtatious Brazil weighs harassment bill. *Washington Post*, p. A14. www.washingtonpost.com, April 15, 2001.
13. Rega, 2000.
14. DaMatta, 1998.
15. www.maria-brazil.org/eat.htm, 2000.
16. DaMatta, 1998.
17. www.maria-brazil.org/eat.htm, 2000.
18. Ibid.
19. www.maria-brazil.org/birthday.htm, 2000.
20. www.maria-brazil.org/biz.htm, 2000.
21. www.maria-brazil.org/at_the_feira_3_.htm, 2000.
22. www.maria-brazil.org/superma.htm, 2000.
23. www.maria-brazil.org/eat.htm, 2000.

Chapter 14

1. Moreira, 1995.
2. Morrison et al., 1994.
3. Althen, 1998.
4. Garcez, 1991.
5. Althen, 1998; Hall, 1959; Morrison et al., 1994.
6. Althen, 1998.
7. Ribeiro, 2000.
8. Handout, courtesy of Professor Tomasz Lenartowicz, University of Texas at Austin, 2001.
9. www.maria-brazil.org/biz.htm, 2000.
10. Althen, 1998.
11. Goslin, 1993, pp. 37, 43.
12. L. Rohter 2000, December 31. Brazil's hot commodity? Not coffee or soccer. *New York Times*, pp. BU1, BU11.
13. Ibid., p. BU11.
14. Santos, 1995.
15. Althen, 1998.

16. D. Tannen, cited in Garcez, 1991.

17. The author's interpretation of negotiation style is based on Pedro de Moraes Garcez's master's thesis (Garcez, 1991), his Ph.D. dissertation (Garcez, 1996), and discussion with Garcez in June 2000. Garcez was a professor at the Departamento de Linguística, Filosofia e Teoria Literaria da Universidade Federal do Rio Grande do Sul [Department of Linguistics, Philosophy and Literary Theory of the Universidade Federal do Rio Grande do Sul] at that time.

18. Althen, 1998, p. 26.

Chapter 15

1. Hall, 1976.
2. Page, 1995.
3. DaMatta, 1998.
4. Page, 1995.
5. www.maria-brazil.org/biz.htm, 2000.
6. Ibid.
7. Ibid.
8. Ibid.
9. Novinger, 2001.
10. Varner and Beamer, 1995.
11. Burgoon et al., 1996.
12. Watzlawick et al., 1967.
13. The discussion of time sense draws on Burgoon et al., 1996; Hall, 1959; Hall and Whyte, 1960; Porter, 1972; Samovar and Porter, 1991; Tixier, 1993.
14. Eakin, 1997.
15. Novinger, 2001.
16. Richard, 1991.
17. www.maria-brazil.org/biz.htm, 2000.
18. R. Gesteland (1998, April). Do's and taboos: Proper etiquette in the global marketplace. *The Rotarian*, pp. 26–29, 59.
19. Riedinger, 1997.

Chapter 16

1. E. T. Hall (1966). *The Hidden Dimension*. Garden City, NY: Doubleday, p. xii.
2. Goslin, 1993.
3. www.maria-brazil.org/intercul.htm, 2000.
4. www.maria-brazil.org, 2001.
5. M. de Carvalho (1964). *Guia de boas maneiras* [Guide to good manners]. São Paulo: Companhia Editora Nacional.
6. Novinger, 2001.
7. Ibid.

8. Ibid.

9. V. Klinkenborg (2000, April 26). The city life: Eye contact. *New York Times*, p. A30.

10. Novinger, 2001.

11. N. Dresser (1996). *Multicultural Manners: New Rules of Etiquette for a Changing Society.* New York: John Wiley and Sons.

12. Novinger, 2001.

13. Burgoon et al., 1996.

14. Samovar and Porter, 1991.

15. L. Di Mare (1990). Ma and Japan. *Southern Communication Journal,* 55, 319–328.

16. Porter, 1972; Tixier, 1993.

17. Althen, 1998.

Chapter 17

1. Pells, 1997.

2. H. Fairlie, cited in Althen, 1998, p. 77.

3. H. Fairlie, cited in Althen, 1998.

4. www.maria-brazil.org/biz.htm, 2000.

5. Ibid.

6. Ibid.

7. Ibid.

8. Ibid.

9. Page, 1995.

10. Hall, 1959.

Chapter 18

1. Moreira, 1995.

2. Ribeiro, 2000.

3. Rega, 2000.

4. Moreira, 1995.

5. Santos, 1995.

6. Garcez, 1991.

7. Santos, 1995.

8. Moreira, 1995.

9. Page, 1995.

10. Moreira, 1995.

11. Rega, 2000.

12. *Washington Post* (2001, April 14). Brazil rediscovers its culture. www.washingtonpost.com.

13. Boas, 1940.

14. Hall, 1959.

15. D. Tannen, cited in Garcez, 1991.

16. Pells, 1997.

17. Novinger, 2001.
18. DaMatta, 1998.
19. Ibid., pp. 16–17.

Glossary

Adapted from Novinger, 2001.
1. Y. Y. Kim, 1991.
2. Barna, 1988; Y. Y. Kim, 1991; Pettigrew, 1986.
3. Porter, 1972.
4. Birdwhistell, 1970.
5. Andersen, 1988.
6. Samovar & Porter, 1991.
7. Carroll, 1987.
8. Varner & Beamer, 1995, p. 13.
9. Tixier, 1993, p. 101.
10. Hall, 1959.
11. Novinger, 2001.
12. Samovar & Porter, 1991.
13. Hall, 1959; Porter & Samovar, 1991.
14. Argyle, 1988; Johnston, 1988.
15. Andersen, 1988; Hall, 1959.
16. Argyle, 1988; Bowman & Okuda, 1985; Inman et al., 1991; R. Jakobsen (1972). Motor signs for "yes" and "no." *Language in Society, 1,* 19–96; W. La Barre, W. (1947). The cultural basis of emotions and gestures. *Journal of Personality, 16,* 49–68; Morrison et al., 1979; Schneller, 1989.
17. Hall, 1959.
18. Tixier, 1993.
19. Andersen, 1988.
20. Samovar & Porter, 1991.
21. Gudykunst & Kim, 1984.
22. Porter, 1972; Samovar & Porter, 1991; V. Terpstra (1978). *The Cultural Environment of International Business.* Cincinnati: South Western Publishing.
23. Porter, 1972.
24. E. Sapir (1949). Time perspective in aboriginal American culture: A study in method. In D. G. Mandelbaum (Ed.), *Selected Writings of Edward Sapir in Language, Culture, and Personality.* Berkeley: University of California Press.
25. Terpstra, 1978.
26. Novinger, 2001.
27. Samovar & Porter, 1991.
28. Y. Y. Kim, 1991.
29. D. Byrne (1971). *The Attraction Paradigm.* New York: Academic Press.
30. Y. Y. Kim, 1991.
31. Barna, 1988; Wedge, 1972.
32. Hall, 1976.

33. Inman et al., 1991; Porter, 1972.

34. Argyle, 1988; Inman et al., 1991.

35. Bowman & Okuda, 1985.

36. Hall, 1959.

37. Barna, 1988; Schneller, 1989.

38. Gudykunst & Kim, 1984; Hall, 1959; Hall, 1969; Hall & Whyte, 1960; Porter, 1972.

39. Hall, 1969.

40. Argyle, 1988; Hall & Whyte, 1960; Inman et al., 1991; Porter, 1972.

41. Samovar & Porter, 1991.

42. Morrison et al., 1994.

43. Burgoon et al., 1996; Hall, 1959; Hall & Whyte, 1960; Samovar & Porter, 1991; Tixier, 1993.

44. Samovar & Porter, 1991.

45. Berger & Calabrese, 1975; Lee & Boster, 1991; Samovar & Porter, 1991.

46. Birdwhistell, 1970.

47. Samovar & Porter, 1991.

48. Barna, 1988; Hall & Whyte, 1960.

49. Torbiorn, 1987.

50. Feinberg, 1989.

51. Burgoon et al., 1996.

52. Samovar & Porter, 1991.

53. Hall, 1959.

54. Samovar & Porter, 1991.

Bibliography

Alder, L. (2000, Fall). Go south young business people. *Texas: The McCombs School of Business Magazine*, pp. 14–15.

Althen, G. (1998). *American Ways*. Yarmouth, ME: Intercultural Press, Inc.

Andersen, P. (1988). Explaining intercultural differences in nonverbal communication. In L. A. Samovar and R. E. Porter (Eds.), *Intercultural Communication: A Reader* (5th ed.) (pp. 272–287). Belmont, CA: Wadsworth Publishing.

Argyle, M. (1988). Intercultural communication. In L. A. Samovar and R. E. Porter (Eds.), *Intercultural Communication: A Reader* (5th ed.) (pp. 31–44). Belmont, CA: Wadsworth Publishing.

Barbosa, L. (1992). *O jeitinho brasileiro—A arte de ser mais igual que os outros* [Brazilian *jeitinho*—The art of being more equal than others]. Rio de Janeiro: Campus.

Barna, L. M. (1988). Stumbling blocks in intercultural communication. In L. A. Samovar and R. E. Porter (Eds.), *Intercultural Communication: A Reader* (5th ed.) (pp. 322–329). Belmont, CA: Wadsworth Publishing.

Berger, C. R., and R. Calabrese (1975). Some explorations in initial interaction and beyond. *Human Communication Research, I,* 99–112.

Birdwhistell, R. L. (1970). *Kinesics and Context: Essays on Body Motion Communication*. Philadelphia: University of Pennsylvania Press.

Boas, F. (1940). *Race, Language and Culture*. New York: Free Press.

Bowman, J. P., and T. Okuda (1985). Japanese-American communication: Mysteries, enigmas, and possibilities. *Bulletin of the Association for Business Communication, 48*(4), 18–21.

Brown-Gort, A. R. (1998). The role of culture in the political and administrative transformation of the Mexican state. Master's thesis, University of Texas, Austin.

Buckley, S. (2000, October 1). In Brazil, a miracle in the war on AIDS. *Austin American-Statesman*, p. J1.

Buckley, S. (2001, April 16). Flirtatious Brazil weighs harassment bill. *Washington Post*, p. A14. www.washingtonpost.com apr15/2001.

Burgoon, J. K., D. B. Butler, and W. G. Woodall (1996). *Nonverbal Communication: The Unspoken Dialogue*. New York: McGraw-Hill.

Byrne, D. (1971). *The Attraction Paradigm.* New York: Academic Press.

CNN.com (2000, August 17). Brazil bandits take crime to new heights on plane. cnn.com/2000/WORLD/Americas/08/17/brazil.hijacking.reut/.

Caldeira, T. P. R. (2000). *City of Walls: Crime, Segregation and Citizenship in São Paulo.* Berkeley: University of California Press.

Carrion, J. (2000, June 16). Palavra do leitor: Orgulho [Letter to the editor: Pride]. *Zero Hora.* Porto Alegre, Brazil, p. 2.

Carroll R. (1987). *Evidences invisibles: Américains et français au quotidien.* Paris: Editions du Seuil. [Available in translation: Carroll, R. (1988). *Cultural misunderstandings: The French-American experience.* (C. Volk, Trans.) Chicago: University of Chicago Press.]

Carvalho, M. de (1964). *Guia de boas maneiras* [Guide to good manners]. São Paulo: Companhia Editora Nacional.

Conway, J. K. (1994). *True North: A Memoir.* New York: Vintage Books.

DaMatta, R. (1995). Do you know who you're talking to?! In G. H. Summ (Ed.), *Brazilian Mosaic: Portraits of a Diverse People and Culture* (pp. 138–142). Wilmington, DE: Scholarly Resources, Inc.

DaMatta, R. (1998). *O que faz o brasil, Brasil?* [What makes Brazil Brazil?]. Rio de Janeiro: Editora Rocco Ltda.

Dias, L., and R. Gambini (1999). *Outros 500: Uma conversa sobre a alma brasileira* [Another 500: A discussion of the Brazilian soul]. São Paulo: Editora SENAC.

Di Mare, L. (1990). Ma and Japan. *The Southern Communication Journal,* 55, 319–328.

Dresser, N. (1996). *Multicultural Manners: New Rules of Etiquette for a Changing Society.* New York: John Wiley and Sons.

Eakin, M. (1998). *Brazil: The Once and Future Country.* New York: St. Martin's Press.

Economist (2001, August 18). Security in Brazil: Bullet-proof in Alphaville, p. 28.

Ellingsworth, H. W. (1977). Conceptualizing intercultural communication. In B. D. Ruben (Ed.), *Communication Yearbook I* (pp. 99–106). New Brunswick, NJ: Transaction Books.

Ertel, L. (2000, June 16). Informe económico [Economic report]. *Zero Hora.* Porto Alegre, Brazil, p. 24.

Feinberg, W. (1989). A role for philosophy of education in intercultural research: A reexamination of the relativism-absolutism debate. *Teachers College Record,* 91, 161–176.

Flor (2000, June 29). Desigualdade cresce no Brasil [Inequality grows in Brazil]. *Zero Hora.* Porto Alegre, Brazil, pp. 50–51.

Flores, M. R. D. Z. (2000, June 8). Palavra do leitor [Letter to the editor]. *Zero Hora.* Porto Alegre, Brazil, p. 2.

Franco, G. (2000, March 29). Sobre o nacionalismo [On nationalism]. *Veja,* Edition 1642, Year 33, No. 13, p. 196. Brazil.

Freire, R. (1998). *Viaje na viagem: Auto-ajuda para turistas* [Travel on the trip: Self-help for tourists]. São Paulo: Mandarim.

Freitas, D. (2000, June 25). Penas de morte [Death penalties]. *Zero Hora.* Porto Alegre, Brazil, p. 23.

Freyre, G. (1956). *The Masters and the Slaves: A Study in the Development of Brazilian Civilization.* (Samuel Putnam, Trans.) (2d English-language ed., rev.). New York: Knopf.

Freyre, G. (1981). *Casa grande e senzala em quadrinhos* [The masters and the slaves in comic strips]. Rio de Janeiro: Editora-América.

Furuichi, S. (1999). On understanding racial inequality in Brazil. Ph.D. dissertation, University of Texas, Austin.

Garcez, P. M. (1991). Conflicting conversational styles in a cross-cultural negotiation. Master's thesis, Universidade Federal de Santa Catarina, Florianópolis, Santa Catarina, Brazil.

Garcez, P. M. (1996). Brazilian manufacturers and United States importers doing business: The co-construction of arguing sequences in negotiation. Ph.D. dissertation, University of Pennsylvania. Ann Arbor, MI: UMI Dissertation Services.

Gesteland, R. (1998, April). Do's and taboos: Proper etiquette in the global marketplace. *The Rotarian*, pp. 26–29, 59.

Gobetti, S. (2000, June 16). Cônsul divulga plano de Cuba para ensinos [Consul discloses Cuba's plans for teaching]. *Zero Hora.* Porto Alegre, Brazil, p. 12.

Gonzalez, F. (2001, April 22). From Brazil, a musician's colorful call. *Washington Post*, p. G01. www.washingtonpost, April 20, 2001.

Goslin, P. A. (1993). *Rau tchu bi a carioca* (*How to be a carioca): O guia alternativo para o turista no Rio* [The alternative guide for the tourist in Rio]. Rio de Janeiro: Editora Livros TwoCan Ltda.

Gudykunst, W. B., and Y. Y. Kim (1984). *Communicating with Strangers: An Approach to Intercultural Communication.* Reading, MA: Addison Wesley.

Gudykunst, W., and S. Ting-Toomey (1988). *Culture and Interpersonal Communication.* Beverly Hills, CA: Sage.

Hall, E. T. (1959). *The Silent Language.* 1st ed. Garden City, NY: Doubleday.

Hall, E. T. (1966). *The Hidden Dimension.* Garden City, NY: Doubleday.

Hall, E. T. (1976). *Beyond Culture.* Garden City, NY: Doubleday.

Hall, E. T., and W. F. Whyte (1960). Intercultural communication: A guide to men of action. *Human Organization, 19,* 5–20.

Hayakawa, S. I. (1958). Communication and the human community. *Etc., 60,* 5–11.

Inman, T. H., A. C. Ownby, H. R. Perreault, and J. N. Rhea (1991). Internationalizing the business communication curriculum. *Business Education Forum, 46*(2), 19–22.

Jakobsen, R. (1972). Motor signs for "yes" and "no." *Language in Society, 1,* 19–96.

Johnston, J. (1988). Japanese firms in the U.S.: Adapting the persuasive message. *Bulletin of the Association for Business Communication, 51*(3), 33–34.

Kim, H. J. (1991). Influence of language and similarity on initial intercultural attraction. In S. Ting-Toomey and F. Korzenny (Eds.), *Cross-Cultural Interpersonal Communication* (pp. 213–229). Newbury Park, CA: Sage.

Kim, Y. Y. (1991). Intercultural communication competence: A systems-theoretic view. In S. Ting-Toomey and F. Korzenny (Eds.), *Cross-Cultural Interpersonal Communication* (pp. 259–275). Newbury Park, CA: Sage.

Klinkenborg, V. (2000, April 26). The city life: Eye contact. *New York Times*, p. A30.

Krich, J. (1997). The girl from Ipanema. In A. Haddad and S. Dogett (Eds.), *Travelers' Tales Brazil: True Stories of Life on the Road* (pp. 336–347). Redwood City, CA: Travelers' Tales, Inc.

La Barre, W. (1947). The cultural basis of emotions and gestures. *Journal of Personality, 16*, 49–68.

Lee, H. O., and F. J. Boster (1991). Social information for uncertainty reduction during initial interactions. In S. Ting-Toomey and F. Korzenny (Eds.), *Cross-Cultural Interpersonal Communication* (pp. 189–212). Newbury Park, CA: Sage.

Lores, R. J. (2000, March 29). E eles culpam o Brasil [And they blame Brazil]. *Veja*, Edition 1642, Year 33, No. 13, pp. 186–195. Brazil.

Mãe (2000). Ano VII, Número 74, front cover. Brazil.

Margolis, M. (1997). Young, down and out. In A. Haddad and S. Dogett (Eds.), *Travelers' Tales Brazil: True Stories of Life on the Road* (pp. 370–375). Redwood City, CA: Travelers' Tales, Inc., p. 372.

Mariani, J. (2000, June 9). As feras no portão [The beasts at the gate]. *Zero Hora*. Porto Alegre, Brazil, p. 21.

Martes, A. C. B. (1999). *Brasileiros nos Estados Unidos: Um estudo sobre imigrantes em Massachusetts* [Brazilians in the United States: A study of immigrants in Massachusetts]. São Paulo, Brazil: Paz e Terra.

Maybury-Lewis, D. (1995). The persistent patronage system. In G. H. Summ (Ed.), *Brazilian Mosaic: Portraits of a Diverse People and Culture* (pp. 153–159). Wilmington, DE: Scholarly Resources.

Mendonça, M., and V. Franco, Directors (2000). *Nascí mulher negra* [I was born a black woman]. Brazil: Global Exchange Video.

Moran, R. T., and J. D. Abbott (1994). *NAFTA: Managing the Cultural Differences*. Houston, TX: Gulf Publishing Company.

Moreira, L. (1995). Living avidly in the present. In G. H. Summ (Ed.), *Brazilian Mosaic: Portraits of a Diverse People and Culture* (pp. 185–188). Wilmington, DE: Scholarly Resources, Inc.

Morrison, T., W. Conway, and G. A. Borden (1994). *Kiss, Bow, or Shake Hands: How to Do Business in Sixty Countries*. Holbrook, MA: Bob Adams, Inc.

Novinger, T. (1996). Intercultural communication: The cultural factors that create obstacles between Mexico and the United States. Master's thesis, Wichita State University, Wichita, KS.

Novinger, T. (2001). *Intercultural Communication: A Practical Guide*. Austin: University of Texas Press.

Page, J. A. (1995). *The Brazilians.* Reading, MA: Addison Wesley.

Pastor, R. A., and J. G. Castañeda (1988). *Limits to Friendship: The United States and Mexico.* New York: Knopf.

Pells, R. H. (1997). *Not Like Us: How Europeans Have Loved, Hated, and Transformed American Culture since World War II.* New York: Basic-Books.

Pettigrew, T. (1986). The intergroup contact hypothesis reconsidered. In Hewstone and R. Brown (Eds.). *Contact and Conflict in Intergroup Encounters* (pp. 169–195). Oxford: Basil Blackwell.

Pike, K. L. (1956). *Language and Life.* Glendale, CA: Summer Institute of Linguistics.

Porter, R. E. (1972). An overview of intercultural communication. In L. A. Samovar and R. E. Porter (Eds.), *Intercultural Communication: A Reader* (pp. 3–18). Belmont, CA: Wadsworth Publishing.

Proença, M. C. (1969). *Roteiro de Macunaíma* [Guide to Macunaíma]. Rio de Janeiro: Editora Civilisação Brasileira.

Rega, L. S. (2000). *Dando um jeito no jeitinho: Como ser ético sem deixar de ser brasileiro* [Finding a way to find a way: How to be ethical without giving up being Brazilian]. São Paulo: Mundo Cristão.

Ribeiro, D. (2000). *The Brazilian People: The Formation and Meaning of Brazil.* (Gregory Rabassa, Trans.) Gainesville: University Press of Florida. (Originally published 1995).

Rich, J. L. (2001, August 16). *New York Times.* www.nytimes.com/2001/08/16/business/worldbusiness/16BRAZ.html.

Richard, C. (1991). *Cultures of the World: Brazil.* New York: Marshall Cavendish Corporation.

Riedinger, E. A. (1997). Once upon a time in Ipanema. In A. Haddad and S. Dogett (Eds.), *Travelers' Tales Brazil: True Stories of Life on the Road* (pp. 18–26). Redwood City, CA: Travelers' Tales, Inc.

Ritzel, L. (2000, July 2). Seis anos do plano real [Six years of the Real Plan]. *Zero Hora.* Porto Alegre, Brazil, p. 22.

Rohter, L. (2001, July 1). Energy crisis is just one more thing for Brazil. *New York Times.* www.nytimes.com/2001/07/01.

Rohter, L. (2000, November 26). Mayor most rare: Sexologist and monied Marxist. *New York Times.* www.nytimes.com 2000/11/26.

Rohter, L. (2000, December 31). Brazil's hot commodity? Not coffee or soccer. *New York Times,* pp. BU1, BU11.

Rubin, T. (2000, June 24). Rio de Janeiro is a town of two worlds. *Austin American-Statesman,* p. A11.

Samovar, L. A., and R. E. Porter (1991). *Communication between Cultures.* Belmont, CA: Wadsworth Publishing.

Sanders, T. G. (1995). The social functions of futebol. In G. H. Summ (Ed.), *Brazilian Mosaic: Portraits of a Diverse People and Culture* (pp. 159–162). Wilmington, DE: Scholarly Resources, Inc.

Santos, J. F. (1995). Bypassing the system. In G. H. Summ (Ed.), *Brazilian Mosaic: Portraits of a Diverse People and Culture* (pp. 142–148). Wilmington, DE: Scholarly Resources, Inc.

Santos, K. (2000, June 18). Entrevista: Renan Calheiros [Interview: Renan Calheiros]. *Zero Hora*. Porto Alegre, Brazil, p. 51.

Sapir, E. (1949). Time perspective in aboriginal American culture: A study in method. In D. G. Mandelbaum (Ed.), *Selected Writings of Edward Sapir in Language, Culture, and Personality*. Berkeley: University of California Press.

Scheper-Hughes, N. (1995). The everyday violence of life. In G. H. Summ (Ed.), *Brazilian Mosaic: Portraits of a Diverse People and Culture* (pp. 194–202). Wilmington, DE: Scholarly Resources, Inc.

Schneller, R. (1989). Intercultural and intrapersonal processes and factors of misunderstanding: Implications for multicultural training. *International Journal of Intercultural Relations, 5,* 175–191.

Selcher, W. A. (1995). Brazil in the world. In G. H. Summ (Ed.), *Brazilian Mosaic: Portraits of a Diverse People and Culture* (pp. 166–171). Wilmington, DE: Scholarly Resources, Inc.

Sitaram, K. S. (1972). What is intercultural communication? In L. A. Samovar and R. E. Porter (Eds.), *Intercultural Communication: A Reader* (pp. 18–23). Belmont, CA: Wadsworth Publishing.

Skidmore, T. E. (1999). *Brazil: Five Centuries of Change*. New York: Oxford University Press.

Soldatelli, R. V. (2000, June 14). Palavra do leitor [Letter to the editor]. *Zero Hora*. Porto Alegre, Brazil, p. 2.

Sowell, T. (1994). *Race and Culture: A World View*. New York: BasicBooks.

Storti, C. (1989). *The Art of Crossing Cultures*. Yarmouth, ME: Intercultural Press, Inc.

Storti, C. (1999). *Figuring Foreigners Out: A Practical Guide*. Yarmouth, ME: Intercultural Press, Inc.

Streeck, J. (1994). Culture, meaning, and interpersonal communication. In Knapp, M. L. (Ed.), *Handbook of Interpersonal Communication* (pp. 286–319). Thousand Oaks, CA: Sage.

Terpstra, V. (1978). *The Cultural Environment of International Business*. Cincinnati: South Western Publishing.

Tixier, M. (1993). Obstacles to internal communication among subsidiary and headquarters executives in western Europe. In P. Gaunt (Ed.), *Beyond Agendas: New Directions in Communication Research* (pp. 101–116). Westport, CT: Greenwood Press.

Torbiorn, I. (1987). Culture barriers as a social psychological construct. In Y. Y. Kim and W. B. Gudykunst (Eds.), Cross-cultural adaptation: Current approaches. *International and Intercultural Communication Annual, XI,* 168–190.

Trezzi, H. (2000, June 18). A escalada da criminalidade: Violência no Brasil triplicou em duas décadas [The escalation of crime: Violence in Brazil tripled in two decades]. *Zero Hora*. Porto Alegre, Brazil.

U.S. Central Intelligence Agency (2000, 9 November). *The World Factbook*. www.odci.gov/cia/publications/factbook/geos/us.num.

U.S. Department of Commerce (1999, July 15). *Brazil: Country Commercial Guide Fiscal Year 2000*. São Paulo, Brazil: U.S. Commercial Service.

Varner, I., and L. Beamer (1995). *Intercultural Communication in the Global Workplace.* Chicago: Irwin.

Veríssimo, L. F. (2000, June 23). A boca do Bush [The mouth of Bush]. *Zero Hora.* Porto Alegre, Brazil.

Wagley, C. (1995). A most personal people. In G. H. Summ (Ed.), *Brazilian Mosaic: Portraits of a Diverse People and Culture* (pp. 148–153). Wilmington, DE: Scholarly Resources, Inc.

Washington Post (2001, April 14). Brazil rediscovers its culture. www .washingtonpost.com.

Watzlawick, P., J. B. Bavelas, and D. D. Jackson (1967). *Pragmatics of Human Communication: A Study of Interactional Patterns, Pathologies, and Paradoxes.* New York: W. W. Norton and Company.

Wedge, B. (1972). Barriers to understanding. In L. A. Samovar and R. E. Porter (Ed.), *Intercultural communication: A reader* (pp. 3–18). Belmont, CA: Wadsworth Publishing.

Wells, G. (1997). Continental drift. In A. Haddad and S. Dogett (Eds.), *Travelers' Tales Brazil: True Stories of Life on the Road* (pp. 67–78). Redwood City, CA: Travelers' Tales, Inc.

Zero Hora, Staff (2000, June 11). O modelo francês [The French model]. Porto Alegre, Brazil, p. 18.

Zero Hora, Staff (2000, June 18). Atividade não é regulamentada [Activity not regulated]. Porto Alegre, Brazil, p. 49.

Zero Hora, Staff (2000, June 18). Eleições 2000: Segurança é maior preocupação do eleitor [2000 elections: Security is greatest concern of the voter]. Porto Alegre, Brazil, p. 10.

Zero Hora, Staff (2000, June 20). A epidemia de violência [The epidemic of violence]. Porto Alegre, Brazil, p. 16.

Zero Hora, Staff (2000, June 26). Onze homicídios marcam o fim de semana no estado [Eleven homicides mark the weekend in the state]. Porto Alegre, Brazil, p. 1.

Zero Hora, Staff (2000, June 27). Unaids destaca sistema brasileiro [Unaids distinguishes Brazilian system]. Porto Alegre, Brazil, p. 40.

Zero Hora, Staff (2000, June 30). Subdesenvolvimento humano [Human underdevelopment]. Porto Alegre, Brazil, p. 24.

Index